Archana Rao

"Strongly recommend"

Admitted to: Darden School of Business

Vibha continues to be a mentor for me even today; providing invaluable guidance every time we meet.

Tanya Mishra

"Very qualified counselors"

Admitted to: London Business School

Each part of the application is carried out by a different counselor who is an expert in his own field, which helps in filling out parts which might have been overlooked earlier.

Ishvarya Raman

"Virtual, yet very personalized"

Admitted to: Kellogg, Duke Fuqua, Tuck, UCLA Anderson

Each application is treated uniquely. My favorite part was the brainstorming sessions. The team took genuine interest to understand my background and helped me tie it to my goals. The entire process was virtual, yet very personalized.

Anik Roy

"Fantastic at what they do!"

Admitted to: Kellogg, UNC Kenan Flagler (25 percent scholarship), Washington University (100 percent scholarship), HEC Paris, Cornell Johnson

Since I already had one MBA, I had to justify my need for a second. ReachIvy did a wonderful job and helped me justify this to the schools I was applying to.

Saee Pansare

"Made the whole process so much easier and more focussed for me"

Admitted to: Yale Silver Scholars Program

I worked with ReachIvy.com on my applications when I was on a time crunch and they just made the whole process so much easier and focused for me.

Payal Tripathi

"Invaluable advice"

Admitted to: Ross School of Business, New York University, London Business School, CEIBS

Having worked with scores of MBA aspirants, they provide invaluable advice to help highlight the most compelling aspects of your profile.

Nunzio Quacquarelli, CEO at QS Quacquarelli Symonds

"Her sessions are greatly appreciated and always see packed houses"

Vibha is a regular panelist at our fairs where she shares 'Top tips on cracking the application process'. Her sessions are greatly appreciated and always see packed houses.

Bindi Dharia, Deputy Director, Centre for Social Impact and Philanthropy, Ashoka University; Board member, Harvard Business School Club of India; President, University of Michigan India Alumni Association

"Can attest to her commitment to ensuring the highest quality of guidance"

Vibha is always eager to help and tries her best to engage the Harvard community in India. She has spoken on many panels for prospective applicants to Harvard; her views are pointed, clear and wise. I have also spoken at ReachIvy.com's panels and seen how thoroughly they approach the admissions process, making it wholesome and fun for applicants!

Praise for the book

Harsh Jain, CEO, Dream11.com, Fortune India 40 Under 40

"Brilliant editors"

Admitted to: Columbia Business School

It definitely helps to have someone like Vibha working with you on your essays because she knows exactly what the thought process of the person evaluating them is.

Neha Singh

"Dependable essay editors"

Admitted to: Chicago Booth, Wharton, London Business School, Michigan Ross

ReachIvy.com used a three-pronged approach towards the goal of getting an admit from selected schools. I would highly recommend ReachIvy.com to any MBA aspirant!

Daniel & Shezaad Zainulbhai (brothers)

Daniel: "Tailored my experiences"

Admitted to: Harvard Business School, Kellogg, Chicago Booth

Without ReachIvy.com I would not have been accepted to the top three B-schools in the world. Vibha and team helped me create a coherent, credible story out of my jumbled experiences.

Shehzaad: "Vibha's expertise is unparalleled"

Admitted to: Harvard Business School

Vibha's expertise in the admissions process is unparalleled. The level of rigor and attention to detail that was put into my essays definitely exceeded my expectations.

Manoj Gursahani, Chairman, USA India Investors Forum; President, Friends of South Africa; Past President, Rotary Club of Mumbai Queen's Necklace

"This book binds together her drive, knowledge and experience"

If I had to describe Vibha in one word, it would be: firecracker! I have facilitated several speaker panels where Vibha has addressed audiences varying from 12 to 75 years of age. She is able to illuminate the room with her in-depth command of her subject and eagerness to share her knowledge. She has a spark that makes her the dynamic woman she is.

Gautam Shewakramani, International Growth Advisor, Quora.com

"...a sure-shot introduction and guide that corrects misinformation around business school admissions"

Vibha's passion for enabling the dreams of many aspiring candidates and her drive to provide genuinely useful, credible and authentic advice is evident. She has been open with sharing her knowledge on Quora, and this book is a culmination of all of this and more—a sure-shot introduction and guide that corrects misinformation around business school admissions from India.

Manish Chokhani, Director at Enam Holdings & Senior Advisor to TPG; Previously MD & CEO of Axis Capital & Alumni Board Member of London Business School

"Vibha and her team play a key role in guiding MBA aspirants"

Vibha and her team play a key role in guiding MBA aspirants. As a panelist at one of their events, I saw the zeal and passion she brings to her role as an admissions consultant. She has been a mentor for my son, assisting with his application to Wharton for his undergrad. Today, as he charts his course forward, Vibha remains an approachable mentor, someone who is vested in his success and future.

BREAK

the

MBA CODE

Fast-track your way into the Ivy League & other top colleges

VIBHA KAGZI

JAICO PUBLISHING HOUSE

Ahmedabad Bangalore Bhopal Chennai
Delhi Hyderabad Kolkata Lucknow Mumbai

Published by Jaico Publishing House
A-2 Jash Chambers, 7-A Sir Phirozshah Mehta Road
Fort, Mumbai - 400 001
jaicopub@jaicobooks.com
www.jaicobooks.com

BREAK THE MBA CODE
ISBN 978-93-89305-44-9

First Jaico Impression: 2020

Page design and layout:
Special Effects Graphics Design Company, Mumbai

Why I Wrote This Book

When I first considered applying to a top school abroad for my undergraduate studies, I was overwhelmed by the range of subjects and schools to pick from and a lack of expert guidance. I did not have a seasoned mentor who could help me understand and evaluate the options, find my fit and navigate the intricate application process. I used the internet as my primary means of research and scrambled to get admitted to Carnegie Mellon University. I had made it to a top-tier university, albeit without much context or understanding of my chosen path.

Similarly, when it was time to apply for my MBA, I wanted to find a top-ranked university where I would have a cultural and intellectual fit, but again I had no one to guide me. This time I was determined to leave no stone unturned in my pursuit. Over four years, I strategically built a 'toolkit' by visiting target colleges, seeking professional guidance, working with friends who were experts in writing, connecting with alumni and conducting extensive research. I finally cracked the code.

After graduating with an MBA from Harvard Business School (HBS), I moved back to India to found ReachIvy.com, a premium education and careers advisory. My objective was to provide students with extensive guidance on studying abroad and on their careers after graduation, from experts who have firsthand knowledge of what it means to earn a degree from a reputed school. I wanted to ensure that other high-caliber students are channeled in the right direction and do not have to suffer the anxiety and confusion I had to endure. Also, there is immense hidden talent within India, which is often buried under social inequalities. I believe that education is a social equalizer, which has the power to elevate you and transform your life. I wanted to establish a platform to bring this talent to the surface by encouraging more students to aim for and get admitted to the most reputed global universities.

When Jaico Publishing House approached me to write a book that would break down, step by step, the whole process of getting into a top business school, my first reaction was, "Absolutely not!" I was reluctant to write a book that would reveal our trade secrets to the world. Our methods, processes and experience are at the core of our business; they are what students pay us for. How could we give them all away in a book? However, after much introspection, I came to the conclusion that no one really "owns" knowledge: it is universal, and everyone should be able to access it. Thus began the journey.

On a more personal note, I wish to encourage more women to apply to top business schools abroad. When I was 26, my parents, like many traditional Indian parents, were eager to see me "settled". When I was admitted to HBS, the news was bittersweet for them since they felt that I would be "too old" by the time I came back to India, and would also be considered "over-educated". I looked them in the eye and said, "Studying at Harvard is a once-in-a-lifetime opportunity; I'd give my right arm for this." And we never looked back. Two years later, they came to Boston for my Harvard graduation. On seeing the campus, meeting my friends and watching me get my degree, their pride and joy knew no bounds.

In India, women are a growing force in an age when glass ceilings are being shattered and new standards are being set in best business practices. At this time, earning an MBA will open several doors for my female readers. At my workplace, I strive to help women overcome their personal challenges and continue working—a feat which has been recognized by the Women Economic Forum and Jobs for Her, who have conferred awards on ReachIvy.com for encouraging women at the workplace.

For all readers, regardless of their educational, professional, economic or social background, I have detailed everything that needs to be done to secure admission at an Ivy League or other top MBA program; *our* trade secrets are now *yours*.

Book Structure

Over the past decade, my team and I have helped thousands of students get interviews and admission at top schools globally, including Harvard Business School, Stanford Graduate School of Business, Wharton School of Business, MIT Sloan, Columbia Business School, Booth School of Business, Ross School of Business, Kellogg, London Business School, Oxford Said School of Business, Cambridge Judge Business School, INSEAD, ESADE, IESE, IMD Switzerland, HEC Paris, IESE, Rotman School of Management, China Europe International Business School, Hong Kong University of Science and Technology, Asian Institute of Management, National University of Singapore and Indian School of Business. Essentially, we have at least one admit at every top global business school.

The book starts with a suggested timeline. The chapters thereafter have been sequenced to provide students a chronological process to follow while applying. From deciding to earn an MBA to securing funding for the program, the book covers it all.

Our advice for each of these steps has been carefully curated by ReachIvy.com's in-house experts who have a diverse range of experiences across different industries and have all studied at top global institutes. More importantly, they have a fine-tuned ability to harness their knowledge about the education industry and their own career expertise to shape strong applicant profiles. We have mastered our craft over the past decade.

Here are major sections that recur through the book:

Busting Common MBA Myths

I have encountered several myths about the MBA degree and the application process itself. For the common applicant who may not have access to an expert counselor, it is easy to fall for such myths and thus fail to secure admission to his dream school. In a bid to present the most effective and realistic method of applying to a top business school, I have dispelled several of these myths throughout the book under this section.

Real People, Unique Skills, Common Errors

To illustrate our method's effectiveness and to help students tackle the myriad admission scenarios, I have included several case studies of students ReachIvy.com has worked with over the years (with the names of the students and schools changed to protect their privacy). These can be found at the end of each chapter. Given that India is a land of a billion people with different backgrounds, I have covered a range of candidates from different fields—from consulting and finance to family business and non-traditional professional profiles (arts, music, dance, etc.)—to ensure you get a wide array of cases.

Insider Tips in a Nutshell

There is a deluge of generic and sometimes incorrect information floating on the internet. I have made sure any false or vague information is filtered out; only direct, specific, professional advice is provided within these pages. This information is consolidated as 'Dos' and 'Don'ts' at the end of each chapter. The key takeaways from each of the case studies are covered in the 'Errors in a Nutshell' section.

Worksheets

I have included 'do-it-yourself' worksheets which will help you plan your MBA journey. I recommend that you use these worksheets to your advantage and fill them in as you read the book. Doing so will help you plan your application process in perfect alignment with my process and will likely fortify your application to its fullest potential.

Each chapter has undergone a rigorous iterative process to ensure the content is accurate and comprehensive. All sections of the book have been scrutinized by ReachIvy.com's in-house experts across functions such as counseling, college selection, essay editing, brainstorming and résumé editing. Thus, we have ensured that reliable and precise information is delivered, directly from practitioners.

This book is my endeavor to ensure that the tools and techniques I have honed over a decade of working on applications can nourish the dreams of millions of deserving candidates over time. Remember, admission decisions are not as cut-and-dried as one may think. Even if you follow my advice verbatim, I cannot guarantee you admission. However, you can definitely change the odds in your favor.

As you embark on your MBA application journey, I wish you all the best. And remember, if I could do it, so can you.

Note: All data presented in the book, including but not limited to Average GMAT Scores, Employment Statistics, School Fees, Acceptance Rates, and Essay Topics, have been updated as per 2018-19 figures. These are all subject to change.

Contents

1

The MBA Dilemma:
To Do or Not to Do

Hi VK,

I work in a top tech firm in India and am confused between getting an MS and an MBA. It would be my first time studying abroad and I'm nervous about making the wrong choice.

Should I do an MBA? If yes, why an MBA and why not an MS? Please help me make a decision.

Amit Tiwari was a techie trying to decide between two master's programs (Master of Information Systems Management and Master of Business Administration). At college, he had headed the robotics club. He had also undertaken several independent projects, which had won awards from his college's Innovation Lab. Amit was then placed at a top tech company as a software engineer. In his second year there, he began leading projects. In his fourth year, he wrote the above email to us.

His inclination towards innovation favored a Master of Science (MS) degree. However, Amit's long-term goal was to launch his own technology-driven firm as opposed to front-running technical operations. His record showed he could effectively lead and manage teams, which pointed to an MBA over an MS.

We first researched various opportunities and courses available at both programs. I also asked Amit to reach out to successful tech entrepreneurs who had earned an MBA. I postponed working on his application for four weeks as I wanted him to be clear about the difference between the two degrees and make an informed decision.

Why did this clarification take priority over working on his applications?

Any master's experience abroad is a milestone and a costly affair. Further, it exacts an opportunity cost along with the monetary cost. While pursuing any post-graduation degree, you willingly forgo up to two years of your career while simultaneously paying a hefty tuition fee. You also invest all your mental bandwidth for one or two years. So, thorough research goes a long way in ensuring that you gain the maximum value out of your decision.

In my case, I gained in-depth understanding beforehand about the colleges of my choice and the program I wanted to pursue. I spoke to several alumni across top schools in the USA, France and Singapore; visited their campuses; attended information sessions to get to the core of 'Why MBA'. This knowledge cemented my decision to go to Harvard Business School. Today, I ensure that the students I work with are similarly informed before they make their choices.

Let us start with the fundamentals and first understand the value of an MBA.

1. Why Would You Want to Earn an MBA?

1:A. To Catapult Financial Growth

Money is a driving force for many when deciding on an MBA. The brochures of top business schools show that fresh graduates begin at a six-figure salary or close to it. Often, graduates draw about twice their pre-MBA salary.

Paras Fatnani, Global Marketing Director of QS, a global company specializing in higher education, points out:

> "An MBA can make one's employability more secure throughout one's career. The QS TopMBA Jobs & Salary Trends Report 2018 showed a 13 percent increase in MBA hiring in 2017 compared to 2016. In addition, MBAs see big gains in salary. Average compensation in the United States and Canada in 2017 stood at $116,300 and in Western Europe at $101,300, which does not even factor in signing bonuses."

However, I suggest you refrain from making financial gain your sole aim and approach the MBA holistically. If this monetary reason spills over to your application, it may put off the admissions committees.

1:B. To Start Your Own Business

The MBA is an excellent choice for budding entrepreneurs, who are offered several options to develop and grow their business skills.

Business plan competitions allow you to formulate your own startup or business idea and present it to venture capitalists. If you win, you receive seed capital for your business, which can range from $20,000 to $100,000.

Some business schools may also allow you to design your own course in any area of interest. Over a semester you can research your business plan and simultaneously earn course credits for it as long as a professor is willing to work with you or endorse you. I worked with a senior professor in the Negotiations Department for a full semester with two classmates; our project culminated in an HBS case study that got inducted into the school's curriculum, making it a phenomenal learning experience.

The Entrepreneurship Club at your business school allows you to network with other aspiring entrepreneurs. You may even find a cofounder for your venture.

The Startup Garage at Stanford, Startup Accelerator at Berkeley Haas, Rock Accelerator and Incubator at HBS are all good examples of the resources that business schools provide for entrepreneurs. These 'entrepreneurship cells' may help you work with mentors, offer you a dedicated space to work on your startup, and assist in exploring funding opportunities. These cells can help make your business idea a reality.

1:C. To Gain International Exposure

Your international exposure begins the moment you land at the airport. For many, it may be the first time leaving home and residing in a foreign land. This requires you to understand the cultural norms of your new home. If you are doing your MBA in France, your experience will be centered around French culture—their language, music, cuisine, etc. These become part of your overall MBA experience. Further, the learning that takes place during out-of-classroom projects and excursions adds to the experience.

Many business schools also have global immersion and exchange programs. This allows students to work for a short period abroad with an organization or on a project of their choice. HBS's FIELD Global Immersion Program, CEIBS's International Exchange Program and Stanford GSB's Global Management Immersion Experience are some examples. Schools may also offer field trips to global locations as part of their course curriculum. For instance, INSEAD's 'Entrepreneurship and Family Enterprise' area includes electives such as Building Business in China, Building Business in India and Building Business in Silicon Valley. Similarly, Kellogg's full-time MBA offers several global opportunities under its Growth Lab, Global Initiatives in Management and field research opportunities, among others. These programs help students gain an international insight into businesses.

Furthermore, top business schools have a diverse student body. Here's a list of the top 15 business schools and their global diversity:

School Name	International Students (percent)	Countries Represented
Harvard Business School	37	69
Stanford Graduate School of Business	42	63
MIT Sloan School of Management	38	49
Cambridge Judge Business School	—	51
Oxford Said Business School	93	62
INSEAD	—	90
London Business School	91	64
CEIBS	36.6	17
IMD Switzerland	—	39
National University of Singapore	66	28
UC Berkeley Haas School of Business	42	39
Yale School of Management	45	51
Columbia Business School	42	—
UPenn Wharton School of Management	33	80

As you can see, global MBA programs have students from various nationalities. Personally, the added perspective has helped me a great deal because my business involves working with students globally. Moreover, meeting and staying with classmates from Hawaii, Argentina, Brussels, Tokyo and Pakistan have given me a rare insight into many cultures.

Most business schools will assign you to a study group. Even within these small groups, diversity is ensured. I was introduced to my learning team on my first day at Harvard. There was a white American boy who had been a consultant at a top firm, a Japanese girl who had worked for the government of Japan and a Hispanic American who had made a career in sports. Our cultural identities led to divergent viewpoints, often leading to heated arguments. Ultimately, these discussions ended up being an incredible learning experience, broadening my sphere of understanding about the world and myself.

1:D. To Help You to Relocate

An MBA can help you move to a different country. It offers credentials that are recognized and accepted globally. The two years you spend earning your MBA will also help you to understand and assimilate into the culture of the region or country you want to relocate to. Additionally, you can use the summer internship to advance your career at your new location. Once you have this work experience, it becomes easier to get recruited as you already have an understanding of the country's work culture.

Depending on your geographical requirements, the career services department of the university and global alumni network can also help.

1:E. To Grow Your Family Business

Every year, several candidates from family business backgrounds apply for an MBA. Many want to gain an understanding of the business world or hone their knowledge further before taking the helm of an entire business.

The resources at a business school for such candidates range from entrepreneurship and family business clubs to more specific short- or long-term programs. Furthermore, MBA programs may offer you electives that train you in family business and enterprise. To name a few, INSEAD's MBA program offers an elective in Family Business Management; HBS's full-time MBA offers Management of the Family Business as an elective; Columbia Business School offers the Family Enterprise and Wealth course.

Similarly, there are initiatives such as Wharton's Global Family Alliance and Darden's Asia Initiative. With these, business schools help to foster learning and understanding of family businesses through research, events and conferences. Exposure to such programs will help you gain insights into the functioning of a family business and teach you how to manage it for sustainable growth. What's more, the global network you build will be of assistance if you are looking to grow your business internationally.

1:F. *To Switch to a New Career*

By and large, more than 50 percent of all MBA aspirants are career switchers who come from one industry and move to a completely different one. For them, the degree is a conduit between two distinct careers. You get exposed to several new sectors through your peers, classes, faculty and guest speakers. Interactions with classmates who come from different backgrounds give you a deep-dive into their career journeys. Additionally, you meet renowned industry and policy leaders who visit your campus. In the same week at Harvard, we had the CEOs of General Electric and Louis Vuitton, the Dalai Lama and Amartya Sen visiting the campus. Inevitably, such combinations lead to many 'aha!' moments which could inspire you to explore a different field of work.

I often get asked by students: "I wrote that I wanted to be a Financial Analyst in my essay, but I have now switched to Product Management. Will the MBA admissions office call me out on this?"

While this is a valid concern, you don't need to worry about what you wrote in your essays in terms of your goals; you can change your mind during the program. Many people do.

Top MBA programs enable you to channel your current expertise to a new field. However, it is important that you have a strong rationale for your switch and an aptitude for the field you want to switch to. I have friends who came from the military and went on to start their own ventures. Similarly, a friend who came from finance moved to the healthcare industry. You have to be smart about using your time at business school carefully and intentionally towards your goal.

1:G. To Enable Professional Development

Professional development is a popular reason students cite in their 'Why MBA' essays, and rightly so. An MBA vastly improves your business and organizational skills. Several non-traditional applicants from the social sciences and performing arts consider an MBA for this same reason. They do this before switching to a business environment or setting up their own businesses. In an MBA program, you learn about business strategy, management, leadership and the nuances of day-to-day operations, which could then be translated to organizational success in the real world.

1:H. To Enable Personal Development

An MBA expedites the development of your personal skills. It is a hands-on degree; lessons and learnings you would imbibe over five years on a job are compressed into an intense two-year curriculum. This intensive experience pushes your personality to its limits. The academic experience develops your communication skills, self-esteem and confidence. You also learn how to manage your relationship with work and manage time effectively as you tread the fine line between managing the course load and having a life outside of it.

The high pressure and competitive environment act as catalysts in encouraging growth, preparing you for the real world.

1:I. To Enable You to Have a Diverse Network

My MBA from HBS did not just confer knowledge and a degree; it enabled me to build a vast global network of intelligent, likeminded individuals. Today, I have peers ready to help me, just a phone call or text message away.

The network I built at HBS has helped me in my business. On

our global advisory board, we inducted Aaron Chadbourne, an HBS classmate who holds three degrees from Harvard. With his depth of knowledge, he has been an immensely useful resource for us. Additionally, as we develop our strategy, I contact fellow entrepreneurs or classmates in Sri Lanka, Seattle, Frankfurt and the Bay Area. They are all able and willing to share their valuable insights.

Here is what Petia Whitmore, Director of the MBA Tour, says about the networking benefits of earning an MBA:

> An MBA is an unparalleled source of boosting your network. It's impossible to overemphasize this point. I graduated a decade ago and have had countless examples of needing a particular piece of insight or connection and I've always been able to find a person, within no more than two degrees of separation, who could help me with the knowledge or resource I needed. Even more importantly, my closest circle of friends and some of my most trusted advisors—I call them my "brain trust" —are all people I encountered as an MBA student. It's the type of ROI that is impossible to precisely calculate but that I consider simply invaluable.

However, attending a school doesn't directly translate to having a strong network. While there will be a diverse set of individuals attending top schools, it requires you to leverage this diversity and build your network actively.

1:J. To Act as an Insurance in Turbulent Times

If your industry is going through turbulent times, studying at business school in this period is a great option. You acquire several new skills and a world of options opens up for you. Even if economic conditions are rough, an MBA works as an insurance and will come in handy when the economy turns around.

2. How an MBA Helps You Impact the World

I know peers from my MBA program who have launched companies that employ over 5,000 people and others who run mentorship programs impacting over 500,000 students. Some have moved to public policy, thereby effecting change at a national level, while others have become well-known writers. While they have branched out to different areas, these are all influencers in their respective domains.

Take the following individuals:

1.   Jacqueline Novogratz, a Stanford GSB MBA who founded the Acumen Fund that tackles global poverty.
2.   Nira Nundy, an HBS MBA who founded Dasra that empowers the underprivileged in India through philanthropic projects.

These are graduates from top business school who have taken a step beyond themselves to impact the lives of others. While an MBA does have an effect on your career, it has a domino effect on the world outside. Over the years, the MBA has produced many change makers in the world. You can also use your MBA degree to create work that positively influences other people's lives.

3. What are the Wrong Reasons to Earn an MBA?

When Rajneesh came to us, he was working in his family's retail electronics chain in Mumbai. The only reason he wanted an MBA was for the prestige of the degree. He repeated this several times during the session. He was a fresh graduate who believed that getting an MBA would translate to a 'fancy tag' against his name. I understood his mindset but decided to help him find deeper motivation.

An MBA does command respect. However, do not treat the degree like an accessory or a mere title. Understand the pros and cons of your choice and then arrive at a decision. This is exactly what we helped Rajneesh do. Over the next three years, he developed an active interest in business and realized his shortcomings. He applied not for a fancy tag but to build the skill set he needed.

However, prestige is just one bad reason. Here are a few others you should avoid:

3:A. Chasing the Bandwagon

Over 291,779 students applied for MBA programs in 2018. Needless to say, the MBA is very popular among students. This has also created a bandwagon mentality. A high number of students enroll in imitation of their peers or due to parental pressure, where the parents think doing an MBA is the ideal solution for them. This leads to disinterested students within programs. Try to understand the merits of doing an MBA given your personal aspirations and constraints. Don't follow the bandwagon blindly.

3:B. An Antidote to a Lacklustre Professional Life

An MBA vastly improves your professional prospects. However, it is not a magic wand that will suddenly make you happy and land you the job you wanted. Recruiting at top business schools is very competitive and you will have to work hard to land your dream job even with an MBA.

3:C. A Filler Between Jobs

If you are between jobs and wish to make good use of this time with an MBA, I will not discourage you. However, you should never let this be your only reason, as business school is not something you do in your free time. You could be changing careers, roles or looking for better opportunities. Whatever your reason, thoroughly question your rationale and ensure that this experience is right for you. Ensure that your rationale is business-oriented. Sometimes, people are unsure of their next career move. On other occasions, they may be unhappy with their current job or existing opportunities. Alternatively, they might have a general urge to get an advanced degree. These are all valid reasons to pursue an MBA.

With the right and wrong reasons for earning an MBA out of the way, let's explore what the program entails.

4. What is the Scope of an MBA Program

The curriculum and scope of teaching at MBA programs varies from school to school. However, let's broadly break these down into the one-year and two-year MBA to give you a flavor of what is taught in these popular programs.

4:A. Two-Year MBA (Full-Time MBA)

Year 1

The first term of an MBA program is usually the most challenging. Many core courses in finance, business operations, leadership, marketing, strategy and international business are taught among others. These are the essentials of business and will form your foundational knowledge. Some business schools allow a few electives in the first year, but the majority focus on a predetermined structure.

The first year also leads into the summer. This means the internship hunt will begin no sooner than half the year has passed. Summer internships are crucial, especially since many come with the promise of a full-time position if you perform well.

Year 2

The second term of a full-time MBA is very flexible. You can take a number of electives as per your interests, with limited core courses in the curriculum. This freedom allows you to specialize in an area of your choice. Here are some examples of electives that schools offer:

1. Technology Strategy
2. Public Policy
3. Globalization and Emerging Markets
4. Corporate Financial Operations
5. Leading Social Enterprise
6. Retailing
7. Negotiation
8. Consumer Behavior
9. Human Resource Management
10. Leadership in Action

These are just a few of the several elective courses that are offered by schools in the second year of a full-time MBA. Most MBA programs that fall under a larger university's umbrella also allow you to take courses from other departments of the university. For example, if you are doing your MBA at Yale SOM, you can cross-register for a course from any other college within Yale University. Some schools even allow you to cross-register for a course at a different university. For example, if you are doing an MBA at MIT Sloan, you can cross-register for select courses at Harvard and vice-versa.

The second year is also when you will be hunting for a full-time job through campus placement drives.

4:B. One-Year MBA (Accelerated MBA)

The one-year MBA or the accelerated MBA program is the two-year program condensed. Most of your time will be spent learning the fundamentals of business, alongside electives that you can pick. One-year MBA programs are divided into 'semesters' or 'periods' (like at INSEAD). These vary from school to school, as they look to impart fundamental business education while providing elective specialization. For example, INSEAD allows students to pick from over 75 different electives spread out across areas such as:

1. Accounting and Control
2. Decision Sciences
3. Economics and Political Science
4. Entrepreneurship and Family Enterprise
5. Finance
6. Marketing
7. Organizational Behavior
8. Strategy
9. Technology and Operations Management

Similarly, prominent one-year MBA programs such as those at Cambridge Judge, Kellogg and London Business School offer a myriad of electives that students can opt for. This course structure with electives weaved into business learning allows you to gain a business specialization in your field of interest.

Summer internships are largely absent owing to the short time frame of the program. However, some schools may make internships available to students through an extension of the duration by two or three months, or as part of the program itself. Examples of such programs are IMD Switzerland, Rotterdam School of Management and Cambridge Judge Business School.

The accelerated MBA is ideal for those with more work experience (six–eight years) looking to advance their business skills in a short duration or for students from an entrepreneurial or family business background. The compact form enables such candidates to earn their MBA and return to their profession without losing too much time.

5. Woman Power: Gender Diversity in the MBA Program

In an increasingly gender-equal world, it is expected that women get equal opportunity to fill leadership spots. The MBA degree produces global leaders, and eyes are set on top MBA programs to work towards this. Over the past five years, the male-female ratio at several top business schools has gradually climbed to 6:4. According to *The Financial Times,* the number of female applicants to business schools has grown to approximately 40 percent of the total applicant pool in 2017. This is seven percent more than in 2013.

While there is still a long way to go to achieve true parity, I believe the wind is blowing in the right direction. More women are interested in business studies now than ever. In fact, the GMAT global average records that 47 percent of the test takers in 2017 were women.

I would strongly urge my female readers to consider an MBA if they are interested in what it offers. An MBA, now more than ever, can help you shatter glass ceilings and enter management positions.

6. What Should I Do? Master of Business Administration or a Different Master's Program?

"The Master of XYZ program vs the MBA" is a question several of my students have grappled with over the years. When should you pick one over the other?

It depends on your long-term goals. Do you want to:

1. Start or develop your own business?
2. Understand various aspects of running an enterprise?
3. Fast-track your corporate career to managing people and having overarching responsibility for a department or function?

If you answered yes to any of the above questions, you should do an MBA over a different master's.

However, do a specialized master's degree if your goal is to:

1. Specialize in your current field
2. Pursue a PhD or research
3. Teach
4. Pursue a technical or domain-specific role

Note that many master's programs do not need any work experience while most top MBA programs will require work experience before you start the program.

7. How Much Work Experience Should You Gain Before Earning an MBA?

Most schools will not stipulate a specific amount of work experience; they will share an acceptable range. However, we have noticed that with at least three years of work experience, you are likely to have both, a higher volume and greater quality of work.

MBA programs are designed to help you transition to leadership. You are expected to absorb business concepts, apply them to real-world situations, and actively contribute to class discussions. This is usually possible only if you have been working for at least two years. Your practical experience can give you enough context and maturity to understand business situations. If you have had several internships and have worked in extremely challenging environments, you could get an MBA with lesser work experience.

Most American business schools will have a class age range of 22–32, with an average age of 27; for European business schools, the age range increases to 24–35, and the average age is 29–30. This translates to five or six years of work experience on an average. If you still want to apply with two years of experience, praiseworthy performance and strong goals should justify your decision. I urge my students to have three or more years of experience to build a competitive profile and be mentally prepared for business school.

At an early age, without much exposure to the workplace, your idea about the future is likely to be uninformed. With at least three years of experience, this changes. You will have encountered the workplace firsthand and developed a fair, realistic idea about your future and your goals.

If you decide to pursure an MBA while still in college, you can consider Yale's Silver Scholars Program, HBS's 2+2, the Young Leaders Program of the Indian School of Business, IESE's Young Talent, Booth's Scholars Programs and other similar programs. To be admitted to these, you need to be a high-performing candidate and apply in your final year of graduation.

Admissions to these programs are highly competitive. You need to be accomplished in the classroom and beyond. It is also recommended that you have strong reasons to do an early MBA. Remember that these programs are highly selective, accepting only 3–11 percent of the total applicants. To have a chance at being accepted, it is recommended that you make your application stand out. I suggest applying the profile-building fundamentals discussed later in this book two to four years before applying.

8. Evaluating Your Options

8:A. Differences Among Two-Year MBA, One-Year MBA and Executive MBA Programs

Program Type	What It Entails	Ideal For	Cons
Two-year MBA/Full	Immersive; allows potential career changers to evaluate their decision and strategize switch. Most full-time MBA programs are structured such that the first year is purely focused on the business curriculum. The second year has a liberal structure, where you can take on coursework from departments in the university outside of business. The full-time MBA enables holistic development. You can also intern during the summer break.	Those with two-seven years of work experience looking to enhance their business skills.	Tuition fee tends to be expensive: more than $150,000. Also exacts an opportunity cost. You will be choosing your MBA degree over two years of salary.

Program Type	What It Entails	Ideal For	Cons
One-year/ Accelerated MBA	Typically lasts between 10 and 18 months. These are intense programs without a summer break; lectures are conducted throughout most of the summer. So not much scope for internships.	Professionals who do not want a long career break. Ideal for people in situations where they can't be away from family for long (in case you are married, have kids, need to support aging parents, etc.).	Less time to network, intense academic learning and no break for internship opportunities.
Executive MBA	May be spread over one or two years, depending on the university. A large section of the class comes from corporate backgrounds and is sponsored by their companies. You can work while doing an Executive MBA, but you could be required to be on campus for some modules.	People further along in their careers. Those who have vast responsibilities at work and are looking to accelerate their careers. The typical age range for the Executive MBA is over 35 years.	Since you will be working while earning your Executive MBA, a hectic schedule is a natural consequence. Balancing your professional commitments with your academic ones becomes important.

Program Type	What It Entails	Ideal For	Cons
Online MBA	Provides a mobile and highly flexible solution to the MBA needs of professionals. However, students and faculty never meet in person, nor do students meet one another.	People who cannot travel, leave their current location or afford traditional MBA programs.	Since classes are virtual, networking opportunities are few. Also, because lectures are recorded and there is no interaction, the completion rates of students are low. Employers may also not find such a degree credible unless it is from a top school.

9. Reality Check: Busting Common MBA Myths

9:A. An MBA Is All I Need to Be at the Top of the Corporate Ladder

An MBA will not instantly translate to career success. It's just one stepping stone. Please form a realistic opinion by connecting with people in your field to understand their trajectories after their MBA.

An MBA is an enabler; it opens up opportunities. Success in the world of business takes an excellent work ethic, analytical skills, intelligence and ambition. Business school helps you develop these skills, but their honing and implementation are entirely up to you.

9:B. As an Indian Engineer, It Is Obvious I Need an MBA

Many engineering graduates in India consider an MBA the next logical step in their careers. However, this line of thinking may not work if you want to pursue a top MBA program abroad.

More than your marks in an entrance exam, top schools consider your rationale for doing an MBA. You will be required to justify to yourself and to the admissions committee why you want an MBA. Think about why you want to make the transition, what this change will mean for your career, how your work profile will change once you have the MBA, whether you really want to steer away from core engineering, etc.

10. Real People, Unique Skills, Common Errors: Analysis and Fixes

10:A. Adil was Confused Between a Master's Degree and an MBA

A: I think I should do an MA in Communications, VK... an MBA is not for me.
VK: You are trying to develop your own business. An MBA is the perfect choice for you!

Adil was a bright-eyed advertising fiend. After working for two years in a leading ad firm, he had begun his own practice with a colleague. Adil had big plans for his company. He wanted to develop his startup into a medium-sized enterprise. He believed that specialization with an MA in Communications would allow him to better develop his business.

This is when he approached me. While I understood his thought process, I pointed him in the right direction to ensure his education was better suited to his long-term goals. This required convincing him that an MBA, not an MA in Communications, was the right choice.

Adil was not convinced. The business concepts and quantitative reasoning modules in business school syllabi scared him and made him resist our advice. However, he was eventually convinced of the merits of an MBA. Alongside an education in business, it would allow him to attend the university's advanced courses in media and design. When he returned, he would have learnt more about advertising and how to grow his business.

He eventually saw the value of an MBA degree and decided to apply to business schools. That year, he was admitted to Kellogg's full-time MBA program.

After his graduation, Adil résuméd with his startup. Over five years after his return, they steadily grew to employ over 250 people in two Indian offices and now manage prestigious portfolios.

My Take

Adil's profile was definitely suited to a MA in Communications. However, his long-term goal was better fulfilled by an MBA. His learnings from business school would allow him to optimally run and develop his company after graduating.

A specialized master's would enhance your understanding of your field. However, that is better for those who wish to pursue research or specialize in these fields. An MBA is ideal if you wish to build you own business or occupy top management positions.

Ensure that your education takes your long-term goals into account and is not a myopic choice.

10:B. Tanisha Is a Model; She Wants to Advance Her Career

T: I have a non-traditional profile, VK… do you think it will pose any problem?
VK: As long as you can build a strong profile for business school and leverage it, not one bit.

Tanisha was a model with nine years' experience. She had realized the short life span of a career in modeling. When she approached me, she was unsure what to do to advance her career beyond its life span.

Through our career-counseling sessions, one thing was clear—fashion would remain Tanisha's passion. So we explored possibilities. She could begin her own fashion brand, be a fashion designer or set up a consulting service to help aspiring models. Upon deliberation, she leaned towards setting up her brand.

However, setting up a business requires an understanding of management, finance and operations. This could be achieved with an MBA. I floated the idea and nudged her in this direction. We decided to apply to business schools in Europe. Since Europe is a global fashion hub, we felt that a European MBA would also help her to leverage internship opportunities in France and Italy. Ultimately, she could return to India and start her label.

Tanisha worked with us over 15 months to build a profile worthy of an international business school. She was successfully admitted to a top European business school the next year. Today, she lives in India and runs a successful online apparel brand.

My Take

Non-traditional candidates like Tanisha, whose careers can run dry after a certain age, greatly benefit from the career advancement capability an MBA provides.

Like Tanisha, over the years we have had writers, actors, academic researchers, doctors, military personnel and even a chef successfully enter business school. While non-traditional candidates might have to work harder, profiles of those who have excelled in their field are always welcome.

10:C. Shirline Wants a Second MBA

> **S: I have lived in India all my life. I am looking for global exposure, but as a starting step would like to move somewhere in Asia. Should I join a multinational corporation with an Asian office and push for a transfer?**
>
> **VK: While that is a solid idea, chances of its success are low. I recommend getting an MBA.**
>
> **S: But I already have an MBA!**
>
> **VK: Yes, but I recommend getting one from abroad, now that you have more work experience.**

Shirline had earned her first MBA from IIM Ahmedabad when she was 22. After five years of working in business development in India, she wanted to relocate to an emerging economy in Asia, preferably Singapore or Malaysia. She had been working for a popular startup in Delhi and had helped it to acquire business of over Rs 3 crore in her first year.

When Shirline approached me, she was unsure how she could relocate. She thought she could move to a large multinational corporation (MNC) and seek a transfer to a location like Singapore, Malaysia or China. While her idea seemed great, I explained that the chances of it working were low. This was because Shirline's experience and expertise lay in the Indian market. Unfortunately, this expertise is not very relevant in another geography.

I suggested that she pursue a second MBA at a top Asian business school to build a global profile. This would also afford her placement opportunities in the country of her choice.

Shirline took my advice and pursued an MBA at INSEAD Singapore. After graduating, she worked in Singapore for two years for a London-based firm and now works at the London headquarters of the firm, traveling to Asia frequently. She is finally living the global life that she wanted.

My Take

Shirline's rationale for getting a second MBA was justified. In India, most top MBA programs start straight out of college. No work experience is required. While this system may be good for a career in India, candidates wishing to relocate globally will benefit from an MBA from a top global business school, as discussed in my point about earning an MBA to relocate.

Moreover, going to business school after working for a few years allows you to benefit more from the degree. Real world experience will make you an expert in your domain and potentially expose you to complex situations and dynamic team structures. You will be able to relate to and participate in classroom discussions and activities given your experience and exposure.

10:D. Uday Wants to Switch Careers

> **U: I have six years of experience in business development but want to switch to marketing, VK. How can I do that?**
> **VK: Consider an MBA. It is the ideal career-change degree.**

When Uday approached us, he was an established business development associate working in a small firm. Over the years, he had helped the business to grow and also worked closely with the marketing team. He enjoyed the world of marketing and developed an interest in the field. Soon, he wanted to switch to a role in marketing.

When he expressed this desire in a career-counseling session, my recommendation to him was to get an MBA. Uday was reluctant at first, mainly because of the cost and time involved. He felt that he could fast-track his career by spending one more year at work. If he chose to attend business school, he would miss out on a major product launch the next year.

While this was a valid concern, he had not weighed his options keeping his long-term goals in mind. While staying back would help Uday to advance his career in the short term, the MBA would make his career switch easier.

Uday saw the merits of an MBA and the avenues it would open up. We worked together over six months and helped him to justify his reasons and reemphasize his interest in the field in his essays. Next year, he applied to five European and American MBA programs and was accepted at three.

In business school, he took advanced courses in marketing and worked on several related projects. He was also the marketing lead in a few business plan competitions. This allowed him to gain an in-depth understanding of marketing. Upon graduating, Uday made a successful transition to a marketing role and now runs his own marketing startup in Chennai.

My Take

Admissions committees are receptive to career-switcher profiles as long as their decision is justified with a business-oriented rationale and their experience is impactful.

However, not all career switches will be aided equally by an MBA. For instance, it is easier to switch from Technical Operations to Product Management than from Professional Athletics to Product Management. However, it is still possible. If you wish to make such a switch, develop a definite plan for it. I cannot insist enough about the relevance of having a solid rationale for an MBA, whether it's a close switch or a far one. Additionally, you should give yourself more time before applying to build a compelling case and plan the journey.

I would encourage career switchers to consider an MBA. This is a totally valid reason.

10:E. *Devendra Wants to Outsource His Manufacturing to China*

D: I want to expand my business in China. What should I do? I want a good understanding of the business environment before I expand.
VK: An MBA will be ideal. You can perceive and adopt their business culture while earning the degree.

Devendra had begun working in his family business after his undergraduate degree in Commerce. He was 26 years old when he met me at an entrepreneurship summit, and wrote to me with his query soon after.

His family business in renewable energy had been growing steadily and he wished to expand its reach globally and set up a manufacturing plant in China to lower costs. Since he had little idea of what the Chinese market was like, he approached me for a solution.

Devendra needed two things for his expansion to be successful. First, an understanding of the Chinese business culture as well as how international business operates. Second, the expansion would require him to have a strong network within China to help him out. I thus recommended that he apply to the China Europe International Business School (CEIBS). Their 18-month MBA program would arm him with everything necessary for the expansion. At CEIBS, he could learn Chinese customs, understand manufacturing and operations in China, and network with others who are in the same boat as him and exchange ideas.

Once this rationale was clear, we worked with him on his applications and he successfully entered CEIBS. By the time Devendra graduated, he was ready to expand his business to China.

My Take

Devendra had a very specific rationale for his choice of business school. This was not the first time I had worked with a candidate like him. An MBA definitely benefits people with a family business who want to expand it to a different country. Since the expansion is global in scale, international business education is necessary to avoid future problems. The international exposure also enhances the candidate's understanding of the economy and business culture elsewhere. And the MBA ensures that you have a strong network of peers in China, ready to help and advise you. All this helps to make the transition smoother and enhances the candidate's leadership and management skills.

10:F. Deepika Wants to Relocate for Personal Reasons

> **D: VK, I need to relocate to Canada. What should I do?**
> **VK: Relocating mid-career requires you to have an advanced degree. Have you considered an MBA?**

Deepika had worked at a top consulting firm in India for over six years. When her sister married and moved to Canada, her parents followed suit. Deepika also wanted to relocate but found it difficult as an Indian professional to straight away land a job in a foreign country.

When she approached me, she wanted to relocate to Canada, but she also did not want to start over on the corporate ladder. Considering her requirements, I recommended that she apply to a Canadian business school. Getting into an MBA program in Canada would allow Deepika to use the university's recruiting resources. This would prevent having to downgrade her role and ensure she got placed adequately.

That year, I worked with Deepika and helped her get accepted at the Rotman School of Management. After graduating, Deepika was absorbed by a top investment bank in Canada. She had successfully relocated closer to her family.

My Take

Wanting to relocate to a different country is a valid reason to pursue an education there. If you are worried that changing geographies would mean you have to start over, an MBA can help. It allows you to spend your years of education in imbibing the local culture and it positions you to find a job locally. It also helps you to earn a degree that is both valid and valued from an international standpoint. Business schools will help you fine-tune your career search and provide opportunities through business fairs, alumni meets and similar activities.

The MBA, therefore, is an ideal choice for mid-career professionals who wish to relocate.

10:G. Avinash Wants to Work on Wall Street

A: VK, I have always wanted to work on Wall Street. Will an MBA help get me a job there?
VK: An MBA degree with a focus on finance will definitely help you towards such a goal.

Avinash had one dream: to work on Wall Street. The high-pressure, high-stakes environment it represented appealed to him. He had a successful stint with BlackRock, which he thought would help him get transferred to the company's Wall Street office. However, though BlackRock is a global brand, Avinash's work was limited to the Indian subcontinent. Thus, such a transfer was next to impossible.

He had already tried applying directly for jobs on Wall Street and been rejected several times. It was not hard to see why. While Avinash was capable, he had focused his time at BlackRock on the Indian equity markets. Though he managed a large portfolio, his skill set was not transferable to New York.

To fix this, Avinash initially wanted to pursue a master's in finance. When I read his profile and his long-term goals, I advised against such a move. A master's in finance was not the most optimal path for entering corporate positions. An MBA with a focus in finance was more suitable as it would prepare him for the role by combining finance education with business education. He could take advanced finance courses to strengthen his quantitative base and get exposed to financial instruments and asset classes prevalent in the West.

Furthermore, studying at top finance schools like NYU Stern and Columbia Business School (CBS) would allow Avinash to work at and intern with Wall Street companies. This would directly help his short-term goal of working on Wall Street as many companies offer full-time positions to students who intern with them.

Avinash took a long time to process my recommendation. This was a complete game-changer and not in line with his plans. However, he agreed eventually, and began working with us on his applications. He entered CBS that year. Today, Avinash holds a senior position in a Wall Street company.

My Take

Specific dreams and goals like Avinash's are also enabled by an MBA. While he was capable of landing a job on Wall Street, he needed to understand the US financial context first. An MBA greatly helped towards this end.

You could have a similar, specific goal, whether it is to work in Silicon Valley or to set up a business in another country. An MBA from business schools specialized in producing professionals in your field of choice will greatly enhance your chances of success.

10:H. Ketan Wants to Build His Social Enterprise

K: VK, I'm just a social entrepreneur… I don't think I need an MBA.

VK: To help influence change in the world, your enterprise needs to be around for some time. How will you sustain it for long without business skills?

Ketan met me after my talk at a business summit. I had spoken about how much my HBS MBA had helped me to grow and sustain my business. Over our chat, he expressed his wish to scale up his five-man social enterprise which helped displaced tribal communities to relocate and sustain themselves.

He was initially resistant to the idea of an MBA abroad. He thought that since his was a social enterprise, business education was not necessary to help him build it. I pointed out that even if its outlook was social, he was still running a corporation and business school would help him to acquire the skills to grow and sustain such an organization.

We kept in touch after our interaction and almost a month later, Ketan approached us for help with entering an MBA program.

I helped Ketan enter Babson's MBA program, where he found a contributor in a classmate. After his MBA, Ketan also started looking for other avenues to fund his enterprise. With the skills he developed through business plan competitions, he successfully pitched to the CSR units of several large corporations for a round of funding. Today, Ketan's enterprise employs over 50 people and is spread across India.

My Take

While social enterprises might be not-for-profit, they still need a sustainable model to survive. This is where an MBA comes in handy for individuals like Ketan as he would learn key business skills and how to efficiently manage day-to-day operations. The program would help transform him into a strong leader for his own enterprise.

Moreover, on-campus competitions allow you to attract funding for your enterprise and prepare you for similar pitches in the future. You might also find a friend at business school who would be interested in your work and offer to contribute or be on the board. Furthermore, some business schools may offer loan forgiveness programs and scholarships for people working in these spaces.

An MBA enriches social entrepreneurs with the skills necessary to sustain an organization that wishes to change the world.

10:I. Pooja Needs to Take over Her Family Business

> **P: VK, I have to take up my family's manufacturing business. I need the right skills and want the team to respect me.**
> **VK: I think an MBA is right for you.**

Pooja was an only child. Her family had a manufacturing business which she would soon have to take over. When she came to us, Pooja expressed her hesitation in doing so. It is difficult to take up and manage a manufacturing business in India as earning the respect of a team which is already in place is an important factor. An MBA from a top business school commands respect and would help her gain instant credibility in the eyes of her employees as someone capable of leading them. If she had more time on hand, Pooja could have pursued a top position at a different firm to build credibility before taking on the business. However, she had very little time as her father's health was deteriorating.

I recommended that she attend a one-year MBA program. Since she was to enter her family business, she would not need internship experience. Moreover, she would only be away from the business for a year and could still develop the required skills. When she returned, she would be in a position to lead the business in the right direction. Thus, the MBA was also an enabler which would solidify her position as her company's head.

I worked closely with her over 10 months, after which she applied to top Asian business schools. After spending a year abroad, Pooja returned to her family business armed with an MBA. Within three years, she was able to expand the reach of her business in India to two more locations.

My Take

I have worked with several people in family businesses like Pooja. For many, taking up the mantle of a large business is a daunting task.

Since many family business candidates start directly at a high position, credibility becomes crucial. Pooja would be leading and providing direction to employees who were up to 30 years older than her. Some would have spent 15 years in the organization. Earning their respect and ensuring she knew how to manage them effectively was important for her managerial success.

An MBA helps you gain business knowledge and a varied perspective on organizational problems. It also helps you develop a like-minded network that you can consult to get through difficult times. Furthermore, the international experience comes in handy if your business has international dealings. This makes the MBA an ideal degree for candidates from a family business background.

Insider Tips at a Glance

DO:

- ✓ Seek an MBA because it fits your long-term goals.
- ✓ Apply, even if you are a non-traditional applicant.
- ✓ Learn about the different types of MBAs and pick the one that is right for you.
- ✓ Aim for top business schools.
- ✓ Garner at least two years of substantial work experience before applying.
- ✓ Consider business school if you want to create large-scale impact.
- ✓ Evaluate the right program duration for you.

DON'T:

- X Go to business school because your friends are doing the same, or without a rationale that benefits your work.
- X Pursue an MBA to fill up your free time.
- X Apply to business school without introspection.
- X Assume that getting an MBA will make you a CEO overnight.
- X Shy away from getting a second MBA.

APPENDIX

Application Timeline

Application Rounds*	Application Deadline	Decisions
Early Action	August–September	October–November
Round 1	September–October	November–January
Round 2	November–January	January–March
Round 3	March–April	March–June
Round 4	March–May	April–May

* Schools can have anywhere from three to seven application rounds.

MBA Costs

Cost of an MBA (studying and living) in top countries in 2018 (all figures in US$):

Country	Average annual cost for MBA at top universities	Average annual cost of living*	Average annual total cost
The United States	62,500	12,000	74,500
The United Kingdom	56,000	13,000	69,000
Canada	40,000	13,000	53,000
Singapore	46,500	20,000	66,500
Germany	3,500	13,900	17,400

* The living costs can be altered based on how and where you choose to live.

2

Profile Building and Positioning: Setting Your Benchmark

This was Tanish Mishra a few years ago. He came from a family that had a manufacturing and logistics business. He had not joined it yet but was gathering experience at an MNC. Seeing his manager set targets, delegate tasks, hire and fire employees, he realized the complexity of being at the helm of a business. This made him realize he would need business education before he could manage his own company. He zeroed in on two schools that he really liked: Kellogg

School of Management and London Business School.

The short answer to Tanish's initial dilemma was this: "You don't have to build a profile around the schools' wants. Harness your strengths and passions and build a profile in line with your long-term personal and professional goals."

I helped Tanish build and position his profile in line with his strengths. He had strong academics, but given his long hours at work, he had scored 680 in his first GMAT attempt. He would need a higher score to make up for his limited work experience and extracurricular profile. Initially, he was unwilling to retake the GMAT owing to his tight work schedule. However, with some nudging, he did so and scored 720.

Since Tanish wished to apply with three years of experience, I asked him to leave the MNC and join his family business right away. He refused at first, since he felt underprepared and lacked the confidence to do this. So I asked him to work under the vice-president (VP) of the company instead of his father, to ensure he learns the business from the ground up.

He began working under the leadership and guidance of the company VP. This shift to the family business was done so that his positioning, 'MNC executive transitioning to take over the family business', was reinforced. This shift would also help Tanish to develop an understanding of the family business.

After these initial fixes, we continued to enhance his profile in line with his positioning, enabling his admission to LBS.

Let's demystify some of these terms for you.

1. What Does 'Profile Building' and 'Positioning' Mean?

Positioning is an overarching message that encapsulates your background, strengths and goals. Examples: 'Indian engineer transitioning to the public sector', 'accomplished musician with a vision to improve patent right for artists', 'female investment banker starting an online cosmetics company', etc. A simpler way of thinking of positioning is as a 200-character tweet or sentence that best describes who you are. Pause for a moment and think of your own positioning statement.

Profile building encapsulates working towards adding activities and experiences to your profile based on your strengths, interests or goals in line with your positioning statement. For example, if your positioning statement is 'teacher wanting to start ed-tech company', show your understanding of technology by taking some UI/UX/coding classes. Take on managerial roles at work to show your entrepreneurial side and showcase your accomplishments in the education sector to indicate your strong sectoral expertise.

Let us now explore how to put these strategies in action.

2. How to Build Your Profile and Arrive at a Positioning Statement

Profile building and positioning are like a chicken and egg situation. How you build your profile may lead to your positioning. Similarly, you could first arrive at a positioning statement and then build a profile.

If you are building your profile first, explore personal and professional experiences and activities in line with your strengths and passions. As you build a repertoire of experiences, a majority of these will get aligned in a certain direction, helping you to organically develop your positioning statement. Some consultants might suggest that you mold your candidacy by 'fixing your profile' in accordance with what your dream school supposedly looks for. My take on this is different. I recommend following your passion and staying authentic to yourself. Through trial and error, try to understand who you are and what is important for you. This introspective approach will augur well for you in the long run and lend honesty to your profile.

If you are clear about your goals and already have a positioning statement, start building experiences and accomplishments in line with it. This will allow you to delve deeper in your chosen direction, build expertise and enhance the authenticity of your positioning statement.

Your profile and positioning must show a trajectory: **where you began, what your future holds,** and **what defining and niche traits you have.** Think of it as building a brand. When you think of Elon Musk, you think "genius tech billionaire". Similarly, when the admissions officer reads an application, he should be able to capture your key traits and build a quick character sketch.

Factors such as your early years, the college you attended, what you studied there, any internships you did, all the extra-curricular, leadership and community activities you have been involved in, your full-time work experience, advanced certifications, projects completed, research you have done and more can all contribute to your profile. The admissions committee (AdCom) will scrutinize your entire background. Every year, every moment is accounted for. Make your time count.

Also, the stories behind the accomplishments make the application more compelling. The AdCom wants to know about the trials, tribulations and triumphs that have made you the person you are. It wishes to know what drives you, what shapes your ambition, what compels you to make a change.

Before we go any further, let's understand what the AdCom is.

3. What is the MBA Admissions Committee (AdCom)?

Business schools employ anywhere from 5-12 professionals who collectively form the admissions committee, hereafter referred to as the AdCom. The AdCom picks between 6 and 20 percent out of thousands of applications that are a perfect match with the MBA program of the school it works for. It ensures diversity of perspective from different countries, races and professional backgrounds in the program; unique skills and backgrounds are also encouraged.

This is not necessarily a group of only MBA graduates but a diverse group of individuals drawn from various backgrounds. It could comprise science, technology, engineering and math majors, PhDs, JDs, social science and humanities graduates. Professionals are drawn from academic, manufacturing, technology, consultancy, finance and other backgrounds. Their collective knowledge empowers them to understand a varied range of profiles.

The AdCom members are accessible individuals who will be happy to help you. I strongly suggest you engage with them at every opportunity; you can even start the process three to four years before you apply for an MBA. Interacting with the members early on and understanding how a school perceives candidates will give you a head start and hold you in good stead when you finally apply. The AdCom members have chosen this profession because they like engaging with bright individuals such as yourself, and in most cases will respond if you try to reach out. Give it a shot!

4. What Admissions Officers Want

There is no objective formula or checklist that will ensure your admission. Instead, your candidacy is a balance between your strengths and weaknesses.

Take Anuradha Roy, a 25-year-old chartered accountant who had also completed her Chartered Financial Analyst (CFA) certification. She had successful stints at top companies. Despite her accomplishments, she had a GMAT score of 690 and needed to take a career break for the next six months for personal reasons. Anuradha was fixated on these setbacks and saw them as detrimental to her application success. She was on the verge of giving up on applying to her dream colleges.

However, with some effort, she was still able to secure admission to a top business school. The AdCom recognized that given her CA and CFA certification, she would be able to handle the rigorous curriculum despite her GMAT score being below the school's average. Her career break was compensated for by a challenging and impactful four-year track record at work.

If a break means you were looking after a sick parent, the AdCom will accommodate this when reviewing your application. Similarly, a low GPA in the first two terms of college, followed by a stellar report card, will also be judged openly, accounting for other factors as well.

MBA admissions is a holistic process, not a linear one.

4:A. How Profile Building Helps the Application Process

1. Profile Building Can Help Your Application Gain Direction

Taking a long, hard look at your profile and questioning yourself on how you can excel in your chosen field will point you in the right direction. It helps you to identify where you lack skills or experience and to determine how you can grow. Solidifying your profile and positioning is the first and biggest step towards submitting a strong application; it sets a framework and foundation for your essays.

2. *Profile Building Can Lend Coherence to a Haphazard Application*

Over the years, I have worked with profiles that zigzag among many professional paths. Take Satish Dubey, for instance. When he began working on his application, he had two years of experience as Head of Technology at a small startup and was on the cusp of becoming a Product Manager at a large online retailer. His ultimate goal was to establish and manage his own technology-enabled NGO. He lacked business skills as he had never worked in a business function and had little display of leadership on his profile. While his experiences were interesting, they did not align well with his long-term goals.

To correct this alignment, I asked Satish to first complete his transition to the role of Product Manager. Once there, Satish had to actively push for projects and lead teams for these projects. I also recommended that he take up certified courses on leadership, management and business fundamentals; this would establish a business inclination in his profile. Next, I asked Satish to volunteer for a startup in the crowdfunding space for social enterprises as a technology advisor. All these suggestions were in line with Satish's core interests and were not simply thrust upon him.

Once this plan was in place, Satish began executing it over the next two years. When he finally applied, he was accepted at HEC Paris, his target school.

Imagine his initial profile without strategic building and positioning going to the AdCom. His application would have been misaligned with his long-term goals and the positioning would not have come through. He had no social enterprise experience apart from working for a year as a math tutor at an NGO. This made his long-term goal seem incongruent with his experience. Profile building helps you tie varied experiences together into a single story and give it the right direction. Further, it gives you a much better sense of your own interests and goals.

4:B. What AdComs Will Look At

1. Brand

Working for or studying at reputed organizations and institutions will have a 'quick-click' effect with the AdCom. Brands can be derived from a degree from a top college or an online certification or working with a well-known NGO or globally recognized organization. As someone who has studied at or worked with a large brand, you get associated with the high standards it represents. Additionally, such brands are recognizable and relatable. Leading business schools show a strong preference for graduates of top colleges and employees of premium firms across sectors.

The absence of a brand in your résumé is not a complete deal-breaker, but its presence can definitely aid you.

Caveat: While working with a big brand does add value to your profile, it is not the end-all. Your impact is what matters the most. You can have significant impact at a smaller organization or family business as compared to being at a junior level at a leading MNC. Opportunities abound in smaller organizations. They allow for more responsibility, greater visibility and therefore more avenues for you to make an impact.

2. Global Exposure

We live in an increasingly globalized world. Like it or not, the leaders of tomorrow will have to deal with global operational, legal, political and strategic business issues. Business schools want to ensure that you will be able to operate in this context. Therefore, having some form of global exposure (academic, professional or extracurricular) on your profile will help your application. This could range from actual on-site work abroad to a cross-borders project in your company while working domestically or even a short-term program from a top university abroad. This exposure will allow you to add more value to conversations inside the classroom and relate with your peers from different geographies.

3. Impact

Showing measurable impact makes your application stand out. For instance, having worked with top brands with limited impact is going to be less valuable than helping a small business develop into a medium-sized one by leading change. In the first case, the candidate is simply a subordinate with a brand. In the latter, the candidate is a change maker, which business schools favor.

4. Personality

Your personality is an amalgamation of the three factors above. The brands you have worked with, your exposure and the impact you make shape you.

Top business schools globally give a lot of weightage to personality alongside marks and experience. You will be given a fair chance if you can showcase diverse aspects of your personality and the impact you have made across your professional and community spaces in a compelling manner. Several people with 740+ GMAT scores and 3.9/4.0 GPAs get rejected by top schools every year. This is because they may not have been able to display a strong personality fit with the school.

What you put in your application says a lot about your personality. Think of this as a way of communicating with the AdCom before the interview.

5. What Comprises Your Profile?

Some of the most common questions I get asked by students are: "Is my profile good enough to be accepted at a top school?" or "Do I have to do community service to get accepted?"

No special weightage is assigned by AdComs to a particular section. To simplify the elements of what comprises your profile, we have divided the profile into five buckets. Each bucket targets a specific type of experience.

5:A. Academic Profile

This includes your educational record, your GMAT or GRE score, academic accomplishments, academic awards you have won, published research work, courses outside of your major and foreign language skills.

If you have moved to a profession that is unrelated to your field of study, have your academic profile reflect this. Take a few certifications or courses in your current field of work.

A strong academic profile is a prerequisite if you wish to apply to elite business schools such as Wharton, MIT Sloan, Stanford GSB and HBS. These schools set very high academic standards and are uncompromising when it comes to your academic profile.

Here is a brief look at the common weaknesses in this area and how they can be plugged:

Gaps	Advice
Low Grades	It is ideal that your college grades rank you among the top 10 percent. Ranking below 30 percent of your class is not ideal; you may compensate for this by excelling in online or onsite courses, pursuing additional diplomas and certification courses, etc. Target a strong GMAT score (710+) to compensate for your college scores and write compelling essays for a winning application.

Gaps	Advice
Low GMAT/GRE score	If you are aiming for top schools abroad, re-take the GMAT/GRE, unless there is something stellar in your overall profile. Target a test score within the range of the college you are applying to.
Not from a top institution (IIT, NIT, BITS, St. Stephen's, JNU and similarly well-known institutions)	Not a deal breaker. Ensure that your academic scores are strong and follow the steps advised for low grades. Online courses from top universities will add a brand to your profile.
Correspondence, online or part-time degree	Getting into a top business school will be challenging but not impossible. Ensure the institution granting you the degree is accredited and connect with the business school before you apply to confirm that they will recognize your degree.

5:B. Professional Profile

This is a record of the places you have worked for, your roles there, and what you achieved in those places. Your professional profile is an indicator of your future career trajectory as well. If you show no major growth in roles, impact, team managed, responsibilities, etc., or fail to explain this well on your application, you are positioning yourself as a stagnating professional. This is a red flag. Business schools look for professionals with steady and/or fast-track careers. They like applicants who have taken on tasks beyond their prescribed roles and are eager to learn and grasp more.

Here is a brief look at the common weaknesses in this area and how they can be plugged:

Gaps	Advice
No international experience	Though not a deal breaker, international experience is valuable on a profile. Explore opportunities at work that could lend this opportunity. If not possible, try to portray exceptional performance in your present role. Vast domestic experience also counts. You could explore opportunities where you are required to travel across India and work in different social and cultural environments.
No strong (Top 5/Fortune 500) corporate brands on profile	Aim to make solid impact at your current workplace so you are not overshadowed by branded peers.
Long gap in résumé	Make the most of your time away from a job. Use it to build your academic credentials. Learn a foreign language, build your extracurricular skillsets, etc. In your application, ensure that you explain how this time was used.
No internships in college	A lack of internships may be viewed as a negative if you have less than two years of experience. If this is the case, ensure your work profile is really strong.
Local experience in family or small business	This is not a weakness, but requires smart profile building and positioning. In a small business, you can show higher autonomy, ability to make big decisions with high stakes, and a broad perspective on running and operating a business.

5:C. Leadership Profile

Leadership roles you have occupied in your lifetime (more emphasis on positions held during and after college) are given weightage in your application. Outside of work, this includes positions held in extracurricular and community service roles. For example, being the Event Head for a festival or Editor of your college magazine counts towards your leadership profile. This reveals how adept you are at managerial and leadership skills.

Often, students have participated in various activities in college without 'leading' per se. Anogh, for instance, had a lot of activities under his belt from his college days due to his varied interests. He was a member of the cricket team, a core member at the college technology fest, and also participated in debates, but never took up leadership roles. Similarly, he had been working for two years at a large company and owing to his junior position was not given leadership of projects.

We asked Anogh to quit the large company and join a startup. Upon doing so, he was hired as Director of Strategy. He now had four people under him, had to manage them and worked directly with the CEO in making critical decisions on strategy. Since he was also passionate about debating, I asked Anogh to lead a vocational club for people interested in public speaking in the city. He did so, and soon advanced the club from having just one to 50 members.

This changed Anogh from being an excellent team player to being an excellent team leader, realizing the challenges and pitfalls a leader must face.

Here's a brief look at the common weaknesses in this area and how they can be plugged:

Gaps	Advice
No leadership experience	Look to lead or take the initiative on projects at the workplace or outside. Speak with your manager and see if you can take on more responsibilities. Also, try to learn leadership theoretically as well, through courses on leadership and management.

Gaps	Advice
Leading a project alone	You may be competing with peers that have led large teams. However, focus on explaining the impact you created and the obstacles you overcame.

5:D. Community Involvement Profile

The line from a John Donne poem, 'No man is an island entire of itself', is true even in the case of your MBA application profile. Individuals who work towards the welfare of the communities they inhabit showcase sensitivity and a willingness to help others. This could be in the form of working at the local animal shelter, with the local municipal body in planning a clean-up drive or something as simple as your involvement with an NGO.

However, do not try to check off the 'community service' box and start volunteering three months before your MBA application. It will look phony. If you are inclined towards impacting your community, pick a cause you believe in and help further it actively and consistently over many years. If your work does not permit time for a community cause, so be it. Do not force fit or fake this on an application.

Here's a brief look at common weaknesses in this area and how they can be plugged:

Gaps	Advice
Worked in a generic volunteering role	You may be working really hard as a fellow or teacher at Teach for India, but there are a thousand more teachers like you. How do you stand out? Highlight specific cases, how you effected change and showed initiative beyond what the role demanded.

Gaps	Advice
No time for community work given long work hours	Work with your company's CSR department and get actively involved with a cause or initiate one.

5:E. *Extracurricular Profile*

Extracurricular activities include anything you have done outside the requisites of your career path or education. This is one place where you can really stand out.

Here, you can add to the depth and diversity of your profile. Your niche hobbies, skills, sports experiences, passions, etc., can set you apart from thousands of other applications.

Here's a brief look at the common weaknesses in this area and how they can be plugged:

Gaps	Advice
I have no substantial extracurricular activities	Take up a hobby and trying to excel at it. For example, if you want to add to your extracurricular activities and improve your public-speaking skills at the same time, join a local Toastmasters chapter.
All my extracurriculars are from my school and high-school days	Do NOT include these unless they are truly EX-TRAordinary feats like breaking world/national/state/city records, competing internationally/nationally/at the state/city level in a sport, and so on.

Now that we know what the AdCom values as traits in incoming applicants, start acting on this information.

6. How to Build Your Profile and Position Your Application

There is no 'one size fits all' approach to building a profile. You have to first assess your strengths and weaknesses. Next, you must gauge how much time you have before the application deadline. Finally, you should strategize how to use this time effectively.

However, before we dive into these steps, let us ensure you understand what profiling does NOT mean.

6:A. Profiling Does NOT Mean Faking It

I understand the pressure to make the best impression on the AdCom. Nevertheless, do not give in to the urge to lie or build an inauthentic profile. Truth will take you farther than lies; here's why:

I. **The AdCom is experienced and can detect lies.** You are not submitting your application to a machine that processes the application based on an algorithm and decides your fate. You are submitting it to the AdCom, which comprises seasoned professionals who have been in the field long enough to be able to spot a lie or a faked trait on an application, no matter how you try to veil it.

II. **Ultimately, it's about your own ethics.** Do not lie and cheat your way into an MBA program. A good ethical code will definitely assist you in your business and in life as well.

6:B. What are the Two Primary Aspects of Profile Building?

What is YOUR personal brand? What do YOU stand for? What are your VALUES, MISSION and VISION? Business schools want you for the brand you bring and the diversity it brings to the class. You can display this effectively through profile building and positioning.

Profile building can broadly be broken down into two parts. First, understanding and reinforcing your profile and its traits. Then, ensuring that severe weaknesses are plugged (for example, failed courses, bad GMAT scores, lack of leadership experience, etc.).

Let us now look at these two components in depth.

1. *How to Strengthen Your Profile*

Direct the spotlight at everything you are good at and aim to actively strengthen it. You can understand these strengths in several ways. Here are a few:

a. Self-Analysis

Self-analysis of your profile and its different buckets is the first and most crucial aspect of profiling. This should come from a truthful place devoid of your personal biases.

To identify your strengths and weaknesses, ask yourself these questions and answer them truthfully.

Strength Analysis

1. What am I passionate about?

2. What are my values as an individual?

3. Is my current career in line with my passion?

4. How does my career inspire me?

5. What individual traits do my answers above display? Can I be seen as someone who can lead? Someone with good interpersonal skills? Someone who is intelligent and excels in academics?

6. How can I strengthen the display of these traits?

Weakness Analysis

1. Am I lacking severely in any of my profile buckets?

2. If yes, how can I plug that gap?

3. How many months do I have to plug that gap?

4. Can my strengths compensate for this gap?

With these answered, you begin to give your profile a definite shape. First, begin capitalizing on your strengths. If weaknesses exist, work actively to plug them; no mental gymnastics you perform will plug them otherwise.

However, since this is a personal assessment, your biases may still cloud your judgment. This could be plugged by approaching a third party, as discussed in the next two methods.

b. Analysis Through Friends, Family and Loved Ones

This should be done only after a self-analysis. Take what you have gathered through the self-analysis to a friend or family member. This will give you a truthful view of your profile and is a great way of eliminating biases that you might harbor about yourself.

However, even an analysis through friends, family members or loved ones could be biased, inexperienced or even uninformed. While they have your best interests at heart, they might not have adequate information to share an informed perspective. You should choose wisely from what you are told.

c. Analysis Through an Unbiased Third Party

Working with an unbiased third party is a sure-shot way of building a profile that is most reflective of you. Professional consultants, given their expertise in the area, are a smart choice. They can give you unbiased advice and help you to build a strong profile.

The only caveat here is that good advice comes at a cost and a high-quality consultant will command a high price for his advice and experience.

2. How to Plug Gaps

After gathering information on what your profile lacks, categorize it into the buckets described in Section 3 of this chapter. For instance, if you lack leadership experience, list it as a weakness in the Leadership Profile bucket. You can use the worksheet in this chapter's appendix for this.

Depending on the nature of the gap, see if it is compensated for by a display of strength in other areas of your profile. For instance, average grades could be justified by emphasizing that you were heavily invested in extracurricular activities at that time. Though this does not remedy poor academic performance, it contextualizes your scores.

Ideally, it is best to tackle the problem at its source rather than providing a justification. For instance, the academic gap can be addressed by providing a strong GMAT score or taking up a course and obtaining marks more reflective of your abilities.

However, balancing your profile is an extremely complicated task and takes years to master. There is no precise formula for cracking it.

6:C. Profiling Needs Patience and Time

Sandeep approached me about three months before the submission deadline. In our first counseling session, I noticed he had no extracurricular activities. Even at his workplace, his progress had scope for improvement. Due to personal issues he scored 660 in his first GMAT attempt. His profile needed improvement across the buckets and would take at least a year to build. So I advised him to wait and apply next year.

His initial reaction was negative since Sandeep and his parents were eager to "finish off" his studies. To this end, they were fine with settling for an obscure business school. I had to explain to them the tradeoff involved in attending an average business school over strengthening the profile and finally entering a top school. Once they were convinced, we worked together over 15 months to address the weaknesses and build a strong profile.

First, I asked him to focus on improving his workplace performance. He spoke with his manager and was given a core role in a company project. Then, I asked Sandeep to retake the GMAT, this time with at least two months of preparation. In his second attempt, he improved his score by 30 points, scoring 690.

After applying some more strategic fixes to his profile, Sandeep was ready to apply. He was ultimately accepted at HKUST in Hong Kong, his dream school.

Filling gaps in your profile should be done with patience. It takes time to convert a weak profile into a strong one. In fact, I advise that you begin building a good profile as early as four years before applying to an MBA program for best results.

However, building a strong profile is not enough. You must be able to position it correctly to have the maximum impact. Let's now explore how you can do so.

7. How to Position Your Profile Effectively: Two Approaches

7:A. Positioning in Line With Your Passion

Aligning your positioning statement with your passion is ideal. This is possible only if you have pursued your core passion through your academic and professional years.

Let's say you are passionate about math. You have scored extremely well in high school, pursued a degree in mathematics, and have since been working in a quantitative role. In the future, you want to start a quantitative hedge fund. In this case, your past, present and future all align with your core passion. This allows you to build a really strong positioning statement around your passion.

7:B. Positioning in Line With Your Strengths

While it is great to position according to your passion, this is not always possible. You might have chosen a professional path tangentially different from your passion.

For example, Nimish had always been passionate about food. He experimented with recipes on weekends and was determined to start his own restaurant some time in the future. Food was definitely his core passion. However, he was a product manager and had studied engineering. His professional strengths were in technology design and UI/UX. Clearly, his demonstrated strengths were strikingly different from his primary passion. In such cases, I recommend sticking to your demonstrated strengths over your passion when determining your positioning statement. Business schools will always seek evidence of accomplishment in fields you claim to be passionate about.

7:C. Positioning With Respect to the School You Are Applying to

I do not recommend this approach as people sound phony when they exclusively cater to a school's expectations and force-fit their actions to align with the school's mission.

However, knowing what the school wants can indicate traits you must emphasize on your application. For instance, if the school says it wants socially minded individuals, like Yale School of Management does, shine the spotlight on such experiences. This will also show that you are aligned with the school's philosophy and interested in what it has to offer. Again, do not just conjure something up to fake an alignment.

8. Why Social Media Presence Is Also Important

In the age of the internet, your profile includes your social media presence. If you wish to make a good impression on the AdCom, keep your social media profiles updated and in check. Keep in mind that AdComs could check these to validate your candidacy.

It is advised that you have a profile that is sober at the very least. Having, for instance, that picture of you drunk, captioned 'The best life is the high life', is not ideal.

You can also use social media to your advantage. For example, if you are interested in a certain area, your Quora, Twitter or Instagram profile and posts could showcase you as an influencer in that field. Your LinkedIn profile and presence also say a lot about your interests. How often you share, post or comment, the people who interact with you, any groups or online communities you manage, etc., could show your genuine interest in a field or topic.

9. Non-Traditional Profile? No Problem!

Traditional profiles at MBA programs have common backgrounds such as finance, consulting and tech professionals. On the other hand, non-traditional profiles include backgrounds in pure humanities (designers, writers, artists, etc.), the performing arts (actors, dancers, musicians, etc.) or pure sciences (doctors, researchers, scientists, etc.).

If you have a non-traditional profile, an MBA can help you enter managerial roles in your field or begin your own enterprise. MBA programs value the diversity that non-traditional profiles bring. However, you will still be evaluated against the rest of the applicants and you must ensure that your profile is competitive.

Here is a table to help you navigate profile building with a non-traditional profile:

Professional	As in other areas, you need to establish managerial and business interests here. If you are a performing artist or researcher, let your professional record reflect it. Also, address how an MBA aligns with your professional goals. E.g., if you are a journalist, talk about the number of articles you have published and the domain of expertise you have picked up that can be directly transferred to your post-MBA goals.
Academic	Strengthen this with relevant short-term courses and certifications from top universities. Also, take courses to strengthen your quantitative skills if your profile doesn't reflect that, or if you are from a non-quant background.
Leadership	While this could be difficult for people like solo artists, take up more responsibility and lead on a project. If you do not have this, don't force-fill.
Community Involvement	Organize/perform a cultural event for a charitable trust if you are a performer; alternatively, get working with an NGO or a cause you care about.

10. Reality Check: Busting Common Profiling Myths

10:A. My Profile Needs to Be Strong in All Buckets

Have you met the person who is always out to please everyone? More often than not, such a person ends up pleasing none. This is true of the application as well. You cannot expect to have the strengths of a financial consultant as well as a techie. If you try this, you will spread your application thin and show a lack of direction and focus.

10:B. My Profile Is Weak, I Am Doomed

While a weak profile should be your top concern, do not use this as an excuse to give up your MBA dream. Your profile includes everything you do right up to the date of being accepted; keep working on it. Use my suggestions and actively seek to iron out any weaknesses without wallowing in self-pity.

10:C. I Have Not Studied at an IIT, I Will Never Be Admitted

Colleges such as IIT, BITS, VIT, NIT, SRCC, St. Stephen's and JNU are premium educational brands. I will not lie; brands like these add value to your profile and schools definitely respect students who have graduated from these colleges. However, many B-schools are open to students not from these institutes. You will not be dismissed for being from a lesser known college. I have helped students who did not attend the top 10 Indian institutes get into the top 10 global business schools. It is possible.

10:D. I Have Not Worked for a Big Brand, My Profile Is Not Competitive

Top schools place importance on the impact you make at your workplace. At a large branded organization, you may have a junior role and therefore limited responsibilities, leading to limited impact. However, at a small unbranded startup, you may have a frontline role driving the growth of the entire business. There is no 'one-size-fits-all' rule when it comes to having a top brand on your profile.

10:E. I Will Be Admitted with Less Than a Year of Experience Because I Was a Topper in College

Kudos to you if you are a topper. It is a significant achievement. However, this does not translate to MBA admissions success. As mentioned before, AdComs look at your holistic profile. Topper status must come with good professional work, extracurricular activities and the other characteristics described earlier in this chapter that constitute a strong profile. If this is not present, the profile is simply not impactful and only has strong academics going for it. If you have only a year of work experience, I would suggest garnering more before applying.

11. Real People, Unique Skills, Common Errors: Analysis and Fixes

11:A. Avanti Tries to Check All the Boxes

A: But VK, doesn't my profile have to be strong across all buckets? VK: No. Keep the spotlight on your strengths and stop trying to force-fill buckets.

Avanti had a quantitative background as a Chartered Accountant but worked as operations head for a fast-growing startup. She also claimed to be a professional dancer who regularly performed across the city and would volunteer at an orphanage on weekends. Avanti was also interested in digital marketing and had completed two online courses for it.

You get the idea. Her profile was fairly strong and well rounded. However, when I was reading her profile, the first question that arose was, "So... what exactly does she want to do?"

Because Avanti was trying to be an all-rounder, she failed to show how all her accomplishments fit one overarching theme, or even her long-term goals.

My Take

Avanti should have been using her time to do relevant coursework in line with her goals and strengthen her profile accordingly. Instead, she chose to do marketing courses while working as an operations head. This would send conflicting messages unless she was trying to transition to a marketing role (which she was not).

Also, if you already have a 16-hour day job and are pursuing dance professionally, then one may question how you excel at all of this. It is not long before such a profile starts sounding fake or too thinly spread. If you are indeed this talented, make sure you can substantiate your claims with recommendations from a credible source who can vouch for your all-round excellence.

Avanti's profile showed a sense of awareness of the community and its culture. This achieved the unique niche of a quant who isn't entirely technical and can be creative. While revisiting her profile during our counseling sessions, her conception as the 'culturally savvy quant' came into being. Once we drew this positioning statement out, we removed focus from things that did not align with her profile, and directed it towards experiences that did.

Do not try to diversify and waver your profile's focus. Stay on message.

11:B. *Deepak Thought It Was Too Late (It Wasn't)*

**D: I am 29, VK… do I have to give up on my business school dream?
VK: Not one bit. Your experience is perfectly ripe for an MBA, in fact.**

Deepak grew up in a district in Bihar before making his way to a top IIT for a Chemical Engineering degree. At IIT, his interests moved towards design, UI, UX and coding. His passions led him to make his career as a Product Manager instead of a Chemical Engineer. He was 29 when he approached us and had not consciously built his profile to earn an MBA.

His MBA aspirations were uncovered during a résumé-editing service, when he asked us if it was too late for him to apply to business school. For American schools, where the average class age is around 27, Deepak was late. However, European and Asian business schools, with an average class age of 29–30, were still open to him.

I put him on the treadmill over the next year and had him report back every six to eight weeks to gauge his progress. I helped Deepak refine his positioning statement and build his profile in alignment with it. Soon, he applied to his target colleges and was finally accepted at ESADE.

My Take

Let's clear this: it is never too late to build your profile. Profile building is not just a means to get an admit. It holds you in good stead for life. In Deepak's case, he graduated from business school at 31 and immediately launched his own design agency. The brainstorming we did gave him a stable vision for the rest of his career. The MBA acted as a catalyst towards that vision.

The minute you realize you want to apply to business school, start taking stock of your profile and figure out how to best structure and strengthen it. Even once you apply, during and after the interview phase, you should continue building your profile.

Professionals late in their careers can still obtain an MBA. It is never too late to work towards this dream.

11:C. *Meghna Was in the Same Company for Five Years: Depth Can Triumph over Breadth*

M: Should I change my company, VK? I have been here for over five years.

VK: That is not a negative! As long as you have been making progress and creating impact at your current workplace, you are in a good spot.

Meghna was concerned that five years in the same company would project her as uni-dimensional. However, she had great depth of experience, considering how deeply invested she was in the industry. She had started off in a junior role but began handling bigger clients in the first year itself. Over the next four years, she saw regular promotions and was even invited as a guest speaker on several industry panels.

I worked with Meghna over a year and helped her to reemphasize her commitment to her industry. We positioned her as an expert in her field. When she did apply, she successfully entered Ross Business School in Michigan.

My Take

Many MBA aspirants seem to aim for a breadth of experience, i.e., having a profile across careers, industries or roles. Albeit beneficial, breadth will not magically get you accepted at a business school. Experience and specialization are not overlooked by the AdCom.

Working in the same company for many years does not act against you. Ensure that your experience is intensive, you have shown steady growth and made an impact instead of trying to aimlessly diversify. I have seen individuals specialized in single roles get accepted into top MBA programs and those with diverse profiles get rejected. The niche category of being a domain specialist can help you add significant value to MBA classrooms.

11:D. Tejal Thought International Experience Was Compulsory

> **T: I have never worked outside India. Can I still make it to a top-tier school?**
>
> **VK: Why not? As long as you have been able to produce results here, you are good to go.**

If you looked at Tejal's profile, you would find nothing wrong. She had approached me in a state of panic three months before the application deadline. Her nagging worry was that she did not have any international experience. This meant that her work was confined to the Indian subcontinent.

My first task was to clear her misconception that a top MBA program would not accept her without any international experience.

My Take

Tejal had a GMAT score of 720 and great scores in her undergraduate courses alongside other certifications. She had also worked with some of India's biggest NGOs in her undergraduate years. She had been running her own startup for the past three years, had completed two rounds of funding, and was on the verge of breaking even. She had excelled at her entrepreneurial venture. Even without international experience, she had a strong profile.

However, Tejal was ready to wind up her successful startup and move to London to pursue a job. Most of my sessions with her were spent convincing her of the merits of her profile even without this international experience. I finally persuaded her to apply to business schools and worked on projecting her entrepreneurial positioning on her essays. She was finally accepted that year at NYU Stern and Columbia Business School.

Tejal's story validates that top schools look for 'what' impact you create, not just 'where' you create it.

11:E. Brands Do Matter

T: But didn't you say impact is the most important factor?
VK: Correct. However, in your case, the impact is lacking and a strong brand can help you to compensate.

Tarun had approached us for a three-school rejection analysis. He seemed perplexed about being rejected by three business schools. In my first conversation with him, Tarun laid out his expectation of entering a European business school, preferably INSEAD, ESADE or Oxford Said.

Tarun had been working at a small startup for four years as a Finance Associate. The startup was deep in the red, still unfunded, and he was one of six employees at the firm. His past experience, too, was with lesser known companies. Though he had four years of work experience, Tarun's profile lacked strong brands and demonstrated limited professional impact.

My Take

Tarun held a job title that sounded impressive. However, he only had domestic experience dealing with transactions of a few lakh rupees and a handful of vendors and clients who were also unknown.

I advised Tarun to transition to a leading financial firm, even if that meant starting a rung lower and not being the head of the department. He would work on higher value transactions, interact with colleagues globally and work directly under the mentorship of the Head of Finance, who would also write his recommendation. When he applied to business schools that year, he was accepted at Oxford Said. While we did work on other areas (community involvement) of his profile, his experience working with a top brand definitely made the biggest impact.

11:F. Wealth Does Not Translate to an Admit

S: VK, my company's turnover is over a billion dollars and my father is among India's leading businessmen. I should have no problem getting accepted at Harvard.

VK: While your family business gives you a great platform, you will still need to prove your personal merit to get into Harvard.

Shrikant was heir to a large family business. He had just returned after earning an undergraduate degree in the UK and was adjusting to the corporate culture in India. A year into his work, he approached me, wanting to apply to business school. Shrikant was under the impression that since he came from a reputed business family, business schools would readily accept him. However, this is not the case.

I had to explain to Shrikant that business schools evaluate candidates on the basis of their personal merits and accomplishments. Regardless of his family's brand, I advised him to not overlook the profile-building phase. To ensure his spot at a top school, he would have to start at the bottom of his family business and work his way up to a senior leadership role. This would take at least three years. Cracking Harvard admissions is no cakewalk.

On my advice, Shrikant started rotating through the operations strategy, business development and finance departments. He realized he had a propensity towards international business development and began working in that function. Soon, he was traveling all over North America and Europe, signing multimillion-dollar deals with large companies. Over time, Shrikant became accountable for the revenue generation of the entire organization.

As I guided Shrikant over four years, I noticed his self-confidence shoot up in tandem with his stellar profile. When he finally did get his admit to Harvard, he knew he had earned it.

My Take

Shrikant's case relates primarily to candidates from business families. A large business inheritance does not grant you instant admission to top business schools. You still have to build a strong profile.

First, find your place within the family business. Join the business in a role that you are passionate about and deliver in that role, like Shrikant did. Additionally, such experience helps you to come to terms with the realities of running a business. This process is both fulfilling and goes a long way in nurturing you as a professional.

12. The Errors in a Nutshell

12:A. *Trying to Force-Fill All Profile Buckets Equally*

Your profile should have an overall theme and must tie in with your long-term goals. Do not populate it with random activities.

Insider Tips

1. Focus on your strengths and emphasize them.
2. Ensure that the activities you choose are congruous with your long-term goals.
3. Don't attempt to check all boxes.

12:B. *Thinking That It Is Too Late to Position Correctly*

Applicants fall into the trap of thinking it is too late to build a strong profile. This is seldom true.

Insider Tips

1. You can build a strong profile, no matter how old you are.
2. We recommend working on your profile until you get your admit letter.
3. Sometimes we also continue profile building until the candidates start their programs.

12:C. *Thinking of Depth of Experience as a Negative*

This is common hearsay about the requirements of a business school. Refrain from believing this.

Insider Tips

1. Your profile does not have to be spread out thinly across roles and industries to get into a business school.
2. Depth of experience can actually establish you as a specialist and allow you a niche status in the applicant pool.

12:D. Thinking You Cannot Make It Without International Experience

It is untrue that international experience is mandatory to get admitted to a top business school.

Insider Tips

1. If you can, definitely work internationally, not just for your MBA application but also because it is an invaluable learning experience.
2. Even if you are located in India, try to work with your global counterparts by exploring cross-border opportunities within your organization or working domestically on international projects.
3. Rich domestic experience is also valued. Impactful experience at large Indian corporations, startup experience or founding your own organization will hold you in good stead.

12:E. Thinking That Brands Can(not) Impact Your Candidacy

Having a well-recognized brand on your profile can enhance it. However, working at a small company with more impact can outdo a job with a brand.

Insider Tips

1. When deciding on employment opportunities, look for companies that will allow you to make a significant impact.
2. When working for a big brand, ensure you are working with your manager to get frontline responsibilities.

12:F. *Thinking You Won't Have to Work Hard If You Are from a Prominent Business Family*

Being from a business background can work in your favor. However, you still need to prove your mettle.

Insider Tips

1. Join your family's business in a role you are passionate about, get decision-making authority and show positive impact.
2. Understand your business to determine how best you can leverage business school for further growth.

Insider Tips at a Glance

DO:

✓ Start working on your profile as early as possible.

✓ Thoroughly analyze and ensure that you frame a strong positioning statement in line with your strengths/passions.

✓ Ensure that your application validates the overall message of your profile.

✓ Identify gaps in your profile.

✓ Work actively to plug glaring gaps and address smaller gaps in your profile.

✓ Know that it is never too late.

✓ Keep your long-term goals in mind.

✓ Seek to work at top brands if your experience has been insubstantial at smaller ones.

✓ Apply when your profile is ready.

DON'T:

X Create an unrealistic positioning statement.

X Look for breadth of experience for the sake of it.

X Be fixated on small gaps in your profile.

X Shy away from connecting with the AdCom.

X Be inconsistent in your profile's messaging.

X Assume business school will accept you just because your family owns a large business.

X Assume that not having international experience will lead business schools to reject you.

X Pick passion over demonstrated strengths when writing your positioning statement.

X Rush your MBA.

X Shy away from business school just because you are a writer or a musician.

APPENDIX

Profiling Worksheet

Use this worksheet to chart your strengths and areas for improvement. Once you have filled this in, begin working on them as discussed in the chapter.

	Strengths	**Areas for Improvement**
Professional	1. ______________ 2. ______________ 3. ______________	1. ______________ 2. ______________ 3. ______________
Academic	1. ______________ 2. ______________ 3. ______________	1. ______________ 2. ______________ 3. ______________
Leadership	1. ______________ 2. ______________ 3. ______________	1. ______________ 2. ______________ 3. ______________
Community Involvement	1. ______________ 2. ______________ 3. ______________	1. ______________ 2. ______________ 3. ______________
Extracurricular	1. ______________ 2. ______________ 3. ______________	1. ______________ 2. ______________ 3. ______________

3

GMAT and GRE:
How to Ace Standardized Testing

Dear VK,

Thank you for helping me build my profile over the past few months. While most other areas of my profile look solid now, my GMAT score is not strong.

I do not want to take the test a third time, VK. How much do business schools care about my scores? Is there a cut-off for specific schools?

Standardized tests like GMAT and GRE are objective markers of your current intellectual aptitude. This is what makes them important for admissions officers at top business schools.

When Adish Raja sent me this email, he was seven months away from applying. His profile was slowly shaping up to be rock solid, but his GMAT scores left a lot to be desired. In his first two attempts, Adish had scored 650 and 670, respectively. He mentioned that he had taken both attempts "casually" since he "did not enjoy taking tests". Understandably, he did not want to retake the GMAT.

However, the GMAT was still an important component of his application. The GMAT/GRE tests your analytical and verbal skills alongside your ability to extrapolate matter and read between the lines. At a business school, you need to be articulate and analytical in your approach to common problems. Whether Adish liked it or not, his application would be judged with the GMAT score.

On my advice, Adish made one last, sincere attempt at the GMAT. This time he was focused and spent six weeks doing rigorous practice for the tests. His hectic work schedule did not allow him much time, but we planned on working around it and putting in at least two hours of work every day. His effort paid off, and his score jumped by 40 points to 710. That year, Adish was accepted at INSEAD and National University of Singapore.

Evidently, prioritizing tasks and having a strategy delivers results. Work on your strengths and weaknesses, figure out a suitable learning method, and keep track of your progress. Some students are able to study the most in the early hours while some work well with peers. For Adish, it was about dedicating a few focused hours every day.

I explained earlier that the AdCom reviews the applications holistically; the GMAT/GRE score is a key metric in the evaluation process. A strong GMAT/GRE score testifies to your intellectual potential and sets you apart from your peers.

However, focusing only on your GMAT/GRE at the cost of your overall profile is not ideal. The GMAT/GRE score is only one data point for the school. You could score higher than the 95th on a test and still get rejected if other parts of your application are weak.

Why do business schools need these test scores? Let's find out.

1. What Admissions Officers Want

Let us first discuss scores. Most top business schools have a GMAT range of 620-780 and a GRE range of 305-330. Their median scores lie around 700 for the GMAT, and 330 for the GRE (refer to the table in the appendix for median GMAT/GRE scores at top global business schools). If your scores match the median score of your chosen schools; you are exhibiting your proficiency in test-taking at the median level acceptable to the school. You do not need to reach a minimum threshold score to apply to top business schools; there is no 'cut-off' where only scores above a certain number will be considered.

Then why do schools ask for the GMAT or GRE test scores in the first place? While each school has its own reasons, let me explain three primary ones:

a. An Objective Scoring of Your Abilities

The GMAT and GRE have binary responses, i.e., each answer is either correct or incorrect. The responses are not qualitative in nature, nor are there multiple correct answers. There is no room for evaluator's bias or judgment when correcting these tests. This ensures that everyone is evaluated objectively on the same metrics.

This objectivity allows various applications from diverse backgrounds to be judged and standardized on the basis of these results. AdComs are frequently inundated with applications from around the world. These are from applicants who have studied various degrees from a multitude of colleges and received scores calibrated in percentages, 4.0 scales, 5.0 scales, grades, on a scale of 10, etc. Sounds overwhelming? Well, it is.

This diversity in the applicant pool can lead to a situation of comparing apples with oranges. How does one compare an 8.9 CGPA from IIT Bombay with a 78 percentage from Beijing University? Is 8.9/10 a better score than 78/100? To add more confusion, how will the comparison change if one score was for economics and the other for aeronautical engineering? Doesn't the program within the college matter when looking at grades? Which among economics and aeronautical engineering is the tougher degree to score in? This further leads to the question, how competitive is the university from which you earned your degree? Is IIT Bombay more difficult to score higher marks in than IIT Delhi? There are many layers to this complex conundrum, making the AdCom's job difficult.

The GMAT/GRE score alleviates this complexity by allowing the AdCom to look at a number that is standardized across all test takers regardless of gender, race, location, etc. All applicants are viewed through the same lens, enabling the AdCcom to make an apples-to-apples comparison.

b. Determinants of Your Success in Business School

AdComs at top business schools need to ensure that students can keep up with the academic intensity of the MBA program; else, they will be doing you and your peers a disservice. While the GMAT and GRE may not be perfect tools, they judge your intellect and understanding of quantitative areas, reasoning and language. A high score does indicate a positive chance that you will be able to keep up with the course load. However, your GMAT/GRE score does not directly translate or correlate to your academic performance at a business school.

c. An Assessment of Your Academic Abilities Outside of Your College Performance

AdComs of top business schools want to see your academic abilities outside of your undergraduate grades as well.

Students I counsel often harbor this worry: "My undergraduate scores don't reflect my true potential. If the AdCom looks at my scores, I will never be accepted."

I have often confronted this doomsday scenario with anxious students agonizing over their poor academic record in college. This could be due to personal problems, extracurricular commitments, misfit with the degree they pursued, etc. However, they have been able to crack top schools by compensating for these low scores through their GMAT or GRE. Since these scores reflect your current academic ability to the AdCom, they could help you compensate for low scores in your undergraduate years.

2. Which Test Should I Take: GMAT or GRE?

Students no longer pick the GMAT only for business school applications and the GRE only for other graduate programs. Many top business schools now accept GRE scores as well. This leaves the average MBA applicant in a pickle: Which test should I take?

To answer this, let us look at the basic differences between the GMAT, GRE as well as CAT.

Criteria	GMAT	GRE	CAT
Acceptance	International business schools and a few Indian business schools	International business schools and graduate schools	Indian business schools
Cost	$250	$205	₹1,800
Scoring	Scored from 200 to 800 in 10-point increments	Scored from 260 to 340 in 1-point increments	Maximum score attainable is 300
Difficulty	Computer adaptive. Subsequent questions get harder as you answer correctly	Computer adaptive, but by section. Subsequent sections get harder as you answer correctly	Each correct answer grants +3 marks, each incorrect answer grants -1 mark
Sections of the Test	Verbal, quantitative, writing	Verbal, quantitative, writing	Verbal ability, data interpretation & logical reasoning, quantitative ability

Criteria	GMAT	GRE	CAT
Section Breakdown	1. Analytical Writing Assessment (1 Question) 2. Integrated Reasoning (12 Questions) 3. Quantitative Reasoning (31 Questions) 4. Verbal Reasoning (36 Questions)	1. Analytical Writing (1 Analyze-an-Issue Task; 1 Analyze-an-Argument Task) 2. Verbal Reasoning (20 Questions per Section) 3. Quantitative Reasoning (20 Questions per Session) 4. Unscored/ Research Section (Varied Number of Questions)	1. Verbal Ability and Reading Comprehension (34 Questions) 2. Data Interpretation and Logical Reasoning (32 Questions) 3. Quantitative Ability (34 Questions)
Score Validity	5 years	5 years	1 year
Maximum Number of Attempts Allowed	8 in total, no more than 5 in 12 months	5 in 12 months, 1 every calendar month	No limit on attempts; capped at 1 in a year

If you look at the table above, you will notice some key differences.

The acceptability of all three tests vary. The CAT has limited scope and is only accepted at Indian business schools. On the other hand, the

GMAT is accepted by all top global business schools and some Indian business schools. The GRE, on the other hand, is accepted at certain MBA programs as well as most graduate programs globally.

The GMAT and GRE scores are valid for five years, but the CAT score is valid for only one admissions cycle. This means that if you want to reapply the next year, you have to reappear for the CAT. Here, I will focus mainly on the GMAT and GRE as you will have to crack these tests to apply to a top global business school.

The GMAT and GRE are open to everyone, and students often ask me which one is 'ideal' for their case. While many counselors would recommend one over the other, based on certain sections, I do not. Your decision should depend on three factors:

I. **Acceptability at the School or Program of Your Choice:** The GMAT is accepted at almost all global business schools. While the GRE has caught up with the GMAT in terms of acceptability at business schools in recent years, I still recommend checking with the schools you are applying to.

Do note that the GRE is also widely accepted at graduate programs at universities. This makes it ideal for people who want to take the test early (one or two years before application), but are on the fence between the MBA and a different master's program. Taking the GRE will keep the option of earning a different master's degree open to you. Many applicants complete a master's and then an MBA within five years of taking the GRE and save the effort and money involved in taking two tests.

For example, our student Tanmay Patel worked for three years after his undergraduate degree. He took the GRE one year after graduating from college, and worked with us on his application for a master's program at the University of California at Berkeley. While at graduate school, he simultaneously worked with me on building his profile for a business school and got accepted into the Cornell MBA program using the same GRE score. In four years he finished two master's programs, having cracked the GRE at his first attempt. This saved him a lot of time, effort, money and anxiety!

II.   **Your Career Choice:** GMAT scores could affect your employability. On occasion, some companies from the consulting and finance fields may ask for your GMAT scores during recruitment interviews. However, this is not the norm. Check if your target companies need you to specifically submit a GMAT score. If they do, I recommend that you take the GMAT instead of GRE.

III. **Your Aptitude:** Take two-three mock tests of both the GMAT and GRE. This will help you determine the format that you are able to maneuver more naturally and score higher in.

Once you have decided which test you want to take, it is time to begin preparing.

3. How the GMAT and GRE Are Structured

While both tests seem similar on the surface, there are several sections within them that vary. Let's have a brief look at the different sections available on the test. Sample questions for each of these sections are available on the official GMAT and GRE websites.

GMAT

1. **Quantitative Reasoning**
    i.   Problem Solving
    ii. Data Sufficiency
2. **Verbal Reasoning**
    i.   Reading Comprehension

    ii. Critical Reasoning

    iii. Sentence Correction

3. **Analytical Writing Assessment**

    i. Analyze an Argument

4. **Integrated Reasoning**

    i. Multi-Source Reasoning

    ii. Table Analysis

    iii. Graphics Interpretation

    iv. Two-Part Analysis

GRE

1. **Verbal Reasoning**

    i. Reading Comprehension

    ii. Text Completion

    iii. Sentence Equivalence

2. **Quantitative Reasoning**

    i. Quantitative Comparison

    ii. Multiple Choice (One correct answer)

    iii. Multiple Choice (One or more correct answers)

    iv. Numeric Entry Questions

3. **Analytical Writing Measure**

    i. Analyze an Issue

    ii. Analyze an Argument

Now that we have understood the formats and uses of the GMAT and GRE tests, let us explore how they are different from their Indian equivalent.

4. When Should I Take the GMAT/GRE?

This question has highly varied answers to it. You can take the GMAT/ GRE any time you are ready. Remember, the score only remains valid for five years. If you take it too early and end up applying after six years of taking the test, your initial attempt will not be valid anymore. However, if you take it too late, then you might be taking the test under a lot of pressure. It is best to plan ahead and give yourself sufficient time. I recommend taking the tests immediately upon your college graduation if possible. Specially if you have already decided on getting an MBA in the future. At this juncture, you are still adept at taking tests and will be able to easily apply concepts learned in college to the tests.

In my case, I took the GMAT just nine months after my undergraduate degree. Since I hold a Bachelor of Science degree, my undergraduate curriculum was quantitatively driven. This made my base in math very strong. Additionally, being a fresh graduate, I was still in the habit of studying and taking tests. This discipline made it easier for me to score well on the test and I did not need to retake the test after my first attempt. If you have been away from studying for two to five years, you might struggle with going back to the books.

Also, think forward and plan based on your workflow when you want to take the test. If you are in a seasonal business, take the test in your low season. If you are taking leave for personal reasons, you can extend it and use it to focus on the test. A career break (time between jobs) is also a great time to prepare adequately for the GMAT/GRE test.

There is always an option to retake these tests if you are not satisfied with your score. For the GMAT, two consecutive attempts cannot be less than 16 days apart. In case of the GRE, consecutive attempts cannot be less than 21 days apart.

You can register for the tests online on the official GMAT/GRE websites. For the GRE, please note that you will be asked to specify whether you are taking the GRE General Test or a Subject Test. MBA applicants are usually required to take the General Test. However, I recommend that you cross-check with your target schools regarding this. After picking the type of test, candidates can schedule their test and pay the fees. Please note that there are no particular dates for either the GMAT or GRE. Slots are available throughout the year at different test centres and you can simply book a slot that is convenient for you.

I also suggest that you begin preparing for the test the moment you decide you want to take it. The earlier your first attempt is from the application deadline, the more flexibility you have in case you want to retake the test.

Once you have decided when you want to take the test, it is time to study for it.

5. How to Begin Preparing for the GMAT and GRE Tests

Preparing for the GMAT and GRE, like any other standardized test, is key. Let's look at some general preparation tips:

1. **Relearning Math and English Concepts Taught in School**
   High-school math and English are going to come handy in both these tests—revisit and refresh these concepts. For the verbal reasoning section, you will be required to revisit grammatical concepts such as sentence structure, tense, subject-verb agreement, modifiers and parallelisms. Similarly, for the quantitative reasoning section, you will be required to revisit math concepts such as word problems, data interpretation, integers, geometry, algebra and statistics.

   Do remember that the GMAT and GRE are both American tests. As Indians, we have been brought up on a diet of UK grammar, and the tests use US grammar. Learning spellings and concepts as per US grammar is also important.

2. **The Importance of Practice**
   Merely learning concepts will not serve you well on the big day. One must also practice and revise them repeatedly

until the day of the exam. The amount of practice you need depends on how good a test taker you are, your learning style, background, aptitude for math and English, your work schedule, target score and other factors.

Broadly, you could need to practice anywhere between 7 to 30 hours a week for two to three months to help you prepare adequately for the test. Additionally, you should do at least one full-length test every weekend.

Daily practice will put you in the habit of studying and taking a test. This discipline will go a long way in ensuring a strong test score. Spending a week doing a full-length practice test every day before your final test day is also recommended.

A great way to kick-start your GMAT preparation is the GMAT test Official Starter Kit that gives students two free practice tests. For the GRE, students can use the official POWERPREP software which also allows you to access two free practice tests.

3. **Familiarize Yourself with the Test's Format**

    When you know the test's format and what questions to expect, you are mentally prepared. You can focus on answering the questions rather than fretting over format or being puzzled or overwhelmed by the structure, interface, design, etc. This will also save you time on the day of the test.

4. **The Art of Guessing**

    Remember, guessing is simply a hack. In an ideal situation, you should be well acquainted with the concepts and not resort to guesswork.

    Also note that there is no negative scoring on either the GMAT or GRE. Each also has several sections where you cannot skip a question if you do not know the answer. Therefore, guesswork can sometimes pay off. When not sure, put in an approximate answer since you have a 25 percent probability of getting it right.

If you are short on time, instead of timing out on the test, try to complete it by filling in all the responses using your best judgment. One out of four times you may make the right guess!

5. Verbal or Quant: Understanding Your Strengths and Weaknesses

Establish your strengths during preparation and prioritize practice accordingly. This can be done via mock tests and preparation worksheets. For instance, if you find yourself scoring well on the quantitative section but low on the verbal sections, begin spending a little more time on the verbal sections.

Let's say you were splitting your time 50:50 between the verbal and quantitative sections. Over a few mock tests, if you realize that your verbal section needs more work, you can begin splitting your time 70:30 between the verbal and quantitative sections respectively. Paying attention to your weak areas and practicing them will definitely improve your performance.

However, do not stop practicing a section merely because it is your strong suit. Continued practice of your strong areas will reinforce them and ensure a good score.

Schools are looking for strong performance across all sections of the tests. A result that is too skewed in favour of one section could raise a red flag.

6. Do NOT Neglect the Analytical Writing Sections

While the analytical writing (AWA) section does not affect your composite score on either test, you should not ignore it. Business schools WILL still receive your scores on these sections. Low scores may not be a deal-breaker, but scoring too low on your Analytical Writing section (<4) will raise a red flag.

There is no shortcut to preparing for the AWA. If you have been an avid reader/writer since you were a child, you will be able to do well naturally on this section.

However, if you are not, I recommend getting into the habit of writing every alternate day for 30 minutes without pause. Clock yourself while writing as well to keep track of how much time you take, and try to improve on this gradually. Practice every alternate day over an 8- to10-week period so that on the day of the test you are well prepared to face this section.

For AWA topics, you can refer to the myriad resources available online that give you a list of topics. Use these and begin writing.

7. **Beating the Clock**

   The GMAT and GRE are timed tests. You might be well versed with the concepts, but your endurance through the three and a half hours matters as well. Take enough timed mock tests to test your mental endurance. When you practice, time your sections so you can keep track of which areas you need to improve your speed on. You must be able to sit through the whole duration of the test without a drop in performance.

8. **Silly Mistakes Can Cost You a Great Deal**

   Confidence is good. Overconfidence and a dismissive attitude are not. Treat each question with the same concentration and double check your answers. Even if an answer seems obvious, think again. The test makers are very skilled and purposely provide answer options that seem correct on the surface. Mistakes affect your final score and a low score may hurt your chance of being accepted by a top school.

9. Joining a Prep Course

You should join a GMAT/GRE preparation course or enroll yourself in a physical coaching class if you are finding it difficult to prepare by yourself for these tests. While they come at a cost, they also ensure that you prepare systematically for a certain number of hours every week. For people whose fundamental concepts are weak or demand honing, preparation courses will also help strengthen them. Additionally, preparation courses will give you access to reference and practice materials along with some tutorials. If you suffer from test-day anxiety, preparation courses might also help you manage it better by simulating a test-taking environment.

GMAT/GRE preparation courses vary by format. Physical classes are typically held for a few months, typically on weekends only. Online classes are self-paced—you can login and study at your convenience.

Coaching classes typically teach the material in large groups and may not cater to your learning style and/or requirements. Online courses are calibrated based on some initial tests the system asks you to take and are hence more tuned to the student's aptitude level. High quality GMAT/GRE physical coaching also comes at a higher cost. Alternatively, digital test prep platforms require you to pay a fixed subscription fee for a personalized study plan. These online platforms come at a lower cost but lack the one-on-one hand-holding element that coaching classes provide.

Ultimately, regardless of the preparation course you choose, once you understand the concepts, you must focus on practice.

10. **On the Day of the Test: Things to Keep in Mind**
   a) Get ample rest the night before.
   b) Do not attempt to cram concepts in the last few moments.
   c) Be confident. You have put in hours of practice and definitely can do it.
   d) Keep an eye on the clock. Do not spend too much time on a single question. Move on with an educated guess if you cannot answer it.

6. What is a Good Score? Should I Retake the GMAT/GRE?

Amey worked with me on his MBA applications a few years ago. He worked at a top consulting firm at the time and had one attempt under his belt with a score of 700. Around five months before applying I had broached the topic of retaking the GMAT and aiming for a higher score. His strong quantitative background indicated that he could score higher if he gave it one more shot. However, Amey was convinced his profile was strong enough already and he need not retake the test.

While 700 is a great score, the median score in his target school was 720. As an Indian male applicant who had worked in consulting (a relatively common profile at top business schools) with limited extracurricular activities, Amey really needed his GMAT score to push his application forward. He chose not to take our advice, however, and was waitlisted that year. Upon connecting with the AdCom, he was given a few instructions, among which was to immediately retake the GMAT. He did, and was able to score 730 on his second attempt. That year, he was accepted from the waitlist.

While the GMAT score was not a silver bullet, it was definitely a decider in his candidacy. Cases like Amey's are a testament to the fact that retaking the GMAT until you hit the median score of your target school can be beneficial. This leads us to ask the next set of questions: Have I scored sufficiently? Should I retake the test?

6:A. How Do I Know If My Score Is Good?

A 'good' score is a relative number. It depends on your background, the schools you are considering, and your propensity towards test-taking. A 'good' score on the GMAT lies in the 650–730+ range. For the GRE, it is recommended that candidates aim for 300–330+. It is important to remember that your scores are a composite of the Verbal and Quantitative sections. While the AdCom will look at your overall score, they will also probe it further to check how you fared in individual sections.

While a school's average score can give you a fair idea of what they expect, you do not have to settle for it. If you want to set yourself apart from the other applicants, shoot for 10–20 points higher than your target school's published average scores.

Now that we know what a 'good' score is, let us find out how many times you should retake the GMAT/GRE, and why.

6:B. How Many Times Should I Attempt the Test?

My short answer to this question is "it depends". There are certain cases in which you might want to retake the GMAT/GRE test. Here are four:

1. **Your first attempt might not have been optimal:** This is mainly because many of us are not used to the format of the GMAT and GRE tests. This could affect your performance in your first attempt. Once you have appeared for the test, you are privy to its nature and better prepared. The second attempt (if you prepare equally well) is likely to be more fruitful, since you would have overcome the anxiety a first-time test taker experiences.

2. **You have scored exceedingly well in one section over the other:** An example of this is if you have scored high marks in the Verbal Section, but poorly in the Quantitative Section.

Your overall GRE score might be 327, but the sub-160 score in the Quantitative Section may be a red flag. I suggest then that you retake the test. In your next attempt, aim to improve your weaker section's score.

3. **You believe you can score higher than in your earlier attempts:** Students often worry about retaking these tests and getting a lower score in their second attempts. However, the GMAT and GRE both allow you to cancel your scores within a certain duration after taking them; thus, you have nothing to lose by retaking these tests. If you score lower than you did in your previous attempt, you can cancel the new score. If you are sitting on the fence about your GMAT/GRE scores and are curious to see if you can improve, retaking the GMAT/GRE could pay off.

4. **You have been waitlisted:** If you score is not at the school's average test score and you are waitlisted, I suggest that you retake the test, aim for a higher score and notify the AdCom about the same. This could improve the chances of your waitlist being converted. However, this varies from school to school. It is suggested that you contact them, enquiring if retaking the test can improve your chances of being accepted.

Some schools may also accept revised GMAT and GRE scores after submitting the application. This comes in handy when you have limited time remaining before a deadline but are unsatisfied with your scores. You can submit a revised score in these cases to improve your chances. However, please check with the school to which you are applying to see if they accept scores after you have submitted your application.

Most schools view taking tests more than once positively. It shows a commitment to improve and when scores do improve, it reflects initiative and drive towards self-improvement on the candidate's part.

Caveat: If you are a good test taker and have already scored your target score, do not follow the herd and retake the GMAT/GRE. Instead, focus on other aspects of your profile. The GMAT/GRE is only one data point, and you must strengthen your professional and extracurricular activity profiles as well. You should know where to draw the line.

7. Interpreting Your Score Sheet

GMAT

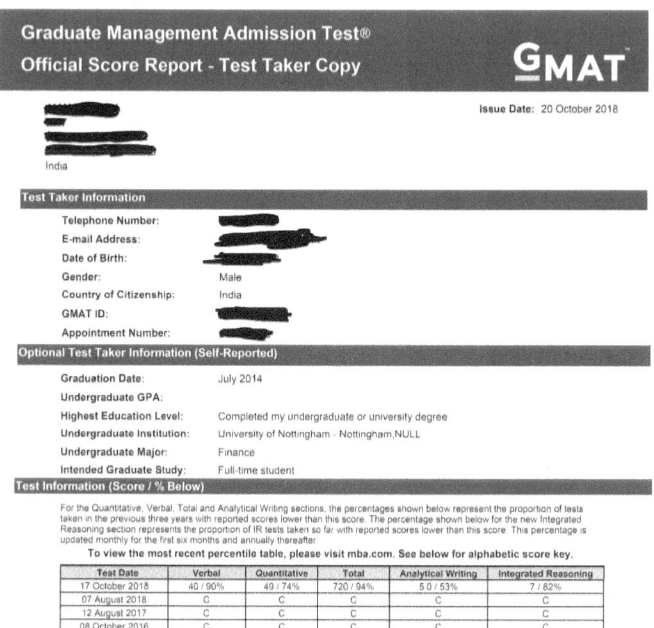

Graduate Management Admission Test®

Official Score Report - Test Taker Copy

GMAT

Issue Date: 20 October 2018

India

Test Taker Information

Telephone Number:

E-mail Address:

Date of Birth:

Gender: Male

Country of Citizenship: India

GMAT ID:

Appointment Number:

Optional Test Taker Information (Self-Reported)

Graduation Date: July 2014

Undergraduate GPA:

Highest Education Level: Completed my undergraduate or university degree

Undergraduate Institution: University of Nottingham - Nottingham,NULL

Undergraduate Major: Finance

Intended Graduate Study: Full-time student

Test Information (Score / % Below)

For the Quantitative, Verbal, Total and Analytical Writing sections, the percentages shown below represent the proportion of tests taken in the previous three years with reported scores lower than this score. The percentage shown below for the new Integrated Reasoning section represents the proportion of IR tests taken so far with reported scores lower than this score. This percentage is updated monthly for the first six months and annually thereafter.

To view the most recent percentile table, please visit mba.com. See below for alphabetic score key.

Test Date	Verbal	Quantitative	Total	Analytical Writing	Integrated Reasoning
17 October 2018	40 / 90%	49 / 74%	720 / 94%	5 0 / 53%	7 / 82%
07 August 2018	C	C	C	C	C
12 August 2017	C	C	C	C	C
08 October 2016	C	C	C	C	C

In the given score sheet, the scores are reported as follows:

Section	Explanation
Test Information (Score/Percent Below)	This is the section where your scores are reported. All your previous attempts are listed. The 'SCORE' reports your score on each of the components. The 'Percent BELOW' reports your percentile.
Test Date	This section reports the dates of all your attempts. In this case, the candidate has made four attempts. While the person has cancelled the previous three scores, the AdCom can still see that he attempted the test four times.
Verbal	The candidate's score on the Verbal Reasoning component. In this case, 49/90 percent means the candidate scored 49 out of 60 which places him in the 90th percentile of all test takers.
Quantitative	The candidate's score on the Quantitative Reasoning component. In this case, 49/74 percent means the candidate scored 49 out of 60 which places him in the 74th percentile of all test takers.
Total	The total scaled score of the candidate in the Verbal and Quantitative components. In this case, 720/94 percent means the candidate scored 720 out of 800 which places him in the 94th percentile of all test takers.
Analytical Writing	The candidate's score in the Analytical Writing section. In this case, 5.0/63 percent means the candidate scored 5.0 out of 6.0 in the AWA section, which places him in the 63rd percentile of all test-takers. Note that this score is not a part of your total score.

Section	Explanation
Integrated Reasoning	The candidate's score in Integrated Reasoning. In this case, 7/82 percent means the candidate scored 7 out of 8 in the IR component, which places him in the 82nd percentile of all test takers. This score is also not part of your total score.

GRE

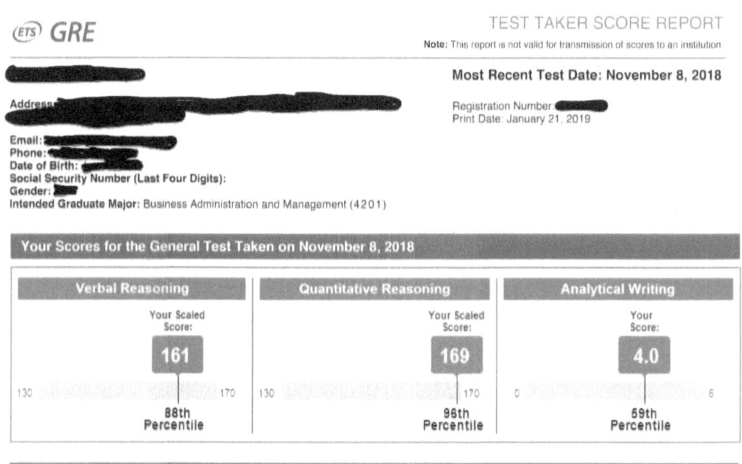

Your Test Score History

General Test Scores

Test Date	Verbal Reasoning		Quantitative Reasoning		Analytical Writing	
	Scaled Score	Percentile	Scaled Score	Percentile	Score	Percentile
November 8, 2018	161	88	169	96	4.0	59

Subject Test Scores

You do not have reportable test scores at this time.

Your Score Recipient(s)

Undergraduate Institution

Report Date	Institution (Code)	Department (Code)	Test Title	Test Date

(ETS) GRE

Most Recent Test Date: November 8, 2018

Date of Birth: ▓▓▓▓

Registration Number: ▓▓▓▓
Print Date: January 21, 2019

Designated Score Recipient(s)

Report Date	Score Recipient (Code)	Department (Code)	Test Title	Test Date
November 21, 2018	HARVARD BUSINESS SCH MBA PGM (4064)	BUSINESS ADMIN & MGMT (4201)	General Test	November 8, 2018
November 21, 2018	MIT SLOAN SCH MGMT MBA (3791)	BUSINESS ADMIN & MGMT (4201)	General Test	November 8, 2018
November 21, 2018	STANFORD UNIVERSITY (4704)	BUSINESS ADMIN & MGMT (4201)	General Test	November 8, 2018
November 21, 2018	U PENNSYLVANIA WHARTON SCH MBA (6802)	BUSINESS ADMIN & MGMT (4201)	General Test	November 8, 2018

Section	Explanation
Your scores for the General Test taken on November 8, 2018	The candidate has scored: 1. 161 on the Verbal Reasoning component out of 170. This places him in the 88th percentile of all test takers. 2. 169 on the Quantitative Reasoning component out of 170. This places him in the 99th percentile of all test takers. 3. 4.0 out of 6.0 in Analytical Writing. This places him in the 59th percentile of all test takers. Please not that this is not part of your composite score.
Your Test Score History	A report of all your attempts. In this case, the candidate has only made one attempt. The score attained (scaled score) in each component and the percentile are shown in the corresponding cells.

Section	Explanation
Designated Score Recipient(s)	This displays the schools that the candidate's score has been sent to. It also displays which departments the score has been sent to. In this case, it is 'Business Admin & Mgmt (4201)', which is for MBA programs. The 'Test Date' cell reports the attempt which has been reported to the given school.

To know your total score on the GRE, you can simply add the scaled score on the Verbal Reasoning and Quantitative Reasoning components. In this case:

161 (Verbal) + 169 (Quantitative) = 330

The maximum attainable composite score is 340.

8. Reality Check: Busting Common GMAT/GRE Myths

8:A. Continuously Retaking the Test Will Lead to Better Scores

Your success on the GMAT/GRE test also depends on factors like how good a test taker you are, how busy your work schedule is, your intellectual aptitude, etc. From experience, I have noticed that after around four attempts, the scores begin to stall.

Instead of taking the test multiple times, I recommend that you prepare well, plan ahead of time, and thus avoid having to take the test multiple times.

Take the tests seriously. Once you do well, you do not have to worry about it for five years. Even if your first admissions attempt is unsuccessful, when you reapply, you can focus on other parts of your profile.

8:B. If I Don't Have a Strong Test Score, I Won't Get In

In the Profile Building chapter, we addressed how each profile is a balance of strengths and weaknesses. A sub-650 GMAT or sub-300

GRE score requires a strong profile to offset it. Students with low GMAT/GRE scores are a minority at top business schools. If you fit in the category of those with an excellent profile, don't fret about an average score. If you have something spectacular working in your favor, the schools may overlook your score.

For instance, Naveen had attempted the GMAT twice, and his highest score was 670. However, he applied and still got a full scholarship to Oxford. The other areas of his profile were strong, and we had worked hard on his positioning statement in his essay. He had dual engineering degrees, one in Electrical Engineering and one in Biomedical Engineering. Naveen had also worked in four countries. Additionally, he had given a TEDx talk and was working on a mobile-application startup on the side. His recommenders were credible and well established. His outstanding profile offset his relatively low GMAT score.

8:C. I Can Study for GMAT/GRE a Week Before the Exam and Still Do Well

It is a tempting thought. However, preparing for the GMAT/GRE, as we covered before, entails much more than just learning the concepts. You have to absorb them and be able to apply them in different contexts. You are also preparing your endurance to survive the 3.5 hours of the test. While you might be able to 'pass' the test, it is unlikely that you will score well. This is why I recommend preparing at least two months beforehand, and putting in daily practice.

8:D. If My Math Scores Are Low, I Won't Get In

This is a common worry, specially among people from non-quantitative backgrounds. Schools will contextualize your scores if you are from a non-quant background and review your application accordingly.

Whereas it is ideal to have a balanced score, some variation is acceptable to the AdCom.

8:E. I Will Not Be Judged Too Harshly on My GMAT/ GRE; I Already Have an Undergraduate Degree in Business

Students from undergraduate programs with a focus on components like business, commerce, math, etc., may fall for this myth. They think they do not need to prove their quantitative skills on the GMAT since they have an undergraduate quantitative background.

Even if you are from a quantitative background, your GMAT/ GRE score will be given equal importance. The same way an arts/ humanities student proves his math skills through the GMAT/GRE, business/commerce/STEM students can prove their verbal/language skills through the GMAT/GRE.

8:F. Since the GMAT/GRE Has No Negative Scoring, I Can Go Wild With Guesswork

The GMAT and GRE are computer adaptive tests. In the GMAT, correct answers increase the difficulty of subsequent questions. These harder questions also carry more marks. The GRE works on a similar concept but with a small difference. It increases difficulty in subsequent sections; difficult sections carry more weightage.

As I mentioned before, there is no direct negative scoring in these tests, but incorrect answers plateau the difficulty of questions you are asked. This reduces the points you earn per correct answer. Consequently, this affects your final score.

Consecutive wrong answers will negatively impact your final score. While guesswork can pay off, do not go wild with it. Prepare well beforehand so you have definite answers for most questions.

Insider Tips in a Nutshell

DO:

- ✓ Make an informed choice between the GMAT and GRE.
- ✓ Prepare at least two months beforehand, for 7–30 hours a week.
- ✓ Relearn your Math and English fundamentals (from 8th grade to 12th grade) if they are weak.
- ✓ Take the tests immediately after college if you can.
- ✓ Use a career break/gap to take the test.
- ✓ Retake the GMAT or GRE if your first attempt was not optimal.

DON'T:

- X Focus exclusively on GMAT/GRE and ignore other aspects of your profile.
- X Compulsively keep retaking the test.
- X Give up on applying to top business schools if you have low GMAT/GRE scores.
- X Go wild with guesswork.
- X Take the test at the last minute just before deadlines.

APPENDIX

GMAT Scores of Top Business Schools Abroad*:

School	Average GMAT Score	Median GRE Score
Harvard Business School	730	328
University of Chicago, Booth School of Business	730	-
University of Cambridge, Judge Business School	696	-
Columbia Business School	724	-
HEC Paris	690	311
INSEAD	709	-
London Business School	708	-
Northwestern University, Kellogg School of Management	732	-
Massachusetts Institute of Technology, Sloan School of Management	728	320
University of Michigan, Ross School of Business	716	320
New York University, Stern School of Business	714	-
Oxford University, Said Business School	690	-
University of California Berkeley, Haas School of Business	725	329
The Wharton School at the University of Pennsylvania	730	325
Yale School of Management	730	-

GMAT Scores of Top Business Schools Abroad*:

School	Average GMAT Score	Median GRE Score
China Europe International Business School	685	-
University of Toronto, Rotman School of Management	658	-
National University of Singapore	662	-
Hong Kong University of Science and Technology (HKUST)	667	-
Melbourne Business School	703	-
IESE	686	-
International Institute for Management Development	680	-
Schulich School of Business	660	-

* Data taken from schools' websites

4

The MBA Résumé: How to Write an Incisive and Impactful Résumé

Writing a résumé is the verbal equivalent of fitting an elephant into a fish tank. It perplexes even the smartest minds.

Take, for instance, Kaushal, a dynamic, passionate and eloquent polyglot with six years of work experience and continuous volunteering work with a tier 1 NGO. He sent me this email at 11 pm on a Saturday night. His two years of consecutive failed attempts getting to top seven business schools had dampened the spirits of this executive from a top consulting firm.

While his profile was impressive, he had little idea about what needed emphasis and what didn't. It was left to me to tell him that résumé writing was not an exact science nor is there a formula to get it right; what you include and what you omit varies from case to case. Eager to fix his résumé, Kaushal signed up with us for our résumé editing service.

The first draft of Kaushal's résumé was extremely detailed and ran into two pages. For his tenure at the top consulting firm, every project had been highlighted. He explained the team structure, the nature of work, the hurdles they faced, and other small details. Additionally, these details were written in paragraphs and not bullets. He had also added a list of personal information such as place of birth, marital status and professional objective, which is irrelevant information for an MBA résumé. The formatting and spacing was also not optimized.

I began by helping Kaushal select only the strongest points from his résumé and omit the rest. After four grueling rounds of editing, his résumé was ready. What we did worked wonders. That year, he was accepted at Chicago Booth School of Business.

Although it was not just his résumé that got him accepted at his target school, the holistic application's flavor was definitely enhanced once his résumé became more reflective of his accomplishments.

Kaushal's fundamental dilemma might ring a familiar tone. Condensing your credentials into one page can be a challenge. We have all been there, looking over each section of our résumé and murmuring, "To keep, or not to keep—that is the question."

Think of your résumé as a snapshot: As a clear image that captures the essence of the scene and gives an accurate description of what has happened.

Another common question I encounter is whether the college application and job application résumé are the same. The answer: "Not at all." Let me elaborate.

1. Why Your MBA Application Résumé Is Not the Same as Your Job Hunt Résumé

Deepesh contacted me in 2014, when his deadline was a month away. To save time, Deepesh was planning to use the CV he had been using for his job applications. It was detailed and up-to-date and hence in his eyes ideal for submission.

"No, I don't have the time for this! I have a ready résumé, I prefer using that instead, please," he said when I asked him to draft a new CV catering to business school. It took that entire session to convince him.

Your MBA application résumé is very different from your job hunt résumé. The difference arises due to many factors: depth and breadth of experience displayed, length of the résumé, focus on academics, tone and, most importantly, intent.

How the Two Résumés Differ in a Nutshell

Points of Difference	Job Application Résumé	College Application Résumé
Who is the reader?	The recruiter	The admissions department
What does the reader want to know?	Whether you have the necessary skills to perform on the job, and the passion for the job you want to work in	Whether you can cope with the curriculum, have the intellectual capacity to learn and contribute to class learning
Who is the ideal fit?	Someone with a strong background in the same field; comes with experience and demonstrated interest in the field. Someone who can get the task done	Does not matter which field you belong to. Must have the potential to lead, perform and grow. Also, whether you demonstrate exceptional leadership skills in any niche area of your choice. People with the hunger for knowledge and the zeal to become leaders in their domain are preferred

Points of Difference	Job Application Résumé	College Application Résumé
What should the résumé showcase?	Technical expertise in the chosen field, command of the subject, and passion; technical jargon helps here	Academic excellence, extracurricular activities that showcase initiative, leadership, creativity, and problem-solving abilities; no need for technical jargon

2. What Admissions Officers (AdComs) Want

Many admissions officers will bring a printout of your résumé to your MBA interview, thereby making your one-page résumé the basis of the interview. To ensure the AdCom can question you on a range of topics, be authentic and ensure that the résumé gives a holistic flavor of who you are.

Sometimes, students fabricate roles and experiences thinking these will not be cross-checked. However, the interviewer is likely to ask you a second line of questions while referring to the document *to double check the authenticity of your presentation.* If you have lied on the résumé, these push-back questions will catch you unawares.

Why are AdComs not happy with long résumés that spill over to multiple pages? Let's do some math here to help you understand.

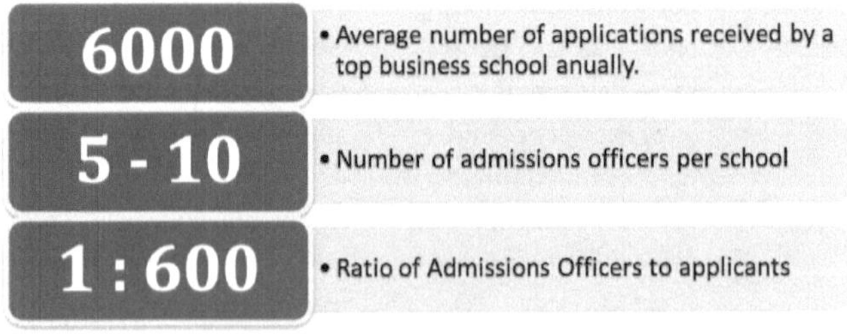

That is only one Admissions Officer for 600 applicants. Moreover, there are other parts of the application such as the essays and letters of recommendation that the AdCom must review. Clock this at an average of at least 30,000 documents (assuming two essays, one résumé, two LoRs) per AdCom, per season, and you will understand why multi-page résumés are not preferred.

Now that we understand why the résumé should be a single-page document, let us discuss how to make your résumé effective.

1. **Provide a Snapshot, Not a Never-Ending Thesis**

    Let the AdCom know what you have done, what you are doing, and how well you have performed. This 'snapshot' should contain each of the following characteristics:

    i.   Short, succinct descriptors
    ii. Minimum jargon
    iii. Clear demarcations between sections and roles
    iv. Point-based formatting

    Caveat: This does not mean applicants should omit specific details to save space. Do not just say:

    - First non-traditional hire

        Also mention in what manner you were non-traditional.
        Similarly, do not just say:

    - Designed key stances and strategies for XYZ

        Also mention what those strategies were, and quantify their impact.

    Here is an example from Kaushal's final résumé:

PROFESSIONAL EXPERIENCE

■■■■■■■■ AND COMPANY   ■■■■, India
Consultant (Implementation Coach - Associate level)   Nov ■■■- Present
Advising senior management of multinationals on a broad range of operational issues and transformational programs
- Built a collaborative 25% annualized ■■■■ increase plan with 100+ cane farmers for leading sugar manufacturer
- Created a 5-year transformation program in business excellence for Fortune 500 building materials company
- Leading a global entrepreneurial venture to build the firm's value proposition in public education transformation

Here, the experience is broken down into four clear points. They accurately capture Kaushal's work with maximum impact, in a few crisp words.

2. **Quantify Your Achievements**
   AdComs love numbers—not because they are math geeks, but because numbers help them assess your impact as a professional. Did you increase the user base of your company's mobile application? Tell them by how much. For example:

   ■ ***Increased user base of ReachIvy.com's mobile application.***

   gives out much less relevant information than saying:

   ■ ***Doubled the mobile application user base from 30,000 members to 60,000 members in a span of three months.***

   This applies to any awards and achievements you mention on your profile as well. Mention the award's name first, what it was for and, more importantly, how selective it was. This allows the AdCom to understand the importance of that achievement.

   Here's an example from Kaushal's final résumé:

   - 1 of 9 out of 1000+ applicants across 75 countries selected for a full-time year-long fellowship as part of leading social venture fund's leadership development initiative with training in leadership, valuation and 9 months field placement

   You can see how quantifying the selectivity of his fellowship helps establish how exclusive it was.

3. **List Technical as Well as Non-Technical Skills**
   Instead of just peppering the résumé with you being an amazing professional, show the AdCom that you have worked for the community, care for human rights, and/or have traveled the country or the world.
   I have seen many students who tend to give all the attention to the 'Professional experience' section of the résumé.

They miss out on other key sections such as 'Community involvement' and 'Extracurricular activities'. This leads the reader to think the candidate is uni-dimensional; the only focal area of their life is work. To avoid this, add activities outside of your professional life as well. As mentioned in the profiling chapter, AdComs are looking for a holistic profile. Your one-page snapshot should capture your overarching profile and personality.

Even if you feel like your tenure has been mostly work, at least save a few lines for your extracurricular/community/ personal activities. **Here's a snap from his final résumé to illustrate how I helped Kaushal accomplish this in his résumé:**

COMMUNITY AND PERSONAL

- Served as advisor to U.N. Secretary-General's Special Envoy (■■ ■■■■) to accelerate ■■■■■ in India
- Facilitated technology and management education for entrepreneurs at Goldman Sachs 10,000 Women Initiative
- Advised ■■■■■■■ Food Bank on warehouse operations; Raised $5500 and collected 3900 pounds of food
- Interviewed by India's leading business magazine – Business Today (Jul, 2013) for career contribution in social sector
- Fluent in 4 Indian languages and conversant in German; Martial Arts (Okinawan Kobudo) advanced level trainer

Even though the section above talks only about five non-professional activities, it provides the AdCom with a holistic view of the applicant.

4. Be Consistent While Formatting

Several applicants make the mistake of submitting résumés that are extremely decorative. They add fancy borders, graphical charts and handwritten fonts, among others. AdComs want résumés that are easy to read and have the same formatting throughout. This includes font size, headings, margins and font style. Keep the fonts uniform and the presentation simple. This will enable the AdCom to focus on content and on discerning your story instead of having to adjust their eyes to the flashy aesthetics of your document.

Would you want to read a résumé that looks like this?

> PROFESSIONAL EXPERIENCE
>
> ████████ – *Designs, manufactures, supplies & erects* ████████,
> India
>
> Manager - Strategy & Planning ___ – Present
>
> • *Led a team of 6 to streamline internal processes like product testing, inspection procedures, product delivery and assembly.*
>
> • *Suggested expeditious and cost-effective solution to in-house manufacturer ____. Spearheaded the process of acquiring*
>
> *approved _____.*

If you want the AdCom to pay attention to your résumé, resist the urge to decorate it.

5. **Customize Résumés to the University's Context**

    Sometimes in the résumé, your impact may be quantified in terms of money (revenue earned, budgets, amount of funding raised, deal size and more). Doing the currency conversion for the AdCom saves them the task of doing it themselves and shows thoughtfulness and effort on your part. For example, if you are applying to a university in Spain, use the euro as your currency metric for all monetary items instead of the rupee. Standardize the entire résumé to one currency.

- Co-led execution of ██ New Product Introduction process from product strategy and planning and manufacturing to roll out of ███, the cheapest car in the world for $2500; successfully drove operational excellence initiatives

- Created a state-wide emergency service public private partnership plan for ████, pitched and won a 3 year, $15M tender with the ████ through the ███████ program.

Above are two different places where Kaushal included a monetary item to quantify his work. As you see, he has standardized the currency to USD ($).

6. **Include Niche Hobbies and Skills**

   Top schools pride themselves on the diversity of their student pool. Having anything new or different, or even uncommon, on your résumé could give you an edge. Do you write a blog? Are you a triathlon runner? Do you play a musical instrument? Add it to your résumé. Anything off the beaten track ***and pursued well in terms of time and dedication put in it, which reflects impactful work,*** wins brownie points.

   Note that schools are looking for hobbies/skills through college and life post-college. I recommend that you do not include an extracurricular activity you did in your high-school days and never pursued through college and life after. The AdComs are largely only interested in what you have done since college.

   Caveat: If any middle or high school achievements are superlative or noteworthy, they should be mentioned. For example, swimming across the English Channel when you were 12, or breaking a world record at 14 would definitely qualify as exceptional feats! Feel free to brag about any extraordinary feats. Remember, I said: EXTRA-ordinary!

   Here's snapshot from Kaushal's résumé illustrating his niche skills (being a polyglot and a martial arts trainer).

- Fluent in 4 Indian languages and conversant in German; Martial Arts (Okinawan Kobudo) advanced level trainer

7. **Stay Authentic**

   Job patterns and roles constantly in flux are absolutely acceptable! AdComs perceive disjointed work experiences as contributors to building an overall personality, developing ability to work with people across sectors and acquiring different skill sets. Don't worry about being judged for your career choices; focus on excelling in whatever you do.

   However, how long you stay in a certain domain and the

impact you make says a lot about your commitment to new endeavors. If you are changing roles and jobs every three months, this could raise a red flag.

Here's Kaushal's final CV, with all these points put into effect:

KAUSHAL ■■■■■

Phone : ■■■■■ Email: ■■■■ Address : ■■■■■■

EDUCATION

■■■■ INSTITUTE OF TECHNOLOGY, ■■■, ■■■   Dec 2008

Master of Science, Industrial Engineering; Graduate Research Scholarship (full tuition); ■■■ Scholar
Winner, 1st prize - ■■■ Business Plan Competition; Recipient of Continental Global Engineering Excellence Internship (1 of 10 from 8 top tier global engineering universities) – ■■■■ expansion strategy

COLLEGE OF ENGINEERING ■■■ (■■■), ■■■, ■■■   Jul 2004

Bachelor of Engineering, Mechanical Engineering, First Class with Distinction (Highest Honors)
Winner of 3 national technical paper competitions on energy; Final year research project selected at ■■ (■■■)
Mayor's Award for State rank 9 of 120,000+ in Higher Secondary Exam; Lead ■■ debate club; ■■ Rowing team
EXECUTIVE EDUCATION: ■■-■■■■■ ■■■■■■■■■■■, Indian School of Business   Feb 2012

PROFESSIONAL EXPERIENCE

■■■■■■■■ AND COMPANY
■■■■, India
Consultant (Implementation Coach - Associate level)   Nov ■■■- Present
Advising senior management of multinationals on a broad range of operational issues and transformational programs
- Built a collaborative 25% annualized ■■■■ increase plan with 100+ cane farmers for leading sugar manufacturer
- Created a 5-year transformation program in business excellence for Fortune 500 building materials company
- Leading a global entrepreneurial venture to build the firm's value proposition in public education transformation

■■■■ FUND   ■■■■■, Mumbai
Global Fellow (Class of 2012)/ Advisor to CEO of portfolio company   Sep ■■■ - Sep ■■■
- 1 of 9 out of 1000+ applicants across 75 countries selected for a full-time year-long fellowship as part of leading social venture fund's leadership development initiative with training in leadership, valuation and 9 months field placement
- Advised CEOS of the fund's portfolio companies on growth strategy, stakeholder management and operational issues
  - Created a state-wide emergency service public private partnership plan for ■■■■, pitched and won a 3 year, $15M tender with the ■■■■ through the ■■■■■■■ program.
  - Conducted due diligence across 6 small enterprises in ■■■■■ and ■■■■■ and shared recommendations with a leading NGO and 2 ■■■■■■ Fund investment teams for a $4M channel partnership

■■■■■■ CONSULTING   ■■■■■■■, United States
Senior Consultant   Sep ■■■■ - Aug ■■■■
Managed teams of 2-3 junior consultants to advise Fortune 500 company CTOS/ IT Directors in technology; Promoted to Senior Consultant (post MBA position) within first review cycle (less than one year). Select casework: -
- Built technology investment business case for Fortune 20 healthcare client CTO with potential to improve ROI by 40 %
- Set up project management office to drive 20 technology and change management initiatives for a leading retailer

■■■■■ GROUP (■■■■■ LIMITED)   ■■■■■■, India
Manager, Auto Projects; Assistant Manager, Production   Jul ■■■■ - Jul ■■■■
- Co-led execution of ■■ New Product Introduction process from product strategy and planning and manufacturing to roll out of ■■■, the cheapest car in the world for $2500; successfully drove operational excellence initiatives
- As Assistant Manager, directly supervised 5 engineers and 70+ line staff as head of trim line of ■■■■■■

COMMUNITY AND PERSONAL
- Served as advisor to U.N. Secretary-General's Special Envoy (■■ ■■■■) to accelerate ■■■■■ in India
- Facilitated technology and management education for entrepreneurs at Goldman Sachs 10,000 Women Initiative
- Advised ■■■■■■■ Food Bank on warehouse operations; Raised $5500 and collected 3900 pounds of food
- Interviewed by India's leading business magazine – Business Today (Jul, 2013) for career contribution in social sector
- Fluent in 4 Indian languages and conversant in German; Martial Arts (Okinawan Kobudo) advanced level trainer

3. How to Break Your Accomplishments Down on Paper

You have introspected and made a long list of your accomplishments. This is what I call a 'data dump', a great first step. Next, you need to clearly delineate the sections and bucket your accomplishments within those sections.

At business school, you are expected to process heaps of information and condense your learnings into a structured format. Let's just say résumé writing is your first glimpse into the world of information management. Writing a great résumé entails breaking it down skill for skill, deed for deed in a systematic manner. Segmenting the résumé into sections means that it is not a wall of text. Instead, it makes the relevant information accessible and readable.

Also, even though this is a résumé for an MBA program, maintain a professional tone. I have often seen résumés which begin with an email address that best describes the candidate as immature. Do away with email addresses such as sandesh_wannaparty@xyz.com and replace them with a simpler, more professional one such as sandesh_awasthi@ xyz.com. Your personal interests are best dealt with in a separate section, and should not reflect in your email address.

3:A. The Sections of an MBA Résumé

1. Education and Academic Honours

- All your educational degrees starting with the most recent full-time degree(s), followed by relevant certifications and fellowships, will come here.
- As a rule of thumb, this is the first section of your résumé. Since you are applying to an educational institution it is important to first showcase your educational prowess.
- Highlight exemplary academic achievements. This could include: outstanding grades, ranking, GPA, scholarships, or

any awards or recognitions you might have received in your school/college/university.

- Do not attempt to convert your college grades to a USA GPA system or any other. Represent your scores as they are. For example, percentages (out of 100), scores out of 10 and/or grades are all acceptable representations of your academic score within your institution.

Here's what a good education section looks like:

EDUCATION

- **H.R. College of Commerce and Economics, Mumbai, India**   Jul ■■■■ - Jul ■■■■
  Bachelor of Commerce

  Current GPA 6.65/7.0; presented "■■■■■■■■■■ Award" by ■■■■■■■■ Committee for highest overall GPA for consecutive years. Ranked 2/249 in my department. Honors Dissertation on the Economics of renewable fuels.

- **Institute of Chartered Accountants of India, Mumbai, India**   Jun ■■■■ - Jul ■■■■
  Integrated Professional Competency Course (Level-2)

CERTIFICATIONS

- University of Pennsylvania Introduction to Financial Accounting   ■■■■ Sep

- Columbia University Economics of Money and Banking   ■■■■ Aug

- Bombay Stock Exchange Mergers and Acquisitions   ■■■■ Dec

2. Professional Experience

- Your professional experience—jobs and positions held—will be a part of this section.
- Ensure that you are not parroting your job role as it was penned in your offer letter.
- Highlight your key achievements, not the job description—in points, and do not forget to quantify your impact.

Here's what an ideal professional experience section should look like:

PROFESSIONAL EXPERIENCE

■■■■■■ Mumbai, India Intern   Oct ■■■■ - Present

- Brainstormed innovative story ideas on XXXXXX; provided XXXX students with in-depth perspective on elections, opportunities for undergraduates and current affairs.

- Authored and published 12+ articles XXXXXX; read by over 100,000 subscribers

- Selected by XXXXXX to write the main feature articles on XXXXXX and the 'Electoral Voting' process

3. Leadership/Community Involvement

> ■ Highlight all non-professional activities in this section—extracurricular activities, volunteering experience and other initiative-driven roles are highlighted here.

> ■ For instance, volunteering at an NGO, a local event or TEDx talk would count towards leadership and community involvement.

> ■ Remember to add experiences where you have led and made an impact over roles where you worked in a subordinate role.

> An ideal leadership and community involvement section could look like this:

LEADERSHIP EXPERIENCE AND COMMUNITY INVOLVEMENT

Team Leader, ■■■■■, ■■■■, India   Oct ■■■■ - Present

- Implemented tools such as ■■■ to track finances; improved ■■■■ by 20%
- Liaised with leading corporates in Finance ■■■■■■
- Executed partnerships with ■■■■■■ for 3 work abroad exchanges in management and finance
- Mentored and trained junior employees in Sales, International Relations, Exchange Delivery and Leadership; effective induction and engagement resulted in ■■■■■ promoted during their first performance review

Teacher ■■■■■■, India   Apr ■■■■ - Present

- Taught English to 100 Middle School and High School children using engaging and fun activities such as flash cards, Pictionary and Hindi to English word association; improved their fluency, vocabulary and built their confidence.
- Organized short skit on ■■■■■ to get 13 students acclimatized to the language.
- Volunteer, ■■■■■ Mumbai, India ■■■■■■
- Fostered creativity in ■■■■■ by visiting schools and hosting workshops on ■■■■■■

4. **Skills and Interests**

- Are you multilingual? Are you a Python whiz? Include this in your skills and interests.
- This also allows you to give the AdCom a look at a side of you not entirely technical— you can highlight the scuba diver, the travel enthusiast and the poet in you here.

Here's what a skills and interests section could look like:

SKILLS AND INTERESTS

Drums

- Trinity Exams - Completed Grade 6 and registered for Grade 7   20■■ - Present
- Performed at school annual day, 2 charity fundraising events, and several other events   20■■ - Present

Languages

- Hindi (Fluent), English (Fluent), French (Fluent)

4. Reality Check: Busting Common MBA Résumé Myths

4:A. I Must Include Everything I Have Done in My Life on My Résumé

It is unrealistic to try to fit all your life's experiences into a single page. Besides being difficult to do in the limited space, this weakens your résumé by drawing attention to everything in general and nothing in particular.

Ensure that you list accomplishments that highlight your top skills to the reader. This spotlight is essential to maintain focus on your core strengths. Keep in mind the rule of thumb: substance over fluff.

4:B. I Must Get Creative with My Résumé

There is no scope for creativity in the résumé in terms of using stylistic devices or being a wordsmith. Always stick to simple, basic vocabulary and do not attempt to impress the AdCom with flowery language—this will backfire.

For example, here is a line one of my students had used in his résumé.

"I motivated my team to burn the midnight lamp and helped them cross insurmountable hurdles, kept the fire of hard work burning until we overcame it all and reached our destination."

Here is my fix: Collaborated closely with the accounts, sales and marketing teams, completing the project two weeks ahead of schedule.

The second example better indicates your role in the team by cutting to the chase; no flowery language is used.

Use punchy, effective words that imply impact and action. More importantly, avoid creative templates, thick borders, images, charts, graphs, over-the-top styling, funky fonts, etc., in your one-page document.

4:C. I Have to Fill a Section for the Sake of Filling It

There is no cookie-cutter approach to writing a résumé. Feel free to create sections based on your profile. If you aren't involved in community activities, don't feel compelled to have a 'community involvement' section just to check a box. I have seen students try to fill the 'community involvement' sections of their résumé with trivialities like:

"Family donations to old age homes every year."

Do not do this. If you don't have points for a certain section, don't make them up. This makes your weaknesses come forth glaringly, and the AdCom will see right through this.

If you are trying to showcase expertise in a certain domain, you can create a new section in your résumé.

For instance, I once had a client, Rahul Tripathi, whose family was actively involved in healthcare. Given his family's legacy, he became interested in the field as well, and was assisting two healthcare startups on the side and wrote regularly for a healthcare journal. To showcase this expertise, we created a separate section specifically called 'Healthcare Initiatives'. This drew the spotlight towards Rahul's expertise and interest in healthcare, an area aligned with his long-term goals.

4:D. My Résumé and LinkedIn Profile Are Separate Things

Your LinkedIn profile is like your 'social media résumé'. It needs to provide information consistent with your résumé.

The AdCom could check your LinkedIn profile to verify your candidacy. Inconsistencies found during this review might raise questions. Ensure that your story/profile is consistent across platforms.

5. Real People, Unique Skills, Common Errors: Analysis and Fixes

5:A. Jai Writes Dissertations

J: What do you mean my résumé has too many words? I thought elaboration was key…

VK: Yes, but your language matters. Long paragraphs for each experience are not recommended.

Jai's first contact with ReachIvy.com was in October 2017, in the form of an email explaining his situation—in 1,375 words. You could use 1,375 words to write: a) A blog; b) A field report; c) An examination essay. His was an email with a simple message to me! Here is a distilled version:

> **I'm a professional data analyst with five years of experience, one published research paper and a family. I applied to HBS, Booth and LBS last year, and was rejected by all three. I need your help.**

I just compressed his email into 35 words by picking out the facts that matter. His résumé reflected his tendency to overelaborate, and thus spilled over four pages.

Key problems in Jai's résumé:

    i.   Verbose

    ii.   No sections or demarcations within the résumé

    iii.   Fluffy language; lack of substance

My Analysis and Fix

1. *The Verbosity*

The excessively long paragraphs that described job roles, extracurricular activity, community involvement or even educational qualifications were fixed in two simple steps. First was to incorporate strong verbs in the résumé. Jai had written:

"Worked on…"

"Responsible for handling…"

"Did an analysis of…"

He could open more powerfully, and assert this position of importance in the project by just using stronger verbs for the actions:

"Pioneered the ..."

"Singlehandedly led..."

"Analyzed market data..."

and so on.

Verbs are key in a résumé: they can really enhance the quality. Refrain from repeating the same verb too many times. Use more apt ones in place of repetitions. I have provided a list of strong verbs for you to refer to at the end of this chapter.

The second step was to use smaller sentences. You do not need to make up complex sentences to impress the reader. Here is an example.

> **"Worked with the marketing team where I helped them to increase the user base of the application by 10,000 users in the mobile space."**

Here is how I fixed it:

> **"Assisted the marketing team in increasing our mobile application user base by 10,000."**

This helps the reader gather what you have accomplished quickly and effectively. Moreover, you use half the number of words giving you space to add more accomplishments on the page.

2. *The Lack of Focused Boundaries within the Résumé*

Jai had five years of work experience and several strong extracurricular activities to his credit. However, he was blurring these two unrelated waters into a verbal sludge. To fix this, we also needed a change in approach and thought process.

First, ensure you have the correct sections in the correct order within your résumé as discussed in section 2:A. All voluntary work that isn't directly related to your career should go under community involvement and leadership.

5:B. Riya Has Little Work Experience

R: Maybe I'll try sometime else, VK… I don't have enough work experience right now.
VK: That's a valid fear… but the thing is, the rest of your profile is truly exceptional. We only have to draw attention to those parts instead. Your goal is realistic too. Business school is not just for high-flying professionals like you think.

Riya, an economics major, had a strong academic record. She had a scholarship and a professor's assistantship under her belt. She was also working on publishing her own research paper and was a university topper. Her GRE score was exceptional, putting her in the 97th percentile of all test takers.

However, she was of the opinion that her work experience was weak and it was the most crucial factor that business schools consider. She had only two years of work experience with a top NGO in India. Her fear led her to move the focus off her spectacular academics and leadership/community involvement to an insipid elaborate explanation of her full-time work experience that took up over three-quarters of her résumé. Her thought:

"How will I compete with my peers who all come with an average of 4½ years of full-time work experience?"

I had to convince Riya that she had to showcase multiple aspects of her profile on the one-page résumé. She had field experience of adopting and assisting villages from areas that were traditionally neglected and in dire need of infrastructure. At college she had had two strong internships and was the head of the cultural council. Her résumé gave this very little importance and relegated these to a few obscure points.

In sum, these were the issues in Riya's résumé:

    i.   Overemphasis on a single professional experience

   ii.   Undermining her academic credentials

  iii.   No focus on her various community activities

My Analysis and Fix

1. Poor Positioning of the Résumé

Riya failed to position herself as a strong candidate on the résumé because she misunderstood what business schools wanted. She was too focused on trying to make her two years of work look glorious, undervaluing her stellar academic record, research, internships and community involvement. Our first advice in any résumé-editing session is:

Focus on your strengths—not on the weaknesses.

I advised Riya to focus on the academic section. Her gold medals and research work were highlighted and given proper descriptors, quantifying the impact of her research. This made her achievements stand out in a clear section and look impressive.

What did we do about the professional section? Trimmed it to the point and focused on the impact she had created. This tremendously helped Riya's résumé as it cut straight to the point and gave room for other aspects to be showcased.

2. Allowing Community Activity to Take a Backseat

Those volunteering opportunities you took, the curation you did at a TEDx event, the projects you led for your college festival, any green initiatives you are involved with at your workspace, are all important aspects. Ignoring them is a major mistake many aspirants make.

Treat the community involvement section of your résumé with importance.

3. Listing Without Detailing

You don't want the details on your application to be at the mercy of the reader's imagination. Explain the scope and impact of your work. Use short sentences with strong verbs and quantify your impact to get your message across. If it's a toss-up between brevity and clarity, go for clarity, even at the cost of a few extra words.

For instance, Riya had merely mentioned:

Head, XYZ Cultural Club   **20XX-20XX**

Here is how we fixed the section in her résumé:

---

1. Managed a team of 15 students to organize over 70 events in a span of 3 months.
2. Increased the number of active members twofold—from 74 to 150—through a series of intensive marketing and PR campaigns.

This shows your work, instead of focusing merely on your title in the organization. The word 'Head' means little if one does not know what you did as the head.

5:C. Anish Uses an Outdated Résumé

VK: So, do you have a résumé ready for review?
A: Yes, I just have to make a few additions—I haven't been job hunting since I graduated.

Anish had been working in his father's business for three years. He promised he would dig out his old résumé, update it and email it to me shortly.

That week, I received his résumé. Anish used numbers in very few places apart from his phone number and dates on the résumé. Even though he had handled the finances of his business, no mention was made of how much money was involved or saved in the projects he had led. Result? Much of the impact he had actually had on the business was lost.

Also, because his résumé was tailored for the job application process (he had applied for an internship in college), it did not bring out the other aspects of his profile or elaborate on his current experience. It completely ignored the fact that Anish had recently ramped up the CSR activities of his business and was actively organizing events to help underprivileged sections of society. Had this résumé made it to the AdCom, it would have severely hurt Anish's chances of being admitted, though he was a strong candidate.

His mistakes were two fairly common ones:

    i.   **Using the same résumé for job-hunting and his MBA application**

    ii.   **Not quantifying the impact of his work**

My Analysis and Fix

1. A 'One-Size-Fits-All' Résumé

As discussed in Section 1 of this chapter, I recommend that you craft a new résumé for the application process. It should lay emphasis on what business schools look for and present a complete, multidimensional picture of you.

2. No Quantification

The result/outcome of a job is what makes it an accomplishment. Yet, several aspirants fail to put down these results on the résumé. For instance, take this descriptor from a résumé a student had sent us:

> 1. **Did an analysis of the viewer activity database and helped formulate new ad strategies that helped increased reach.**

This tells the reader what was done, but can you gauge the impact of the work? No. Merely using words like 'increased' is vague. Look at how much more of a punch it adds with numbers put to the work:

> 1. **Analyzed the activity of 1 million viewers and formulated new ad strategies that tripled the reach to 45,000 from 15,000.**

By putting numbers like these to your achievement, you solidify your impact in a role or project.

For people with unconventional backgrounds in music, art or sports, this kind of quantification might seem difficult at first. However, you can still put a number to the reach of your work, the concerts or exhibitions you presented it at, the gigs you performed, the awards or medals won, teams coached (and prizes won by the team under you), and so on.

5:D. Akanksha's Résumé Is a Scrapbook

A: Do you think my résumé looks good, VK?

VK: Yes, it's artistic… great choice of fonts and illustrations. That's not what the AdCom wants, however.

When Akanksha's résumé made it to us, it looked almost as decorated as an Indian bride. Highlights were in bold red; there were graphs and bar charts to showcase her different skills in relation to one another. The font size also changed from one line to the next haphazardly.

While visually appealing, her résumé did not fit the requisite format for an MBA résumé.

Her mistakes in sum?

    i.   **Inconsistent and overly done formatting**

    ii.   **Focus on visuals over words**

My Analysis and Fix

1. Inconsistent and Overly Done Formatting

Poor formatting and extravagant graphical elements make a résumé harder to read and portrays the applicant as unprofessional. Substance always wins over style. Keep it simple. You do not need the font Algeria for that header; Times New Roman will do just fine. The focus should be on bringing out your accomplishments.

Use the same style of pointers across the résumé. Do not keep switching between bullet and arrow pointers, for instance. You might think this makes your sections stand out, but it really is just confusing to the reader.

Moreover, inconsistent and extra-formatted text with graphics consumes more space than consistent, neat formatting. To avoid such formatting errors, you can head to ReachIvy.com and use our Résumé Builder tool. It is automated and will save you a lot of time and hassle.

6. Errors in a Nutshell

6:A. Verbosity

Remember, you are writing a one-page résumé, not an essay.

Insider Tips

1. Use bullet points instead of big paragraphs.
2. Compose short sentences.
3. Limit yourself to 4–5 bullet points per position held.
4. Use action verbs for greater impact. However, refrain from using the same verb more than twice.

Before

- Calculate, facilitate and produce specific data as per client requirements such as statement of accounts, capital gains statements, AIF Category 3 returns, folio generation, converting units to demat form and lien and mark format, difference in returns between the Institutional Plan and Direct Plan, whether Ultra Short category is better than the Arbitrage category and direct equities is better than the mutual fund

After

- Acquired and advising 50+ new investors-calculating annualized returns, preparing their treasury plan, educating about various schemes and communicating macroeconomic; resulting in over 8Mn USD additional investments in the company's schemes
- Assist the 30+ national sales team by generating and circulating a daily industry comparative return reports, identifying specific sectors with surplus money, tracking new deal flows and producing special industry specific reports
- Trained and supervised 2 summer interns and guided them through rigorous internship projects on ■■■■■ and balance sheet analysis that led to better pitching products to clients and in-depth analysis of clients' treasury investments

6:B. Lack of Focused Boundaries within the Résumé

Remember to create sections based on your strengths in your résumé. Do not let sections overlap; use the sections to project your varied strengths.

Insider Tip

1. Ensure you have correctly divided your résumé as per the demarcations discussed in section 3.

Before

PROFESSIONAL EXPERIENCE

▮▮▮▮ Investment Managers — XXXX, India
Trainee, Institutional Sales Team — August 20XX- Present

- Tapped and handling more than 110 million of first time investor money in equity, liquid and non-liquid debt mutual fund category
- Strategized to target clients based on specific sectors, over 200 million new investments received
- Fast Growth Trajectory- out in the field after a month- Relationship Manager to 50+ new clients
- Generate daily industry comparative return reports that are sent to the institutional and fixed income investment team nationwide
- Cleared NISM-Series-V-A: Mutual Fund Distributors Certification Examination- 86%
- Recommended ideas for waste management at the pan India Level to recycle plastic and paper
- Calculate, facilitate and produce specific data as per client requirements such as statement of accounts, capital gains statements, AIF Category 3 returns, folio generation, converting units to demat form and lien and mark format, difference in returns between the Institutional Plan and Direct Plan, whether Ultra Short category is better than the Arbitrage category and direct equities is better than the mutual fund

Startup – ▮▮▮▮ Lateral Thinking Classes — Present

- Teaching children (Age-group:8-18 years) - thinking out-of-the box, critical reasoning, mind-mapping and collaboration

▮▮▮▮ University — XXXXXX, India
Associate, Office of Admissions and Financial Aid — March 20XX

- Assisted in building a new centralized admissions process and instrumental in developing campus connect for potential students

▮▮▮▮ (Founded by ▮▮▮▮ Alumni) — XXXXX, India
Officer on Special Duty — October 20XX - Present

- Instrumental in project 'Evolution' where we transformed the sanitation facilities, infrastructure, drinking water and dish washing area of the municipal schools through corporate donations of 0.5 mn INR per school, 180 schools have been already renovated
    - Collected approximately 285 mn from corporate donors such as ▮▮▮, ▮▮▮ Bank, ▮▮▮ Finance, etc.
    - Created a self-assessment analytical model that has been implemented in and is benefitting over 180 local municipal schools
- Led the initiative '▮▮▮ Force' in approximately 50 colleges in the State along with the State Minister of Higher & Technical Education, Women & Child Development, to collect necessities and distribute them to benefit thousands of underprivileged children
- Actively involved in the launch of '▮▮▮▮' Campaign in the memory of the late President of India (Dr. A.P.J. Abdul Kalam) where we collected 85000 stories from 95 different schools all over India
- Collaborated a holistic scholarship program '▮▮▮' where we awarded financial aid to +250 students of municipal schools (9th-12th Graders)

▮▮▮ India Private Limited — Ahmedabad, India
Financial Advisory Intern — Summer 20XX

- Assisted with business valuations, financial statements analysis, corporate governance assessment and M&A deal structuring
- Helped develop target acquisition lists for the clients

▮▮▮ Industries — Ahmedabad, India
Import-Export Division Intern — Summer 20XX

- Interacted with the banking institutions for establishing Letters of Credit as part of purchasing and supply chain process
- Gained familiarity with regulatory, transaction and production requirements for exports of dyestuff and polymers

ADDITIONAL INFORMATION AND INTERESTS

- Volunteered at ▮▮▮ Association- Increased their revenues by 100% and Facebook Engagement by 15 fold to create awareness

After

PROFESSIONAL EXPERIENCE

▮ Investment Managers — Mumbai, India

Trainee, *Institutional Sales Team* — Aug 2016 - Present

- Acquired and advising 50+ new investors-calculating annualized returns, preparing their treasury plan, educating about various schemes and communicating macroeconomic; resulting in over 8Mn USD additional investments in the company's schemes
- Assist the 30+ national sales team by generating and circulating a daily industry comparative return reports, identifying specific sectors with surplus money, tracking new deal flows and producing special industry specific reports
- Trained and supervised 2 summer interns and guided them through rigorous internship projects on Alternate Investment Fund and balance sheet analysis that led to better pitching products to clients and in-depth analysis of clients' treasury investments

▮▮▮▮ Private Limited — Ahmedabad, India

Financial Advisory Intern — May 2014

- Analyzed corporate financial statements by calculating business valuations and forming a data set with predetermined benchmarks and variables to study peer dynamics to develop target acquisition lists for potential Mergers & Acquisitions deals
- Prepared and circulated in the entire department an official report on 'Insider Trading' due to strict corporate governance laws

LEADERSHIP EXPERIENCE

▮▮▮▮ Lateral Thinking Classes, India — Feb 2016 - Feb 2017

- Successfully structured and conducted 2 batches and workshops, 40+ students (Ahmedabad & Mumbai)-taught thinking out-of-the box, critical reasoning, mind-mapping, brainstorming and collaboration through various activities using word-of-mouth and closed social media marketing

General Secretary, Student council, ▮▮▮ University — Jun 2014 - Apr 2015

- Planned, executed and oversaw 5+ city, state and national level events by mobilizing 50+ students- assigning responsibility, mentoring, motivating, monitoring of performance, giving constructive feedback and managing internal conflicts

Team Leader, ▮▮ Research Project, ▮▮▮▮, India — Jun 2014 - Apr 2015
- Devised and incorporated specific systems and enforced clear role division to manage internal team conflicts (10 members) that improved work culture, articulation of ideas and implementation, resulting in winning the research competition

COMMUNITY INVOLVEMENT

Officer on Special Duty, ▮▮▮▮, ▮▮▮▮, India — Oct 2014 - Present
- Formalized the municipal school empowerment program, raised 4.41 Mn USD from corporate donors such as ▮▮▮, ▮▮ Bank, ▮▮ Finance and created a self-assessment analytical model benefitting 180+ municipal schools
- Led a team of 10+ senior colleagues- initiative '▮▮ Force' in 40+ colleges to collect necessities and distribute them to benefit 1000+ underprivileged children and - '*Udaan*' that awarded financial aid to 250+ municipal school students
- Composed and reviewed the website content and partnered with media partners and celebrities for 'Make your Mother Smile' campaign, in memory of the late President of India (Dr. A.P.J. Abdul Kalam)-collected 85000+ stories from all over India

Volunteer, ▮▮▮ Association, ▮▮▮▮, India — Jun 2013 - Aug 2013

- Boosted revenues by 100% by working with differently-abled people through redesigning and revamping product portfolio mix
- Accelerated Facebook Engagement by 15 fold by optimising paid marketing, streamlining content and word-of-mouth

As you can see in the highlighted sections, the applicant had put activities that contributed to leadership experience and community involvement in the professional experience bucket. By separating these out, we were able to shed light on these areas.

6:C. *Listing Job Titles without Detailing*

Merely listing roles and responsibilities makes your résumé look like a shopping list.

Insider Tip

1. Add a point-format description for each job title that lets the reader know what work you have done, how you did it, and what impact you had.

Before

- Volunteered at ■■■ ■■■ ■■■■ - Increased their revenues by 100% and Facebook Engagement by 15 fold to create awareness

After

Volunteer, ■■■■■ Association, ■■■■■, India   **Jun 20■■ - Aug 20■■**

- Boosted revenues by 100% by working with differently-abled people through redesigning and revamping product portfolio mix
- Accelerated Facebook Engagement by 15 fold by optimising paid marketing, streamlining content and word-of-mouth

6:D. *No Quantification*

Just stating the work you did at a job says nothing about the impact you had, nor does it help establish how much skill you possess.

Insider Tip

1. Put a number to your achievements. Quantifying accomplishments will ensure that the résumé reflects your skills.

Before

Class Representative, IIT, Delhi, India   August, 20■■ – July, 20■■

- Elected by 150 students to become the voice of the class.
- Organized various sports and cultural events for teambuilding resulting in close bonded alumni base

After

Class Representative, ■■■■ - ■■■, India   August, 20■■ – July, 20■■

- Campaigned for CR elections; Elected by 150 students to become the voice of the class.
- Organized fresher's night with budget of $3k and team of 7; Getting 15 performance entrees and 300+ party guests.

6:E. Allowing Community Work to Take a Back Seat

You are trying to establish yourself as a well-rounded individual with leadership potential, the ability to work in a team, and initiative to give back to the community; have your résumé reflect that.

Insider Tip

1. If you have been involved in community work, please highlight it in a clear section.

Before

- **Mentor at ■■■■■■■■■, ■■■■, ■■■■, India**
- **Founded a Non-profit, ■■■■, measured implementation of ■■■■ in 10 villages.**

After

COMMUNITY INVOLVEMENT

Mentor, ■■■■ ■■■■ ■■■■■ ■■■■■ (■■■), ■■■, ■■■ ■■■■, India   Feb 20■■ – Present

- Facilitated setup of a ■■■■ by working closely with ■■■■■ and local partners, and hiring 3 employees
- Designed the outreach programs to enrol 1120 learners in 1 year, the highest among all 545 DLCs of ■■■ across India

Founder, ■■■■, Non-profit, ■■■■ ■■■■, India   May 20■■ – Aug 20■■

- Built a 45-member volunteer team, by pitching the idea in 5 local colleges, to run social audits of govt. schemes; led them to measure implementation of ■ ■ ■ (■■■■ ■■■■) in 10 villages

6:F. Inconsistent or Overly Done Formatting

A well-formatted résumé will look neat and draw attention to what matters in minimal space.

Insider Tips

1. Keep headings, font size, spacing and font styles consistent throughout the résumé.
2. Use bullet or arrow pointers, not both.
3. Be consistent in whether you are using full stops at the end of bullet points.

Before

LEADERSHIP AND SERVICE

Volunteer Consultant – ■■■ Lead, ■■■■■, ■■■■   May 20■■ - Present

Chosen as 1 of 30 selected from a global application pool of approx. 400 applicants (Tier 1 consulting firms)

- **Engineered a business plan to pilot a Virtual Business Advisor (VBA) system to provide operational and management support to wet mills in ■■■■■■ ■■■■■■– included in depth desk and field research, development of efficiency models.**
- **Conceived and developed a VBA iPhone application demo for presentation to funding partners based on outcome of business plan.**
- **Currently providing post project pro-bono advice on the ■■■■■■■■■ ■■■■project on strategic, execution and tool development.**
- **Invited to give a TEDx Talk on the work in ■■■■■■■■■ in November 20■■ – did not engage as measurable data on outcome and impact was incomplete.**

After

LEADERSHIP AND SERVICE

Volunteer Consultant – ■■■ Lead, ■■■■■, ■■■■   May 20■■ - Present

Chosen as 1 of 30 selected from a global application pool of approx. 400 applicants (Tier 1 consulting firms)

- Engineered a business plan to pilot a Virtual Business Advisor (VBA) system to provide operational and management support to wet mills in ■■■■ ■■■ – included in depth desk and field research, development of efficiency models.
- Conceived and developed a VBA iPhone application demo for presentation to funding partners based on outcome of business plan.
- Currently providing post project pro-bono advice on the ■■■■ ■■■■ project on strategic, execution and tool development.
- Invited to give a TEDx Talk on the work in ■■■■■ in November 20■■ – did not engage as measurable data on outcome and impact was incomplete.

6:G. One Résumé for All Purposes

Business schools and recruiters look for different things in their candidates.

Insider Tips

1. Craft a new résumé for your MBA application which showcases your holistic strengths.

Insider Tips at a Glance

DO:

✓ Maintain the length of your résumé at one page.

✓ Use bullet points instead of big paragraphs.

✓ Condense your accomplishments into crisp sentences.

✓ Limit yourself to 4–5 bullet points per position held.

✓ Use action verbs for greater impact.

✓ Ensure you have correctly divided your résumé into clear sections.

✓ Add a point-format description for each job title.

✓ Quantify your accomplishments.

✓ Treat all sections with equal importance.

✓ Maintain simple, consistent formatting throughout.

✓ Use the résumé like a 'sales tool'.

DON'T:

Χ Write a multi-page résumé.

Χ Harbor misconceptions about what sections business schools prefer.

Χ Lie or concoct information.

Χ Use buzzwords and jargon.

Χ Decorate your résumé with graphs and pie charts.

Χ Repeat the same action verbs.

Χ Mix-up different sections.

Χ Use the same résumé you did for your job application.

APPENDIX

List of Action Verbs You Can Include:

Achieved	Administered	Advised	Assisted	Audited	Budgeted	Built
Coached	Collaborated	Constructed	Coordinated	Decreased	Delivered	Designed
Developed	Directed	Edited	Enacted	Established	Evaluated	Expanded
Facilitated	Fixed	Formulated	Generated	Guided	Headed	Hired
Implemented	Improved	Increased	Inspected	Instructed	Interviewed	Launched
Launched	Learned	Maintained	Managed	Marketed	Manufactured	Monitored
Negotiated	Operated	Ordered	Organized	Oversaw	Planned	Predicted
Prepared	Presented	Programmed	Proposed	Purchased	Recommended	Recorded
Recruited	Reorganized	Reported	Researched	Reviewed	Scheduled	Set up
Solved	Started	Supervised	Taught	Tested	Tracked	Trained
Updated	Upgraded	Utilized	Verified	Widened	Worked	Wrote

Résumé Template

FIRST-NAME LAST-NAME
Phone: +91-123-456-7890 • **E-mail:** youremailid@domain.com • **Address:**

EDUCATION

Academic Institution, City, Country   **Years attended**
Degree/Qualification name in full
Any Awards/Honors Received:

Academic Institution, City, Country   **Years attended**
Degree/Qualification name in full
Any Awards/Honors Received:

Include any Summer Schools or Advanced Educational Programs here

CERTIFICATIONS

Company/Organization you received it from - Name of Certification and (if relevant)   **M/Y end**

PROFESSIONAL EXPERIENCE

Company/Organization   **City/Place, Country**
Designation   **Month & Yr of starting – Present**
- Chronological order of responsibilities (in descending order – start with most recent)
-
-

Company/Organization   **City/Place, Country**
Designation   **Month & Yr start – Month & Yr end**
- Chronological order of responsibilities (in descending order – start with most recent)
-
-

Company/Organization   **City/Place, Country**
Designation   **Month & Yr start – Month & Yr end**
- Chronological order of responsibilities (in descending order – start with most recent)
-
-

LEADERSHIP EXPERIENCE

Designation, Name of Project, Company/Organization, City/Place, Country   **M/Y start – M/Y end**
- Chronological order of responsibilities (in descending order – start with most recent)
-

                                                          M/Y start – M/Y end
Designation, Name of Project, Company/Organization, City/Place, Country
- Chronological order of responsibilities (in descending order – start with most recent)
-

COMMUNITY INVOLVEMENT

Designation, Name of Project, Company/Organization, City/Place, Country   **M/Y start – M/Y end**
- Chronological order of responsibilities (in descending order – start with most recent)
-

                                                          M/Y start – M/Y end
Designation, Name of Project, Company/Organization, City/Place, Country
- Chronological order of responsibilities (in descending order – start with most recent)

SKILLS & INTERESTS

- General skills you possess along with proficiency level/grade of accomplishment
- Languages Spoken: Rate according to level of fluency (Native/Fluent/Beginner)
- Any hobbies you have pursued seriously along with proficiency level/grade of accomplishment

Résumés That Have Worked
Admitted to: Harvard Business School

■■■■ ■■■■■■■■■

+00 00000 00000   ■■■, ■■■, ■■■■, ■■■■, ■■■■, ■■■■ - ■■■■, India   ■■■■■■@xyz.com

EDUCATION

■■■■■■, ■ ■ ■ ■ ■ (■■■■), ■■■■, India   Aug 20■■ – Jul 20■■
Dual Degree (B.Tech, M.Tech), **■■■■■■■■■■■■■■■ ■■■ Engineering** (CGPA: 7.9/10)
Minor, Innovation & Social Entrepreneurship (CGPA: 9.7/10)
- Received the ■ ■ ■ ■ ■ (1 of 8 from over 100 students) for outstanding overall performance (20■■)
- Awarded an Institute Silver Medal for ranking 1ˢᵗ in the ■■■■■ (20■■)
- Presented an Institute Silver Medal for ranking 1ˢᵗ in the Innovation Minor (20■■)

PROFESSIONAL EXPERIENCE

■■■■■■■■■■■, ■■■■■■   Jan 20■■ – Present
Associate, Research & Analysis Unit   ■■■■■, India
- First hire in a new unit operating out of the ■■■■■ ■■■■focusing on research, analysis & strategy.

■■■■■ ■■■■■■ ■■, ■■■■■ ■■■■■   Jun 20■■ – Dec 20■■
Project Manager, Chairman's Office   ■■■■■■■■, India
- First hire in the Chairman's Office, a new core team responsible for identifying new opportunities & executing new projects.
- Established Chairman's Office; recruited 15 Associates from top-tier firms & colleges in India and set up PR, HR teams.
- Leading 5-member team & working with senior bureaucrats in 20 Government Ministries to improve the quality of public services using analysis of citizens feedback; findings used in the Prime Minister's monthly meetings on structural reforms.
- Launched a first-of-its-kind dashboard for the Prime Minister's Office to track citizen feedback across the country, currently being implemented; developing similar dashboards for many of the Prime Minister's flagship schemes as well.
- Guided 4-member pre-launch team of ■ ■ ■ ■ ■ ■ (■■■■■■■■, ■■■■■■), a $100 mn scheme within ■■■■■■ to improve MSME competitiveness. Designed the pilot & implemented key components including operations, marketing & recruiting.

■■■■■■■ & ■■■■■■   Oct 20■■ – May 20■■
Business Analyst   ■■■■■■■, India
Rated 'Distinctive' (top 10% of batch), first BA in 2 years to receive the rating.
- **E-Commerce:** Advised operations & strategy teams of one of India's Top 3 e-commerce companies to achieve GMV and margins targets for key arms of the business
  - Set up planning teams for the client to plan purchasing & track sales of estimated GMV of $1 bn across 15 categories.
  - Developed framework & model to define overall strategy for the client; developed long-term goals & near-term work-plan for client's priority businesses.
- **Pharmaceuticals:** Conducted commercial due-diligence of a $500 mn Pharmaco for an international Private Equity firm.
- **Public Health:** Advised an international aid agency in creating a strategy to eradicate ■■■■■ ■■■■■■.

COMMUNITY INVOLVEMENT

Volunteer, Pro-Bono engagements, ■■■■, ■■■■■■, India   Oct 20■■ – May 20■■
- Reoriented vision for ■■■■■■■, 30-year-old theater group in Pondicherry, and created long-term plan to achieve financial sustainability. Conducted multiple workshops for upper management to help build this capability.
- Advised a tech start-up developing products for autistic children on vision, recruitment & growth strategy.
- Counseled the Director of ■■■■■■■, a ~100-year-old classical arts institution in XXXXX. Led workshops to redefine the organization's mission & vision. Designed & executed initiatives to help the organization achieve profitability.

LEADERSHIP EXPERIENCE

Co-Founder and Executive Editor, ■■■■■■■ – Official News Body of ■■■■■, ■■■■■, India   Aug 20■■ – Jul 20■■
- Co-founded ■■■■■■■'s first online news body; profiled by ■■■■■■ ■ ■ ■ (2011) and regarded as one of the top student news bodies in India in terms of content & readership.
- Expanded team size from 8 to 30, formalized four-tier hierarchy, instituted standard recruiting processes that continue today.
- Guided correspondents in writing articles that have defined key ■■■■■■■ policies and stances, including positions on homosexuality, suicide counseling etc.

Core Member, Sponsorship and PR, ■■■■■■■■ '11 - Technical Festival of ■■■■■, ■■■, India   Mar 20■■ – Oct 20■■
- Led 800 students as part of 20-member core team to run one of Asia's largest tech-festivals with over 10,000 participants.
- Managed 85 students across 5 teams to raise $125,000 from partnerships with over 40 corporations across India.

EXTRA-CURRICULAR ACTIVITIES
- **Business Plan Competitions:** provide affordable drinking water to villages in India. Received funding interest from investors
  - Winner, ■■■■■ – International B-Plan competition by ■■■■■ University with over 150 teams globally, 20■■.
  - Winner, ■■■■■– National B-Plan competition by ■■■■■■■■ with over 120 teams across India, 20■■.
- **Quiz:** Winner/Finalist in over 15 inter-college and intra-college quizzes hosted at ■■■■■■.

Admitted to: London Business School

■■■■■■■■■■■■■■■

■■■-■■■, ■■■■■, ■■■■, ■■■■■ ■■■■■, India; +00-0000000000; ■■■■■■@xyz.com

EDUCATION

■■■■ Fellowship (■■■), ■■■■■■, ■■■■■, India   July'■■ - June'■■

■■■ is a one-year multidisciplinary postgraduate diploma program that selects 200 fellows across country. It is delivered in collaboration with University of ■■■■, ■■■■ College, ■■■■■■ University and other renowned colleges.
Post Graduate Diploma in Liberal Studies, GPA: 3.39/4; Graduated in Top 10% of Batch

■■■■■■■■■ of Commerce (■■■■■), ■■■■ University, ■■■■■, India   July'■■ - July'■■
Bachelor of Commerce (Honors); Graduated with First division and in Top 10% of Batch

Academic Honors:
- **Two National Merit Certificates** (20■■, 20■■), for being among the top 0.1% of all candidates who appeared in India (CBSE)
- **Merit Scholarship – ■■■■■** Scholarship (2015); **■■■■■■** Scholarship (20■■,20■■)

PROFESSIONAL EXPERIENCE

■■■■■ ■■ (■■■■), ■■■■ ■■■■, ■■■■■■ ■■■■, India   Jul '■■ - Present
A government organization set up by ■■■■■■■, ■■■■■■ and ■■■■ and led by ■■■■, former ■■■■■■■■. It is the national accreditation body & sets standards across public & private sectors.
Chairman's Office | Project Manager
- Managed India-wide transformation program for **■■■■■, ■■■■■**. Identified 55 projects across 9 themes, assigned roles and restructured work flows - decision making based on 5 as against earlier 40 signatures, monitored metrics and milestones; decreased project turnaround duration by 67% (9 months to 3 months) and led to implementation of 10+ projects in 1 year
- Increased Non-Fare Revenue of **■■■■■■** by 72% (USD 9.1 Billion in 2016 to USD 15 Billion in 2017) by preparing and implementing 6 policies that focused on less price sensitive customer segments and addressed key concerns of industry
- Led a team of 30 people and 150 contractors to execute the on-ground comprehensive assessment of ■ ■ ■ ■ ■ (■■■■■■) for **■■■■■**. Carried out project across 407 train stations, covering all 29 Indian states. Quality of work delivered led to renewal of the engagement – similar assessment for all 8,000 stations and 200 priority trains
- Developed technology platform (Dashboard) and review framework for **■■■■** and **■■■■■** to monitor key outcomes for 30 federal government ministries; review led to identification of 15 key strategic initiatives
- Initiated collaboration with ■ ■ ■ ■ ■ ■ ■ (■■■■) and ■■■■ ■■■■ ■■■to bring best practices in implementation of quality control in India
- Generated partnerships and grew revenue from consulting and project implementation services by INR. 60 Million. Served as key contact and relationship manager to 5 government departments and ministries

■■■■■■■■ ■■■■■■ Limited, ■■■, India   Jul '■■ - Jul '■■
Associate Solution Advisor
- Performed risk assessments of key government ministries within 5 nations across the African and Asian continents; results used by leading Grants Funding Agency in its Official Development Assistance (ODA) decision-making process
- Spearheaded project aimed at addressing regulatory compliance requirements and implementing effective compliance management process for **■■■■■**; recommendations accepted for 5 countries analyzed - Chile, Brazil, Costa Rica, US and India
- Executed projects for Fortune 500 clients across Public Sector and Consumer goods industry, assisting them in analysing their business processes, identifying key risks and advising risk-mitigation strategies to enhance operational excellence; increased India integration with clients across the Asian, Australian, North and South American continents
- Advised one of the biggest private Oil and Gas companies based in Canada in the vendor contract compliance space; project involved leading coordination efforts with close to 500 client vendors spread across the globe; Quality of work delivered led to renewal of the engagement for the following fiscal (USD 1 million)
- Prepared internal **■■■■■■■** model to benchmark key business processes of Public Sector clients; model adopted by member firms (150+) globally; insights of model used to win Federal Government departments of Australia and US
- Recognized as top performing Consultant by Management – awarded highest rating among 150 consultants (Advisory function)

COMMUNITY INVOLVEMENT

■■■■ ■■■■ ■■■■ – ■ ■ ■ ■ ■ (■■■■) | Lead Intern (16 hours/week)   Sep'■■ - May'■■
■■■■, program based at University of ■■■■ – ■■■■■, sends top talent to work with government organizations to implement innovative solutions to important development problems
- Collaborated with MA (Funded by USAID, DFID & TDB), a grants funding platform, to increase application base for India; Augmented the existing application base to more than 1.3 Million organizations by re-strategizing communications policy

■■■■■■, ■■■■■■, India| Volunteer (40 hours/week)   June'■■ - Jul'■■
- Planned and executed medical camps and health awareness drives in villages of **■■■■■**; 200+ patients examined in the drive

Admitted to:
National University of Singapore,
China Europe International Business School &
Indian School of Business

■■■■■■■■■ ■■■■■■■
P: +91-■■■■■■■ • E: ■■■■@xyz.com • A: ■■■■■, ■■■■■, ■■■■■

EDUCATION

Institute of Chartered Accountants of India   20■■ – 20■■
Chartered Accountant

■■■■ ■■■■ College of Commerce and Economics   20■■ – 20■■
Bachelor of Commerce (Honours); Graduated with First Class

CERTIFICATIONS

Decision Making for Managerial Effectiveness, ■■■■■■   20■■
Fundamentals of Quantitative Modeling, ■■■■■ ■■■■■■■■■   20■■
Basics of Credit Appraisal, ■ ■ ■ ■ ■ (affiliate of **■■■■■■ ■■■■■**)   20■■

PROFESSIONAL EXPERIENCE

■■■■■■■■ Consultants Pvt Ltd   **■■■■■, India**
Director   **Aug 20■■ - Present**
- Advising India's largest consumer durables company on restructuring debt of ■■■■■■ under ■■■■■■■ ("■■") scheme of the government through 115 acres of affordable housing project

■■■■■■■■ Infotech Ltd   **■■■■■, India**
■■■■■■ Manager   **Nov 20■■ - Jul 20■■**
- Prepared and analyzed monthly financial plan for the company, successfully used it to secure USD 500 Mn in short and long-term financing from a syndicate of lenders including foreign banks
- Lead a team of three to set-up and automated Forex back office department and spearheaded changes in hedging framework for Handsets business; Reduced manual dependency to 1 person and saved USD 10Mn in hedging costs

■■■■■■■■■■■ ■■■ Pvt Ltd   **■■■■■, India**
Co-founder   **Dec 20■■ - Present**
- Established a 1Mn sq. ft granite manufacturing unit in partnership and generated sales of ~USD 0.6 Mn and profits of ~USD 0.07 Mn within 1 year from the commercial operations date
- Acquired 50% stake in a granite mine by structuring the deal, saving ~USD 0.3 Mn;
- Introduced granite scanning technology in ■■■■■■ district, India to improve efficiencies and eliminate the need of intermediate agents; Project unsuccessful and hence had to discard the technology

■■■■■■ ■■■■ Bank Ltd   **■■■■■, India**
Associate Relationship Manager – Large Corporates   **Oct 20■■ - Nov 20■■**
- Rescued ■■■■■■ largest client from becoming a Non-Performing Asset by expanding the project scope from USD 1.1 Bn to USD 1.8 Bn and streamlining deal terms with subordinate Indian and US hedge fund lenders
- Co-led and appraised one of India's largest Food Grain Handling Co. and arranged debt financing of USD 75 Mn

■■■ ■■■■■■ & ■■■■■ and Co.   **■■■■■■, India**
Industrial Trainee & Article Assistant (Part of CA course)   **Jun 20■■ - Jun 20■■**
- Assisted in preparing credit rating notes for Indian companies and in audit of ■■■■■■■■■■ of India

COMMUNITY & LEADERSHIP EXPERIENCE

Individual Capacity
- Developed 10 free stay facilities for poor patients in ■■■■■■ and successfully lobbied the state government to build additional rooms; Project inaugurated by Health Minister of **■■■■ (20■■)**
- Light House Project: Mentoring 5 students from highly vulnerable section of the society on improving Math and English skills; academic scores of 3 students in these subjects improved ~50% **(Nov 20■■ to present)**
- Discussed my idea of reducing Child labor in the unorganized sectors of India with National Spokesperson of Indian National Congress and Chairperson of Organizational Behavior and HR Management, **■■■■■■■ (20■■)**

INTERESTS

- Travelling - Been to over 15 countries such as the UK, Australia, New Zealand, China, South Africa etc.
- Adventure Sports - Participated in Bungee Jumping, Shark-Cage, Scuba Diving etc.

5

College Selection:
How to Find Your 'Perfect Match'

Dear VK,

I want to build a business in India. Despite that some colleagues have suggested that I apply to American business schools while others praise European business schools. Why should I go abroad if I want to stay in India in the long term?

This conflicting advice is a lot to process, and I am very confused. Please help me out!

Selecting the right college is a complex, multi-layered task. Many people do not pay attention to the nuances of college selection. You will be spending 12–24 months of your primary years, in addition to up to $250,000, at the institute. Make your time and money count.

When Ayushi wrote to us, she was facing a serious dilemma. She had six years of experience in consulting (focused on financial services) and planned to start her own financial advisory firm. When she discussed her post-MBA goals with me, I assessed that she needed to develop key skills in management and entrepreneurship, build a strong global network and ideally incubate her company while at business school, taking advantage of the entrepreneurship centers that many top B-schools have. Going to a top-tier school in the United States or Europe might also help her find a strong co-founder or advisor.

At the same time, studying in an Indian or Asian school was cheaper and could save her money that could be deployed as capital for her company. Further, staying within the region could help her build a strong domestic network that could come in handy when scaling up. Then, of course, there was the question of doing a one-year versus a two-year program. Through my counseling session, I brought up all these issues and we examined all our options, before finally compiling our shortlist.

I bring up Ayushi's case for one simple reason: going into this chapter, I want the reader to let go of any preconceived notions. The American, European, Asian and Indian business schools each have their pros and cons. Location deeply influences the MBA experience and is a vital factor to consider. However, location is just one among several factors. The quality of the faculty, teaching methods, curriculum, cost, duration, brand, career opportunities, class size, alumni and other variables also need to be considered to make the right choice.

Another important tool that many applicants rely on heavily is rankings. Remember, these are published by various organizations that use vastly different methodologies. While rankings can give you a broad list of colleges, I suggest not to take the numerical ranking too seriously since these change annually and vary significantly by publisher. Look beyond geography and rankings. Consider the eight different factors I will explore later in this chapter.

Am I making too big a deal about something basic? Why is selecting the right college so critical? Let's find out.

1. The Importance of Choosing the Right College

When I was looking for a college to apply to, I sat in classrooms to understand the teaching methodology and classroom vibe and to get a pulse of the various campuses. This is when I began to understand what 'finding your fit' means.

Let me elaborate on one aspect of fit: housing and student life. I stayed on campus with a friend at INSEAD who was sharing a house with three other friends. While it was a beautiful, cozy residence, I felt disconnected from the campus and the energy of living in an on-campus residence. Being close to Paris, a major commercial hub in Europe, and the opportunity to experience French culture first-hand while getting an MBA in one year were aspects I would lose out on.

Similarly, when visiting Columbia Business School, I stayed with a friend who lived in a beautiful high-rise apartment in NYC. While I loved the buzz of being in New York, this again gave me a sense of being disconnected from the main campus. Enjoying the exhilaration of studying at an Ivy League institute while living in the Big Apple was a big tradeoff to make.

When I visited Harvard Business School, I realized that I preferred the compact and integrated nature of the HBS campus where my dorm room was a two-minute walk from the classrooms, all connected via underground tunnels. The HBS teaching methods, the strong brand recognition and other factors tilted my decision towards HBS.

It is important to note here that my friends were extremely happy with the choices they had made. They enjoyed the privacy and autonomy that comes with living away from the main campus and were enjoying the several benefits their MBA programs offered. There is no standard formula for picking a college nor is there a uniform choice for everyone. It is an extremely personal decision that is based on multiple variables.

Picking the right college is critical. Here are three reasons why:

1:A. You Get an Educational Experience That Fits Your Requirements

A component of college selection is looking at the teaching methods and courses offered by the college. Doing so helps you select a college which teaches in a manner most effective for you. We all learn differently from one another. Some might prefer the hands-on nature of experiential learning. Others might find lectures a better mode of soaking in information. When you select a college that is suited to a style you have experienced and/or are comfortable with, you will be able to take the most learning back from your MBA. Consequently, you will be able to translate these learnings into real-world action more effectively.

1:B. You Increase Your Chances of Being Accepted at Your Target Schools

Top global business schools are also judging whether you are a good fit for their program. First understand the school, review its class profile and see if you fit the overall class profile (available on their website). Class profile contains parameters such as age, average GMAT score, number of years of full-time experience, etc. If you are broadly within the averages mentioned on their websites, you know this school is a potential target for you. If you don't, eliminating the school may be a good option. Also, the research (speaking to alumni, visiting the college, meeting the AdCom, etc.) that you put into truly understanding the college will aid you with your applications, as many programs will ask why you want to attend their program, in the essays or interviews.

Colleges are gauging your self-awareness when you say you are a 'perfect fit' for them.

1:C. Prudent College Selection Prevents You from Overshooting

Comprehensively researching the schools you want to attend will prevent you from aiming for schools that might not be within your reach. I am not saying you cannot overcome odds. I only ask you to be realistic about them. For instance, you cannot expect to enter the top three business schools with a 630 GMAT and an ordinary professional experience. It is not worth investing the time writing the essays and applying to these schools that are super-competitive and look for extraordinary candidates. It will only lead to a rejection that will then lead to heartburn. Seeing the college's class profiles will allow you to gauge its requirements and make your shortlist. Remember, most top schools reject over 85 percent of the candidates who apply to them. The schools are super selective.

2. How to Choose the Right College: Factors to Consider Beyond Rankings

MBA programs worldwide are ranked every year by research companies. These give you a baseline idea of how good a school is in comparison to others. However, they are not indicative of whether a given college is a good fit for you. There are several other factors at play. Over the years, many students who contacted me on being rejected had picked colleges based only on their world ranks. They did not look at the campus culture, teaching methods, class sizes, geography, program structure or other factors. This led to a mismatch in what the candidate expected versus what the school offered. When the mismatch came through in the essays and interviews, it led to a rejection.

Why are we asking you to look beyond rankings? To understand this, let's look at how popular ranking systems work.

How Popular Rankings Work

The two most popular MBA ranking lists are provided every year by QS and *The Financial Times*. Both use different methodologies to arrive at the lists they release. It is important to note that the methodology can change over time. Certain factors from the benchmarks they follow to rate colleges may be added or dropped every year.

Some of the factors the rankings take into consideration include academic reputation, employer reputation, research produced by a given university, salaries, career assistance to students, value for money, quality of the faculty, diversity and more. Each ranking agency determines the mix of factors it wants to consider and assigns a weighted average that it deems accurate, leading to some level of 'creator bias'.

Therefore, I suggest looking at other aspects while shortlisting your colleges.

Here are 10 factors to consider when selecting an MBA program:

2:A. Accreditation

This is the first sign of quality for a top business school. Accreditations attest to the legitimacy of the degree you will be earning. Checking for accreditation should be your first step. Christophe Coutat, founder and CEO of the Advent Group, agrees:

> **"Considering only accredited MBA programs is step one. Accreditation serves as a stamp of quality guaranteeing high academic standards. The top three international MBA accreditation bodies are AACSB, AMBA and EQUIS. On the other hand, media MBA rankings should be considered after obtaining a deep understanding of their methodologies and only in cases where they reflect your essential MBA selection criteria. Ranking should never be viewed as the single selection criterion."**

2:B. Location

Students typically think about location as the country in which the business school is situated. "I only want to study in the USA." "I want to be in Europe." These are commonly heard statements at MBA events. I urge you to think deeper. Within a given country, is the campus located in a small town, rural area, suburban area or a large metropolitan city? This factor can make a big difference. Students who are used to small towns might find the city experience overwhelming. This could also work the other way around, where people from large metropolitan areas end up in small towns and find they miss the bustle of city life.

When considering location, you can also take into account the major industries located in the area. Choosing a location which is central to your industry could offer excellent opportunities to work closely with them during the MBA or during the summer break.

If you have family or relatives in a particular location, you may also pick a college that is in close proximity to them. You may consider staying with them to offset the living costs. Even if you are staying on campus, having someone related close by may come in handy in an emergency.

Additionally, understand the weather and climactic conditions of the location. If you are unable to withstand bitter winters, you may want to rule out some locations entirely.

Lastly, I advise you not to think of any one location as superior to the other. Top-notch MBA programs can be found across the globe. Consider geography in conjunction with other variables and make your decision.

2:C. Campus Culture

Campus culture consists of the spirit and vibe of the college environment and the mission of the MBA program. The clubs on campus, extracurricular activities organized by the student body, other social activities on campus, the student body's diversity, all comprise campus culture. It lends a college its distinctive vibe. Some generic examples of campus culture can be 'collaborative', 'sports hub', 'research-centric', 'quantitative orientation', 'tech orientation', and so on.

You want to find a campus whose culture most complements you. If, for example, you have an analytical orientation and enjoy being in a very quantitative program, you might want to go to similarly oriented schools such as MIT Sloan School of Management or the Tepper School of Business. This will ensure that you attend college with similarly minded individuals. Also, the curriculum and classes will be structured to suit a quantitative mindset. Fitting in with the culture of the school is one of the factors I give a lot of weightage to.

2:D. Cost of Attendance

You must definitely consider how much you can afford to spend on your education. Tuition fees vary significantly from one geography to another and also depend on duration of the program. If money is a factor, your choice of college may vary significantly on the basis of that parameter.

Personally, I recommend looking at financing the MBA not just in terms of the cost of attendance but also by evaluating the long-term Return on Investment (RoI). For instance, Stanford GSB has a $120,000 cost of attendance and the median salary of graduates is anywhere upwards of $115,000. Similarly, it takes around $45,000 to attend NUS and the median salary of graduates is upwards of $65,000. The cost of attending and salary earned are typically directly proportional to each other. I advocate keeping the long-term perspective in mind when calculating the RoI on your program.

Additionally, scholarships play an important role in determining how much you end up paying. Some colleges offer special scholarships and some organizations provide grants to students going to certain colleges.

For instance, I worked with Sneha, who was accepted at both Wharton and Michigan Ross. Wharton ranks very high in most rankings and is considered a top-league school. However, she chose Michigan Ross as it gave her a 100 percent scholarship on tuition fees, effectively giving her a free education.

Picking a large financial grant over a top-brand school is a very personal choice. For Sneha, taking the offer from the school that offered her a scholarship relieved her of the worry of having to finance her education. Following in her footsteps could be a huge relief for aspirants who wish to go to a top MBA program but cannot afford it.

On the flip side, I have worked with several students who have chosen to go to top-ranked schools despite the high costs involved. They considered the MBA an investment and were comfortable making this investment owing to the significant RoI involved.

Finances can also vary based on the geography you pick. Programs located in places where living costs are high will drive up your expenses. It will be prudent on your part to factor in living expenses as well when picking a college.

Chapter 10 delves into how to plan your finances.

2:E. Teaching Methods

Teaching methods at schools are case study-focused (Harvard Business School), lecture-centric (Carnegie Mellon), and experiential learning-based (Cornell Johnson). Most schools will use a combination of the three methods, but they may be skewed heavily towards one of the three. Factor in which mode of teaching you enjoy, helps you learn faster, and best suits what you aim to gain from business school. Then make an informed choice.

I have seen many Indian students who have thrived in a 'lecture-centric' environment, where the professor is the dominant speaker, struggle initially with a 'case-based' method where the students become the dominant voice in the classroom. There is always an adjustment period when students transition from one methodology to another.

In my case, sitting on a case discussion at Harvard made me realize that I wanted to partake in the passionate interchange among classmates leading to a high-energy discussion. Students were encouraged to freely express divergent viewpoints. This atmosphere of discussion really appealed to me. I was further pleased to know that all classes at HBS were taught in a similar manner. Every class was taught in the form of a case discussion with students engaging with one another and the professor mainly playing the role of facilitator.

Once again, this teaching style may not appeal to you if you enjoy a formal student-professor relationship. I understand that voicing opinions loudly and strongly in a public setting is not for everyone. I advise you to choose a school that best suits your ideal mode of learning.

2:F. *Program Structure and Duration*

The program structure and duration vary highly between the traditional MBA, one-year MBA, executive MBA and online MBA. Pick the structure and duration that best fits your professional needs:

1. Are you two–seven years into your career but want a comprehensive business education? The traditional MBA is for you.
2. Do you want to avoid the long career break a traditional MBA imposes, or come back to manage your family business? Look into the one-year MBA.
3. Are you a seasoned professional deep into your career? The executive MBA might be what you are looking for.

See our section on the different types of MBA (Chapter 1, Why MBA) to know more about the structure and duration of different programs. Understand the requirements, eligibility, pros and cons of various program structures and then make a decision.

2:G. Alumni Network

A strong, responsive alumni network is often overlooked by students. It provides you with a network of brilliant, accomplished individuals who are ready to help you. Moreover, a dynamic alumni body speaks volumes for the quality of the school. A good school impresses a sense of belonging and camaraderie among its students. Check to see how large and active the school's alumni chapters are across the world.

I would suggest that you reach out to some alumni to gather more information about the college. Judge how their career trajectories have been and see how responsive they are to helping you. These interactions will reveal the quality and strength of the alumni network.

2:H. Class Size

While it may seem insignificant at first, the class size becomes an important factor as the program advances.

A large program may afford you diverse and plenty of networking opportunities. However, the trade-off in programs with a large class size is the intimacy of the program itself.

On the other hand, a smaller class size allows you to build a stronger bond with your peers. You are also likely to receive focused attention from professors since there are fewer students. The trade-off is that smaller programs afford you fewer networking opportunities.

It all boils down to what you prefer. Is it a small, close-knit community? Or a large, diverse one?

2:I. Brand

The brand of an MBA program is an immensely valuable asset; it stays with you like a shadow, through life. To evaluate whether the brand is strong, try to gauge the reach of the college by asking the following questions:

1.   How many people know this college in your home country?

2. Do potential employers value this college?
3. When you talk to your peers, how many of them are eager to apply to this college?

These are simple dip-stick questions for you to ask to self-evaluate a program's brand.

Personally, the Harvard brand allows me to make an instant connection on email, on a phone call and during face-to-face meetings. It opens doors that would others have been inaccessible to me. I have seen from experience that anytime I have reached out to anyone senior (not just other Harvard alumni), they are open to setting up a meeting or a phone call purely on the basis of the reputation of my alma mater.

Brands also transcend geography and culture. I have seen the reactions of taxi drivers in Morocco, tour guides in Turkey, and even a restaurant waiter in Bombay. On mentioning that I studied at Harvard, their jaws dropped in awe—everyone knows Harvard. The brand recollection is extremely strong and my credibility is instantaneously established.

You might assume that the brand of your MBA program comes in handy only when looking for a job. This is not the case. The brand also helps me as an entrepreneur when I'm recruiting people to join my team. People associate the Harvard brand with leaders who will be result-oriented, passionate and deliver a fulfilling work environment. This is a big draw for top talent. Needless to say, as a study-abroad and career consultant, the MBA from Harvard has lent immense credibility to my venture as Harvard is considered the gold standard for MBA programs.

Pick a strong brand so that your MBA experience is worthwhile. The credibility of the brand will directly transfer on to your personal profile and most definitely help you in your future endeavors.

2:J. *Placements*

When shortlisting colleges, employment is another factor to consider. Jobs can be viewed through two lenses—industry and salary range.

Industry is the 'speciality' area of study/industry of the college in question. For example, universities like Stanford or UC Berkeley are considered to be 'tech schools'. A large part of this perception is influenced by their geography, as they are situated on the West Coast of the US. Similarly, schools on the East Coast like Columbia Business School are renowned for their 'finance' focus. However, I suggest you avoid boxing the colleges into these industry segments.

Tech schools offer enough exposure to finance and vice-versa. Sure, they do have a locational advantage, being around top technology companies. However, many top business schools circumvent the locational challenge by organizing visits to industry-specific locations (For e.g., Wall Street for finance, Silicon Valley for tech). This allows students from universities away from these locations to have similar exposure as students from universities close to such a location.

Additionally, data proves that you can easily get placed in the technology sector even if you attend a finance-focus school such as NYU Stern. Consider this table:

School Name	Tech Placements	Finance Placements	Consulting Placements
Stanford GSB	33 percent	31 percent	18 percent
UC Berkeley	38 percent	15 percent	25 percent
Columbia Business School	16 percent	32 percent	34 percent
NYU Stern	16.5 percent	34 percent	28.4 percent

As you can see, schools renowned for one industry or sector or area of study have a sizeable placement result for other fields as well.

The major takeaway here is that even if you go to a school that specializes in a different industry or sector, you can still get placed in your preferred industry or sector. We will cover this in detail further in the chapter.

Salary is another factor to consider when trying to evaluate placement options. The median starting salary at global business schools allows students to offset the cost of attending business school within three years of graduating. Allow me to illustrate this using a table:

School Name	Annual Cost of Attending	Median Salary
Stanford GSB	$120,000	$115,000–$151,000
London Business School	$107,000	$106,000
Rotman School of Management	$121,000	$57,000–$116,000
National University of Singapore	$45,795	$65,042
Indian School of Business	₹30,41,000	₹22,14,684
IIM Ahmedabad	₹25,00,000	₹23,00,000

As seen above, the median salary correlates to the cost of attending the program.

These are the major factors one must consider when picking an MBA program. My advice is to keep biases away and play devil's advocate when debating your choices. Doing so will ensure that you find a college best suited to you sans any biases.

Moreover, looking at these factors in isolation is not ideal. You must assign weights to each of them based on your personal preferences to arrive at your final list.

3. How to Use These Factors in Combination to Determine Your 'Right Fit'

First, take into account at what point you are in your career; this will help you pick a program structure and duration. Then, take into account what you wish to gain from your MBA and how you want to learn; this will help you determine geography, class size, teaching methods, alumni network and placements. Further narrow down the list by taking into account your preferences and personality; this will allow you to determine the ideal campus culture and class size. Finally, ensure that the schools you have selected are reputed. Once you have taken these factors into consideration, you will have a shortlist of colleges that you can apply to.

For example, here's why Sandeep Kagzi, principal at Warburg Pincus, a leading private equity firm, picked Stanford:

> "I did not look at the rankings when exploring my options. I believe that college selection demands a balanced approach. I preferred the smaller class size at Stanford, owing to closer bonds it would help me build with my batchmates. Furthermore, Stanford's culture, which offered an open-minded approach to career paths, was refreshing and appealed to me."

You must be wondering how one can learn about the culture of a campus. The most obvious way is to read online. Let's explore some other ideas.

4. How to Gather Information about Colleges: Going Beyond the Internet

I always ask my students to be wary of basing their decision solely on the information available on the school's website. This is because if you were to skim through enough university webpages, you will find a recurring pattern. Terms like 'top university', 'best faculty', 'collaborative environment' and 'state-of-the-art infrastructure' are peppered in their descriptions. While these claims may be true (they are 'top schools' for a reason!), they may not give you a deeper sense of the school. The onus to dig deeper is on you.

1. *Talking to AdComs*

AdComs often visit different countries and locations before and during the admissions season. This allows students to have one-on-one interactions with AdComs from different schools around the world. I strongly suggest you attend such events happening in your vicinity. The AdComs are very receptive to questions by potential applicants and will give you a fair idea of the college experience. They will have the most up-to-date information on new courses, faculty members and even the latest admissions statistics. They are by far your most informed source of knowledge when it comes to understanding the college. Read the appendix at the end of the book to learn what AdCom members have to say about their colleges.

However, it is important to ask smart questions. Sometimes, students limit their interaction with a college's AdCom to questions about program duration, structure, program requirements, finances or tuition fees. This information is usually available on their websites.

Ask an advanced question. Make it insightful and specific to your case. Questions about campus culture or the program's advantages to your profile are prudent to ask. Ask for their opinion on how the college can impact your specific profile, help you make that career switch, or if the college can help you specialize in a certain area. These questions will help improve your understanding of the college.

2. *Taking a Campus Tour/Interacting with Current Students*

If possible, I always suggest that students take a one-day campus tour of their shortlisted colleges. This can be done on a short vacation or work event abroad as well, since campus tours do not consume much time. However, they do tell you a lot about the college and you will be able to determine whether you like it there. Campus tours are typically conducted by current students and give you a great chance to interact with someone currently enrolled in the program. Conversations with current students will help you glean from a student's perspective a general sense of the campus culture.

Some campus tours may also arrange for a meeting with the professors or allow you to sit in a class. This will allow you to experience the teaching methodology and class dynamic.

On most campuses, students are permitted to bring guests along. If there are no official campus tours, try to reach out to a current student who will be able to invite you for a class visit.

I understand that campus visits may not always be feasible. Even if you are unable to visit the campus, you can connect with current students to learn more. Find a current student on LinkedIn and strike up a conversation conveying your interest in applying to their program. Many campuses have official Student Ambassadors who volunteer to speak with prospective candidates and help them. Make the most of these opportunities to continue exploring.

3. *Talking to Alumni of the Program*

You could also approach alumni of the program you wish to attend. Having graduated from the college you are considering applying to, they will be able to guide you. They can provide insights into what life after the MBA looks like and the types of opportunities available to you once you graduate. They can tell you how the MBA influenced their personal and professional life, how active the alumni clubs are, and how the alumni network helps them.

Investing some time and energy into researching the schools in such a comprehensive manner will definitely pay off.

5. How Many Colleges Should I Apply To?

There is no limit to the number of colleges you can apply to at a given time. It all boils down to the time you have and the effort you wish to put in. Typically, I ask my students to pick anywhere between five and seven prospective colleges. Doing so ensures a good variety of colleges (ambitious, realistic and safe) while not spreading their efforts too thin.

On the flip side, applying to just one or two colleges requires you to be absolutely sure you are a right fit with the college. The downside to this approach is that you severely limit your options. In my case, I was very focused on only applying to two schools and hence I applied to only those and secured admission to both. However, I did this because I was 100 percent sure of the colleges I wanted to apply to given the extensive research I had done. On checking the class profiles, I ensured I met the school's requirements as well. This may not be the case for you and thus I do not advocate my strategy for everyone.

I suggest you pick a number of colleges you are comfortable with. Factor in the time and effort required per application, and determine what works best for you.

6. Reality Check: Busting Common College Selection Myths

6:A. The College You Graduate from Does Not Matter, the Degree Is All That Does

A reputed business school is recognized globally by millions of employers. It has a strong brand, a track record of excellence, and offers the best education available. Moreover, top schools deliver far more value than an average business school.

Why do students opt to go to average business schools, then?

Many students break down their lives into a 'study phase' (age 0–21) and 'work phase' (age 21–60) with no overlap. Due to this binary mindset, many want an MBA right after graduation, regardless of which school is offering it to them. Consequently, such students end up settling for average schools since they don't meet the eligibility for top schools. Applying to an average school guarantees an easier admit. However, you miss out on the myriad benefits top schools offer.

The quality of education and the peer group are the primary differentiators between top and average business schools. These factors work together and compel students to constantly push their limits and reinvent themselves. The quality of education develops you intellectually, and the peer group drives you to work harder and develop a strong work ethic. This combination helps students achieve their long-term goals. Average MBA programs do not offer this. Since the bar is set low for incoming students, you may not find the same diversity, intellect and drive among your peers in these colleges. Additionally, the alumni network and your peers at top business schools are more likely to be influential people who may be able to help you out in the future.

An average MBA will also exact the same opportunity and monetary cost for a lower return on investment. Thus, you should ask yourself: is it worth paying the same for a less impactful experience?

6:B. If I Study Away from Silicon Valley/Wall Street, I Won't Get a Job There!

This is untrue, as we have already seen earlier (refer section 2:J). Location is a key metric to evaluate when picking your college. However, it should not be considered by itself. Most finance, consulting and tech companies scout for talent globally. In other words, they recruit at all top colleges. Moreover, most top colleges have begun organizing visits to the Bay Area, New York, London and other technology and financial hubs for students to be able to network with organizations in these different geographies.

7. Real People, Unique Skills, Common Errors: Analysis and Fixes

7:A. Karan Underestimated His Profile

K: But VK, aren't these colleges good? Why should I reject them?
VK: These are good colleges, but you have the potential to enter better MBA programs. Why settle for less?

When Karan approached me, he was exhausted from the admissions process. He had spent a lot of time and effort on his applications. Karan came to us saying he had been accepted at five schools and wanted our help picking the one that he would attend.

However, when I reviewed Karan's profile, I noticed that he had underestimated himself. He had two published books and a top post at a leading media company alongside a range of accomplishments. He had a profile worthy of a top-ten business school but had applied only to lower-ranked ones. We asked him to reject all the five schools he had been accepted at and reapply the next year. Though resistant initially, he took our advice and reapplied the next year and was accepted at Duke's Fuqua School of Business.

My Take

Over the years, I have encountered many candidates underselling their profiles. While I appreciate humility, I strongly believe you must get the education you deserve.

Many professional counselors play safe and suggest colleges that you will be able to easily get into, to ensure their success rate goes up. However, I strongly encourage taking some risk and applying for competitive programs as well. Do not undersell a strong profile. Like I have said earlier, the MBA is a one-time experience. You should get the most you can out of it by attending a school that complements your calibre.

7:B. Aman Overestimated His Potential

A: VK, if I get my MBA, it must only be from HBS, Stanford or Wharton.

VK: I appreciate the ambition, but this is… unrealistic.

Aman had a profile for a top business school. However, cracking the top three MBA programs is no cakewalk. With a 680 GMAT, three years of work experience and a 6.5 undergraduate CGPA, these schools were out of Aman's reach. While we could build a stronger profile in a few years, the clock was ticking and Aman wanted to apply immediately. I suggested he apply to other schools, but he was adamant and only applied to HBS, Stanford GSB and Wharton. Sadly, Aman was rejected at all three.

Next year, he reapplied with us. We helped him apply to three other top-tier schools after carefully shortlisting realistic schools where he stood a strong chance at getting admitted. When he applied that year, he secured admissions at two of these.

My Take

Ambition is good, but you must be realistic about your chances. Understand your profile and apply to schools within your reach.

7:C. Sonali Thought Her Silicon Valley Dreams Would Only Be Fulfilled on the West Coast

S: VK, I want to work in Silicon Valley. I will only go to a college on

the West Coast. The others are of no use to me.

VK: Good thinking, but you could work in Silicon Valley with a degree from other top-tier colleges as well.

Sonali was a product manager at a top firm in Bangalore. She was an IIT Delhi graduate and had dreamed of working in the Bay Area all her life. She wanted to get an MBA to make this dream a reality. While I understood her perspective, I explained that graduating from a college in a certain location does not restrict you to that location. The brand of a good global business school is recognized across the globe. Therefore, I asked her to apply to other top-tier schools across the country, in addition to those in the Bay Area.

She was ultimately admitted to Northwestern University's Kellogg School of Management, far from her target location. After graduating, Sonali was recruited by a technology firm in Boston. While she was excited about the job, she was disappointed about the location and sent me an email. I urged her to be patient and focus on excelling at work; she would be able to move to the West Coast eventually. This happened two years later when her organization opened an office in the Bay Area and chose her to lead operations there. Remember, the credentialing and training that a top MBA provides is very strong and empowers you to transition seamlessly between roles and locations.

My Take

While the location of your program does play a role, limiting your options on the basis of a target work location is not ideal. Top tech firms are known to scout for talent all over the world.

The credibility of the MBA degree transcends geography, and Sonali's case testifies to this fact.

7:D. Shyam Has Two Admits and Faces the Acceptance Dilemma

S: VK, I have been accepted at both Harvard and Stanford. I can't decide! Please help me pick one…
VK: Congratulations. They are both top schools, but with vastly different class sizes. Have you taken that into consideration?

In Shyam's mind he had just cracked two top-tier schools that he valued equally. In my eyes, both Harvard and Stanford would give him vastly different experiences.

One of the many ways these schools differ is by class size. I explained to him that in his first-year classroom, HBS will have anywhere between 90 and 100 people, with the program having over 900 students overall. On the other hand, Stanford has a much smaller class size, and half the overall number of students (around 400) in comparison to HBS. The learning and social experience at Stanford are strikingly different from those at HBS.

Stanford would provide a more intimate connection with peers owing to the smaller class size. However, the large class size at HBS would bring interactions with a larger, more diverse student body. Moreover, HBS would give him a larger alumni base (over 85,000) as opposed to Stanford (about 30,000) upon graduation.

We asked Shyam to factor in the class amidst other variables when making his decision. Shyam decided to attend Harvard, owing to the large class and large alumni base which he thought would be handy in the future. He wanted to return to India, where HBS has a very large and active alumni base.

My Take

Class size is an important factor to consider because it truly impacts your classroom experience. You could prefer the vast networking opportunities at a top school or the few, intimate ones at a small school.

Take into consideration the trade-offs between attending one over the other and see what best fits your requirements.

7:E. *Selwin Needed to Expedite the MBA*

> **S: VK, I have to return to India in two years to help my family business. It is now or never.**
> **VK: I understand the urgency. We could pick a one-year program and apply next year.**

Selwin's family had a logistics business in India and a new head office was in the works. It would begin operations in two years. Selwin wished to earn his MBA and return to manage the business.

However, upon reviewing his profile, I realized it was not ready yet. He would need at least another year to build it to a level acceptable at top business schools. When I told him this, he immediately said he did not mind settling for an average school, if that meant getting his MBA early. In his mind, the two-year MBA was the only option, and it was now or never.

I suggested Selwin work on his profile for a year to fortify it. I showed him a list of one-year MBA programs from top schools and explained that since he didn't need a job after business school, a one-year program would work well for him.

He was an engineer, and his focus in his MBA was to understand the tenets of leadership, operations and management, which the one-year degree would provide him. Moreover, Selwin would not have to compromise on school quality if he took this alternative. Though initially resistant, Selwin saw the merit in our suggestion.

We worked on his profile for a year and Selwin ultimately entered Babson's 12-month MBA program, focused on entrepreneurship.

My Take

Selwin was on the verge of compromising on quality to earn his degree early. If you are from a family business background, the one-year MBA would serve you just as well. Since you will be returning to your family business, you might not need the recruitment and internship opportunities and the one-year program would provide you with the same knowledge.

Pick a type of program depending on your personal situation, one that will meet your distinctive individual needs. The full-time two-year MBA is not the only program out there. There is a plethora of options to pick from.

7:F. Mayank And Vineeta Wanted to Earn Their MBA Together

M: VK, we would like to go to the same business school together.
VK: I understand that you want to attend the same school, but note that your careers paths are unique.

Mayank and Vineeta were newlyweds. They had approached me for help in applying to business school, and were looking to go together. However, upon reviewing their individual profiles, I realized they had vastly different career trajectories.

Mayank wanted to enhance his family business and set up an investment office in Singapore. Vineeta, on the other hand, who was fluent in Mandarin, wanted to combine her MBA with a cultural immersion experience in China and find suppliers for her expanding furniture business. I explained to them that they could benefit from the resources available at different schools based on their goals.

Initially hesitant to take this step, they ultimately agreed that it was in their best interests. Mayank entered National University of Singapore's MBA program and Vineeta, CEIBS in China. They ensured their relationship remained stable through frequent visits to each other. At the same time, they grew individually through their experiences at their respective campuses.

My Take

Going to business school together may work for some couples. I am not suggesting otherwise. However, in cases like Mayank and Vineeta's, earning the MBA at different schools was the optimal route. Their career paths were clearly different, and so was their requirement from an MBA program.

Business school is an individual experience, even if you attend as a couple.

8. Errors in a Nutshell

8:A. Underestimating Your Potential (Underselling Yourself)

Some students are hesitant to apply to top MBA programs because they think they won't be accepted at them.

Insider Tip

1. Do not play 'overcareful' when it comes to college selection. Pick a healthy number of top programs that you think you will fit in.

8:B. Overestimating Your Chances

Students sometimes overestimate their profile's merits and shoot for colleges that their credentials do not warrant.

Insider Tips

1. Be realistic about your chances.
2. Apply to a broad list of colleges.

8:C. Thinking That You Will Only Be Recruited in the Location You Graduate From

While picking schools in a certain geography to match your field of interest may help, do not limit yourself.

Insider Tip

1. You can also pick colleges away from your dream work location. Top firms scout for talent globally, and you will be able to make the transition if you have strong MBA credentials.

8:D. Not Considering Where the Campus Is Located

Your MBA experience will also be shaped by the activities around the college and whether it is located in a city or a semi-urban location.

Insider Tips

1. Factor in whether the college is a city, semi-urban or rural campus.
2. Consider personal constraints and preferences; then pick a college that best addresses them.

8:E. Disregarding Class Size

Class size determines the amount of networking opportunities available, the amount of personal attention you can expect to receive from professors, and the strength of the alumni base.

Insider Tip

1. Factor in the trade-off between attending a school with a large class size as opposed to a smaller class.

8:F. Disregarding Program Structure

Different types of MBA programs cater to different personal, professional and educational needs. Evaluate sensibly.

Insider Tip

1. Refer to the table comparing popular program structures and pick one that best fits you.

Insider Tips in a Nutshell

DO:

✓ Be smart about selecting a college and consider other factors while picking your perfect fit.

✓ Use sources other than the internet to gather information about schools you want to apply to.

✓ Talk to the AdCom, current students and alumni to gather information not available on the website.

✓ Be realistic when drafting your shortlist.

✓ Consider where the college is located (city/semi-urban/ rural campus).

DON'T:

X Blindly pick a college because it is in the top five.

X Pick a college just because your friend is also headed there.

X Limit your options because of your ideal post-MBA job location.

X Underestimate the merits of your profile.

X Settle for an average college just because they give you a scholarship.

APPENDIX

College Selection Worksheet

Use this worksheet to list potential colleges. In the cells provided under each factor, score the college in question on a scale of 1–5 (where 1 is unsatisfactory and 5 is ideal). Use this list to then select schools that are to your liking.

Sr. No.	College Name	Brand	Location	Finance	Campus Culture	Teaching Method	Structure +Duration	Alumni Network	Class Size
1									
2									
3									
4									
5									
6									
7									
8									
9									
10									
11									
12									

Top International MBA Programs Map

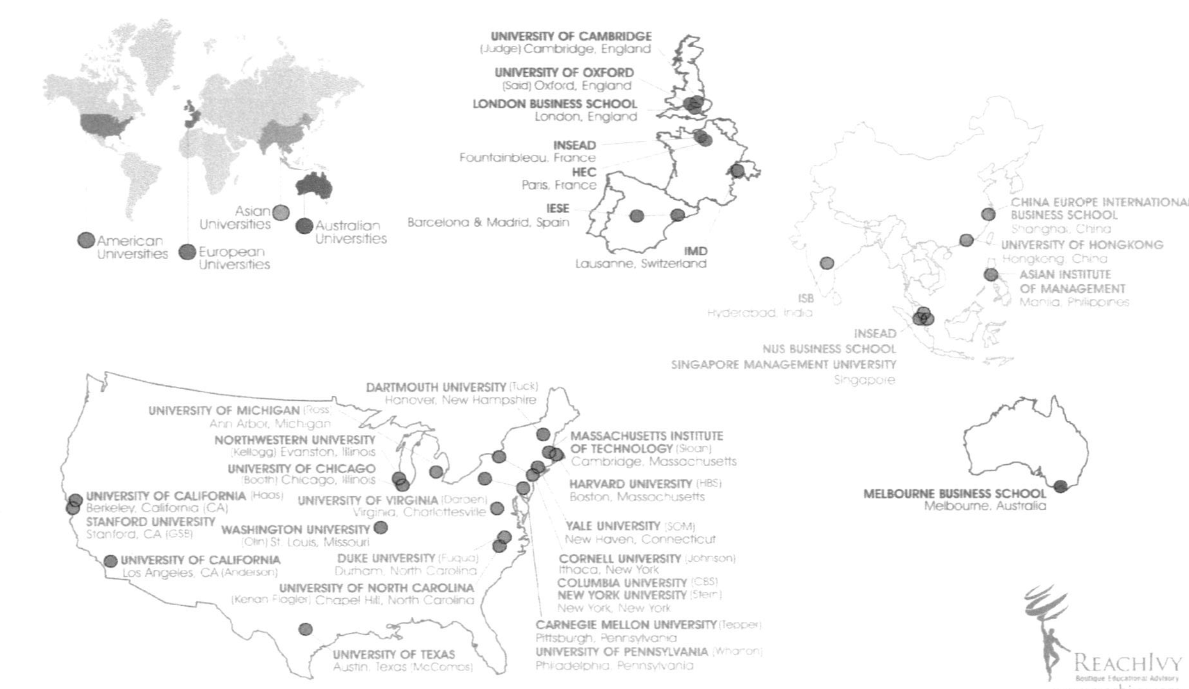

6

Application Essays:
How to Use Structure, Language and
Emotion to Craft a Winning Essay

Hi VK,

For most of my life, I studied and worked towards building my career in banking. Now, I'm ready to apply to business school.

I am confident about my profile but worried about the essays. As an Indian male from the finance sector, I know I face stiff competition and the essays should help me highlight my accomplishments. However, I am clueless how to proceed. Please help me out!

Anup Singh was an accomplished banker who had started as an analyst and worked his way up the ladder to become an associate. He was also a Chartered Accountant. The next logical step for him was getting an MBA to expedite his access to management positions in the sector.

He realized that despite his credentials he needed razor-sharp essays to pull his application to the top of the pile. Being more quantitatively abled, Anup was worried his essays would fail to impress.

To help him, I first explained why business schools ask for an essay.

Through the essays, the AdCom mainly tries to:
1. Judge your ability to communicate effectively through writing.
2. Understand how you stand out from the crowd through your life experiences.
3. Get a deeper understanding of you and your traits beyond the accomplishments on your résumé.

In an essay, the spotlight is on you, the candidate. It is a prime opportunity to showcase how *you are different from other applicants*. Anup was one among the several male Indian bankers who would apply to business school that year. How would he stand out? What was the story behind his credentials? This information would come through only if his individual experiences were expressed well.

We went through about six essay-editing rounds wherein we built a trajectory leading up to his decision to pursue an MBA and his plans thereafter. That year, he successfully entered Georgetown University's McDonough School of Business.

What made Anup's essays work? Let's find out.

1. What Admissions Officers Want from Your Essay

Every year, schools release the topic(s) that you have to base your 100–1,000 word essays on. While these may differ from one school to the other, the template of these questions can be bucketed into six broad categories. Here, I will detail these categories and explain how to approach them.

The number of essay prompts and prescribed word limit varies by school. For instance, HBS asks for just one essay which has no word limit. On the other hand, Chicago Booth requires you to respond to two mandatory essay prompts (250 words each), one optional essay prompt (300 words) and an additional essay (300 words) if you are a re-applicant. These requirements change annually; the schools release the essay topics and word limits towards the first week of June every year.

If you have multiple essays to write, remember this: each essay demands a different answer. It is advised that you do not repeat your ideas, content, accomplishments or experiences across essays unless absolutely necessary.

With that cleared, let's address what the six different categories of essay topics are, and what you are required to write therein.

1:A. *Why This School?*

If you took my advice from Chapter 5 (College Selection) and chose schools that are a 'perfect fit', this essay should be a reiteration of the facts that led you to pick the school. Think about questions like:

- How will this school help you achieve your long-term and short-term goals?
- What resources will help you achieve them?
- What difference does it offer that will help you achieve the end you want?
- What values of the school resonate the most with you?

Here are two examples of this question type:

School Name	Essay Topic
MIT Sloan School of Management	Please submit a cover letter seeking a place in the MIT Sloan MBA Program. Your letter should conform to a standard business correspondence, include one or more examples that illustrate why you meet the desired criteria above, and be addressed to Mr Rod Garcia, Senior Director of Admissions.
UPenn Wharton School of Business	What do you hope to gain professionally from the Wharton MBA?

Please note that AdComs are also looking to understand what *you* bring to the table. Ensure that you add how you can enrich the school's student body and add to its diversity.

Depending on the exact question asked, either focus on what you will gain from the school or what you can add to the school. For example, in the MIT cover letter, you should add what you can **bring** to the school. In contrast, the Wharton essay requires you to detail what you wish to **gain** from the school.

Avoid making your 'Why this school' essay seem like a paraphrased version of the content on its website. Instead, pick what resonates with you and discuss it in a personal context.

In such an essay, the AdCom is looking for two things specifically:

1. **An essay that shows the applicant is focused and has done thorough research.**
2. **An essay that displays a strong fit.**

Here is a simple checklist to follow:

1. Be well informed about the school you are applying to.
2. Use specifics to describe why you chose that school.
3. Explain how you wish to use its resources.
4. Elaborate how you can contribute to the classroom.

You must be able to convince the AdCom that there is a strong match between the business school and you. Also, it must be convinced that you will actively add to the classroom experience and benefit from it.

You will need to link your goals to the business school you are applying to and explain how specific courses, faculty members, clubs, excursions, internships, travel opportunities, etc., at the school directly align with your goals.

Including this information showcases that you know exactly what you want and reassures the AdCom that you are not submitting a generic essay and that you will truly make the most of all the opportunities the business school has to offer.

Do not copy and paste the same essay to multiple schools. This is a huge blunder and will be considered a red flag by the AdCom.

1:B. What Are Your Long-Term and Short-Term Goals and Why MBA?

This is a common question that targets your career path and your rationale for wanting to earn an MBA. Here are a few ways this question may be asked:

School Name	Essay Topic
Dartmouth College (Tuck)	What are your short- and long-term goals? Why is an MBA a critical next step towards achieving those goals?
NYU Stern	What are your short- and long-term career goals? How will the MBA help you achieve them?

In this essay, you must illustrate the key events in your life that have helped you formulate your goals. Then describe your goals in detail (short term: next five years; long term: five to 15 years). Next, mention why the MBA is the next logical step in your career. Specify the skills you need at this point which the MBA can provide. Finally, talk about how it will help you attain your goals.

Please submit an essay that has experiences, not merely assertions.

Remember, a personal story will create an impact and make the essay memorable. Claims of having ambition and goals are hollow until your experiences bring them to life. Illustrate through personal stories what made you choose your goals, describe key turning points in your career that led you to this juncture, and/or provide an emotional rationale for wanting to work for a specific cause or industry.

Showcase key milestones in your personal and professional journey in this essay. **Join the dots between your past, present and future.**

You do not have to speak only about your triumphs. The trials and tribulations you faced and the challenges you overcame all lend to your identity and build your character.

Here is a table to help you list your key life experiences and link them to your goals:

Reason for Wanting an MBA	An Experience That Led You to This Reason	How the MBA Can Help
1.		
2.		
3.		
4.		
5.		

After elaborating on your journey so far, you must specify your goals. Ensure you goal is SMART: Specific, Measurable, Attainable, Realistic, Time-based. Each time you write down your goals statement, ensure it meets the 'SMART' criterion.

A vague statement such as the one below conveys very little:

"I see myself as a motivational speaker and entrepreneur in the future."

Let's make this goal SMART:

"Within the next five years, I envision returning to India and setting up a public-speaking academy to train the next generation of impactful motivational speakers."

Here are a few questions to ask yourself to formulate this essay.

Goals Questionnaire

1. What does your career trajectory look like up to this point?

2. What drives you to work in this field or industry?

3. What is the current and future potential of your chosen field or industry?

4. What is the problem or gap in your chosen field or industry?

5. How will you address this problem or gap?

6. What location do you see yourself working in?

7. What specific company, role, function do you see yourself in?

8. How exactly do you plan to achieve and execute this goal?

9. How does the MBA contribute to your goals, in both the short and the long run?

1:C. Personal or Identity-Based Essays

Sometimes schools may ask you questions that determine your personal values and traits. These may be about your priorities, sacrifices and commitments, among other aspects. These essays help the AdCom to get a glimpse into your identity, personality and values. Let's look at a few variations of this question:

School Name	Essay Question
Yale School of Management	Describe the biggest commitment you have ever made.
IMD Switzerland	Describe yourself in 200 words or less.

Remember, one way to write a stellar personal essay is:

Use simple, personal experiences, not tall tales or exaggerated stories.

Do not spice up or try to make your experiences melodramatic. You run the risk of sounding fake and the AdCom will detect this. Stick to the facts and write a strong essay on the merits of your real experiences.

Also, ideally, pick one experience and dive into its depth rather than writing about multiple experiences. Typically, the word limit for these essays is less than 500. So, detailing only one personal story and highlighting the values and lessons learned from it is more impactful than scattering the limited words available in multiple stories.

Another common mistake is that students tend to insert quotes by eminent personalities to make a point. I recommend against this.

For example, let us look at this student submission:

Ethical business practices are extremely important to me. As Mahatma Gandhi, who fought for the freedom of India with integrity, rightly said, "Honesty is the best policy."

The above statement only makes a claim without backing it up with any personal experience that would validate it. Did you come across a situation in your personal or professional life where you had to make a tricky ethical choice? This is a good place to talk about it. Look how much more of an impact the same statement has when you incorporate a personal story.

How I fixed it:

"In 2011, I was working with my college to help raise funds for a festival. We had already managed to raise over $2,000 of the $2,500 budget. During a sponsorship meeting, the representative of a popular brand offered to give us $1,000 but did not want us to account for it in our books. I could have easily used the cash to make all our payments as it was a large sum of money. While this was tempting, I took a strong

> *stance against such activity since it was an 'off-the-record'*
> *transaction and thus illegal. [...]"*
>
> Substantiating your essay or viewpoint with real-life examples
> makes your submission a legitimate 'personal essay'. It adds the
> 'human' aspect that such personal essays demand. Quotes by
> Gandhi, Mandela and JFK are too common and best avoided.

1:D. Evaluating an Experience

These questions will ask you to pick a life experience and discuss it within a given context. Questions pertaining to risks taken, leadership stories, major accomplishments, etc., may be asked.

Most students have several interesting experiences and are unsure of which to include. Here are a few questions you can ask yourself when deciding:

> **Goals Questionnaire**
>
> 1. Is this experience recent?
>
> 2. Which of my experiences best fits my answer to the specific topic? You may have a stellar life experience you want to highlight in your application, but if it is not in sync with the essay topic, use another experience. Do not force-fit it here.
>
> 3. Was this experience significant in my life journey?
>
> 4. How can I compress this experience into the requisite word limit?

Once you have answered these questions and picked an experience, begin detailing its nuances. However, do not get caught up in the details of the experience alone. There is an introspective part to the essay as well. You have to bring out your personal traits, lessons learned, shift in mindset, etc., through the experience.

Here are two 'evaluate an experience' essay questions:

School Name	Essay Topic
Goizueta Business School	The business school is named for Roberto C Goizueta, former Chairman and CEO of The Coca-Cola Company, who led the organization for 16 years, extending its global reach, quadrupling consumption, building brand responsibility and creating unprecedented shareholder wealth. Mr Goizueta's core values guide us in educating Principled Leaders for Global Enterprise. Provide an example of your leadership—professional or personal—and explain what you learned about yourself through the experience.
UC Berkeley Haas	Describe a significant obstacle you have encountered and how it has impacted you. *OR* Describe how you have cultivated a diverse and inclusive culture.

Here is what differentiates a winning 'evaluate an experience' essay from a mediocre one: **an effective breakdown of the experience.**

Whenever you are adding an experience to your essay, it is important to break it down into the STAR and Learning format. This means breaking the experience down into the situation (S), task (T), action (A), result (R) and learning. I will explain this technique in depth later in the chapter, when I discuss brainstorming.

The Result and Learning are important for this essay type as it indicates your self-awareness. Were you able to perceive what went wrong or worked in your favor? What did you take away from the experience? How will it help you to grow professionally or personally?

Such a breakdown will help you to sequence your essay effectively and show a logical and progressive buildup to your story. Such structuring will aid the essay's readability and coherence.

1:E. *Optional or Additional Information Essay*

Sometimes schools will provide space for an extra essay and limit its scope to "describe any extenuating circumstances or choice of recommenders". In this case the essay must be limited to what is defined in the question. In other cases, the schools may provide an open-ended space to "use the essay to share anything else you would like to".

If that is the case, you can:

1. **Emphasize a strength or value:** You could use this essay to discuss a personal experience that you have not brought up in the other essays. This strategy comes in handy specially when the other essays you are required to write are 'Why MBA' or 'Why This School', essays that have limited scope for you to emphasize your strengths. However, do not brag; keep the tone humble and showcase how you have learnt from your experiences rather than listing one accomplishment after another.

2. **Explain a professional gap:** If you have a gap in your work experience (typically anything longer than three months) you must explain it in this essay. Discuss why you took the break and what you did in that period.

3. **Discuss a red flag in your profile:** Here you could talk about a rough academic patch when your grades suffered. Discuss what you learned from the situation, how you overcame the problems, and how you improved your performance subsequently. A positive reflection of a seemingly negative experience augurs well for you.

1:F. Creative Essays

Some schools may also ask you to include a creative essay, such as '25 random facts about me', a PowerPoint presentation, or a video essay. These questions will often require you to unleash your creativity and answer accurately. Again, ensure there is no overlapping experience or value from your other essays.

Here are a few examples of creative essay topics:

School Name	Essay Topic
Cornell Johnson	Table of Contents Essay You are the author of your Life Story. Please create the table of contents for the book in the space provided or upload it as an attachment. We value creativity and authenticity and encourage you to approach this essay with your unique style. Alternative submission formats may include a slide presentation, links to pre-existing media (personal website, digital portfolio, YouTube, etc.), as well as visually enhanced written submissions.
Chicago Booth	View this collection of shared Booth moments. Choose the moment that best resonates with you and tell us why (a set of images is provided).

The one key element of a winning creative essay I would like to emphasize: focus on impactful content, *not* on high production values.

You get points for the idea and thoughts, not so much for the visual or technical finesse of your submission. Don't drive yourself crazy making a studio-produced video; neither do you need to recruit the services of a professional filmmaker or graphic designer. The idea behind creative essays is to break the essay-writing mode and allow students a new medium to channel their creativity. Focus on substance more than on style.

Strictly adhere to the time limit or length of the PowerPoint presentation or word count prescribed by the school. I will discuss the importance of this later in the chapter.

2. How to Conceptualize Your Essay

2:A. How to Brainstorm Your Strengths and Goals

Essay brainstorming is a method we have devised at ReachIvy.com and made effective over several iterations over the past decade. It has helped many students write winning essays and secure admits to top schools.

Brainstorming is akin to meditation and should ideally be done in isolation. You could get away for a few days (long flights or free time at airports due to delayed flights are great options too!) and spend some time with yourself and your brainstorming sheet. Think about experiences to fill the sheet up. This first part is called 'personal introspection'.

The next part involves constructing the essay—'carving content'. Here, you will be trimming your list of experiences and deciding where and how to incorporate them in your essay. To do this, I recommend reading through your listed experiences and essay topics and asking yourself a series of questions to decide which experiences to use for which essay. List your experiences in parts of the Profile Buckets we discussed in Chapter 2 (Academic, Professional, Leadership, Extracurricular Activities and Community Involvement).

Now you begin planning how these experiences can be added to your essays. All your experiences should tie in to send out one message through the essay.

This exercise will enable you to pinpoint experiences that you want to add in your essays. This allows you to have a visual summary of your life's experiences in one place. Once you have listed out your experiences, reorder them based on how impactful each was.

You can use the brainstorming sheet provided below for maximum effect.

Professional Experience	Year of Occurrence	Relevant Essay Topic
1.		
2.		
3.		
4.		
5.		
Academic Experience		
1.		
2.		
3.		
4.		
5.		
Leadership Experience		
1.		
2.		
3.		
4.		
5.		
Community Involvement		
1.		
2.		
3.		
4.		
5.		

Extracurricular Experience

1.		
2.		
3.		
4.		
5.		

How do you brainstorm experiences effectively? We recommend using the STAR and Learning method. For each of your experiences, list out the Situation (S), Task (T), Action (A), Result (R) and Learning. Here is what each of these terms means:

Situation

The situation is the starting point of the experience. It is the context to your story. It should hook your reader and make him want to read on. The situation should not take up more than 10 percent of the essay.

Let's say you are talking about how you tackled low traffic on your company's website. A plain opening would be: "There was low traffic on the company website, so I began tackling it." Instead, set the situation up to be more exciting and show the scope of the issue on hand. You could mention the number of previous efforts to fix the traffic, the amount of money being burned to fix the site, the number of people deployed on the project, how much business the company was losing daily, etc.

With this in mind, a better way to present the situation would be:

> *"Our customer engagement reports showed a 19 percent decline. At company events, more and more clients told us they were unaware we had a website. This explained the low traffic on the website. I began tackling the issue at once. I had three months till our next review."*

Task

What do you need to do in light of the situation? What key challenges do you face? Explain the complexity of the task at hand by introducing the stakeholders who were involved, the location of team members, the budgets available, etc. This should comprise approximately 10 percent of the recounting of the experience.

For instance, once you have ascertained that there is low traffic on the website, you cannot just say, "So I started to make a plan and execute it." You have to be more specific. You might say:

> *"First I had to get to the root of the problem. It either lay in our content management platform or the SEO was sub-optimal. I would have to work closely with our 15 member digital team spread across three offices to begin devising a plan."*

Action

The 'action' is the part where you can shine. You tell the reader your role in the experience. What was your contribution to the experience? This is the meat of the essay. The action should take up at least 50 percent of the retelling.

If you formulated a plan, you have to tell the reader how it was put into action. A line merely stating that "I put the plan into action and it worked wonders" will not do. This does not give enough information about your role in the experience.

Instead, review this:

> *"Over the next two months, we doubled our SEO efforts, closely monitoring our budget and where it was being spent. The process was a slow, tedious one. I kept the team motivated with the small triumphs along the way, taking it one page at a time. With some critical research into our keywords,*

> *we replaced all the non-performing ones with content-specific words. We fixed over 70 pages of our website by switching servers and making it more mobile-friendly, improving our Alexa rank by almost 80 points."*

This detailing pulls the reader in. You also portray your specific skills when you give details like these. Additionally, you are established at the helm of the team, as an able leader.

Result

What were the results of your action? Did your plans succeed? Or did they not? Again, use specific details to point the result out. This part should not take up more than 20 percent of your story.

For instance, you cannot just write, "After doing all this, the project was successful. We increased our webpage traffic." This tells the reader nothing other than the fact that the project was successful. It does not have an impact. Instead,

> *"Soon we were the highest ranked content page on Google search results for our services. The traffic increased from 1,000 clicks per month to over 15,000 clicks per month— 15 times more than the previous number."*

The above line solidifies the impact of your actions. It brings to the fore that your plan worked. Moreover, this outcome is a testament to your skill as a professional.

Learning

The learning is an important part of any experience. What did you learn from tackling the situation? How does this affect your future actions?

Telling the reader your learning shows what you imbibed from the experience. Additionally, it showcases your ability to introspect and that you can overcome similar challenges. This should comprise the final 10 percent of your essay.

You could say:

> *"I learnt the importance of being able to adapt and of being diligent. I continued to maintain our efforts on our online platforms. The constantly adaptive nature of the internet has since kept me and my team on our toes, looking out for ways to further optimize our webpage."*

This shows your key takeaway from the experience. It establishes that you did not mindlessly just complete the task on hand. Instead, you overcame a challenge and emerged wiser from the experience.

This is the STAR and Learning method. Take a moment to recollect your own experiences in a sheet like this:

Experience	Situation	Task	Action	Result	Learning

2:B. How to Interpret Essay Prompts

Let us begin by looking at this question from McCombs University:

> *"We will learn a lot about your professional background through your résumé and letter of recommendation. We want to get to know you further. Please introduce yourself."*

Read this question five times over to understand what the AdCom wants from you. It should be a very deliberate attempt at answering the specific question asked. My recommendation is to read and interpret the question literally. I have noticed that sometimes, in trying to portray a specific experience, students miss out on answering the question. For example, when in school you were asked "What colour is the sky", you would answer, "The sky is blue." Similarly interpret and answer the question literally.

For instance, in the given essay topic (250 words), the broad instruction is to introduce yourself. Words such as "professional background", "résumé" and "letter of recommendation" imply your work profile. The key sentence here is "we want to get to know you further". This means they want the essay to steer clear of work-related experiences that have already been mentioned on your résumé or letter of recommendation. Use only personal experiences to introduce yourself. They are looking to get to know fun things about you, personal quirks, your values, your belief system, etc. Anything other than your professional persona!

2:C. *Conceptualizing the Essay: Establishing Character*

Ensure that you have a variety of experiences in your essays. Global business schools want candidates who are multi-dimensional. Being accomplished at work is good but will come off as one-dimensional. It is recommended that you establish your character and personality via the essays.

You could showcase the following:

1. **Work Ethic:** Your willingness to take the initiative and go above and beyond.

2. **Emotional Intelligence:** Your ability to understand others' feelings, empathize with them and act accordingly.

3. **Contextual Intelligence:** Your ability to apply your learned skills to a variety of situations and adapt to challenges that come your way.

4. **Maturity:** The culmination of the aforementioned traits in your character.

Establishing these qualities will showcase you as a complete individual.

2:D. Branding Your Application

Go back to the positioning statement you created as recommended in Chapter 2 (Profile Building). Use this as a brand statement. Ensure that all experiences you add to the essays and the viewpoints you express are congruous with this positioning statement. Doing so will make your application consistent in its message and bolster the AdCom's understanding of your profile.

For instance, let's say your positioning statement is 'Business developer who wishes to begin his own sports management company'. To validate this, you should include experiences that tie your business interest with sports. Did you compete in sports? What problems have you identified in the industry? Why would you like to begin your own sports management company? How will you tackle the problems you have identified? How does business school tie in with this goal?

Answering these questions will lend your application a coherent branding. Your goals will be made clear, and so will the context that led up to you having these goals. While on the topic of coherence, let's address another important point.

2:E. Remaining Consistent Throughout the Essay

You cannot make a claim in one paragraph and contradict it in the next. Consistency also comes from being able to back up your experiences and goals with concrete examples.

Beyond this, consistency at the micro-level is also important. You cannot say "I have always been an introvert" and then talk about how you were captain of the debating team. This discrepancy may cause eyebrows to be raised. Consequently, the AdCom will question the veracity of your claims.

2:F. Answer the Question; Do Not Go Off on a Tangent

Stick to the message in your essays. Speak only about what is asked, do not go off on a tangent.

Let's say the essay topic requires you to detail a challenge at your workplace and how you tackled it. Do not meander and talk about your interest in sports or explain why you want to attend this business school. Address the problem, your actions and the result. This topical consistency will ensure that your essay is short and succinct. When working with a tight word limit, going off-topic is not recommended.

Once you have conceptualized your essay, it is time to pen it down and edit it to perfection. Let's explore how.

3. How to Write the Essay and Proofread It

3:A. Use the Active Voice

Using the active voice helps you avoid longwinded sentences and makes your essay less technical and verbose. This ensures clarity and aids comprehension. Let us take a simple sentence and view it in the active and passive voices:

Active Voice:

I worked as a Product Manager at Tiny Man Infosystems.

Passive Voice:

A Product Manager is what I worked as at Tiny Man Infosystems.

As seen here, the active voice makes far more impact. The passive voice is also wordy. A 10-word sentence is written in 12. This may seem like a small number, but it adds up in a essay of 250–500 words.

3:B. Avoid Use of Humor

Humor is interpreted differently by different people and you never know how others will react to a joke. What may seem funny to you may be seen as rude by a member of the AdCom.

Furthermore, people from different geographies may have different senses of humor. Unless you are confident that your joke will not be misunderstood, I recommend that you avoid using humor.

A common tendency is the use of self-deprecating humor. I recommend you avoid this as well. For example, take a statement like this:

> *"I was late as always (learnt it from Joey), but managed to secure the deal and acquire funding."*

The above statement showcases a negative trait. Moreover, your portraying it in a positive light is indicative of an immature personality that thinks this is normal behavior.

3:C. Use Logical Paragraph Breaks to Separate Ideas

I have often noticed that students tend to follow the standard three-paragraph format of writing essays. This usually comprises an introduction, body and conclusion. However, the three-para format is not always recommended. It may only work in some situations (specially shorter essays).

If you are writing a longer essay, or talking about varied ideas or experiences, it is important to separate them. Mashing different, unrelated experiences or ideas in your essay is sub-optimal. You have creative liberty when you write the essays; use it!

3:D. Talk in Specifics

When you are writing your essay, do not include generic information, specially when talking about the school itself. A common example is:

"Since I am interested in XYZ college, the number of clubs there will help me further develop my skills, fuel my passions and challenge my intellect."

This sentence adds little to the overall essay. It does not answer WHICH club, or HOW the given clubs will fuel your passions or challenge your intellect. Instead of a line like this, pick a specific club at the school and do your research on it. Also address how the said club will help you to explore and develop your interests and passions.

3:E. Open With a Bang!

Ever heard the proverb 'First impressions are the most lasting'? I strongly believe in this, at least when it comes to the MBA essay. To open with a bang, you can:

1. Begin with a personal thought or learning that connects best with the essay topic.
2. Use a numerical goal or target that your manager had given you and work backwards.
3. Start with an experience that best introduces you as a candidate (this could be personal).
4. State a doomsday scenario and then build your essay from this low point.

Such openings will grab the reader's attention and a good start will help your essay to stand out among the thousand others.

3:F. Sleep on It

To have the time to sleep on your essay, you should begin writing it at least a month in advance. When you write, ideas are fresh in your mind. Moreover, your focus is spent on expressing it in written English.

If you hit a roadblock, call it a day and "sleep on it". This is essentially putting away the task of writing, editing or proofreading the essay until the next day. Sleeping on your essay will allow your mind to process the information you are ruminating over for your essay.

Also, since the essay is fresh in your mind right after you have written it, editing it immediately will be sub-optimal. You may miss key errors, typos and inconsistencies.

However, do NOT use this as an excuse to procrastinate. Sleep on an essay only if you are facing a problem conceptualizing or editing it.

3:G. Get an Opinion from a Third Party

Ask a relative, well-wisher or consultant to read the essay you have written. Doing this is recommended because, as the writer, you already know what you are trying to express. Only a reader will be able to tell you if that is coming through. For maximum effectiveness, give the reader the essay topic and ask the following:

1. Does my essay address the topic clearly?
2. Can you understand the idea I am trying to express?
3. Are there any inconsistencies?
4. What personal qualities does this essay reflect?

These questions will help to direct their thinking and let them spot any glaring issues in your essay.

I recommend that you find an experienced professional who is proficient in editing and knows the nuances of sentence correction and grammar. Look for graduates in English language or literature from top schools, professional writers, published authors and expert advisers. These individuals have a finely trained eye and an understanding of the skill set required to write impactful essays to be able to guide you to ensure that your story is conveyed in a concise and impactful manner.

4. When Should You Begin Writing the Essay?

There is no short answer to this question. As an admissions consultant, I have seen students take anywhere between two months and two days to come up with the perfect essay. There is no right time to begin writing. It all boils down to personal preference, your work situation and your skill level.

You can begin to brainstorm and list your experiences as early as one year before applying. Review and add more to the sheet as you go on. This is the first phase of brainstorming.

The second phase, which entails actually penning your essay, begins two or three months before your deadline. Taking into consideration your work situation, family commitments and other concerns, figure out how much time you have to write your essay. Once you have clarity and have introspected enough, begin writing the essay.

Generally speaking, keep a safe buffer. Closing your application work a week or two before the deadline is ideal. Keeping it for the last minute and rushing the essay is bound to result in errors.

As a rule of thumb, keep aside at least two months to write your application essays. The two months will allow you plenty of buffer time between your drafts. In turn, you will be able to make as many revisions as needed.

5. Reality Check: Busting Common Application Essay Myths

5:A. Using Big Words Will Make Me Seem Intelligent

A business school's primary motive is not to evaluate your vocabulary through the essay. It is to gain insights into your candidacy. Simple language that conveys a clear message is often the best way to communicate.

There is another major risk in using big words. You might use them in the wrong context. Specially avoid using ad hoc synonyms that technology allows you to find on the click of a button these days. Let's take a simple example of the word 'food':

Original Sentence

"I ate food."

If you simply Google "food synonyms", among the results is 'subsistence'. If you replace 'food' with subsistence, the sentence reads:

"I ate subsistence."

It becomes apparent that the candidate looked up a synonym and used it without thought. Do not do this. Some words can only be used in certain contexts.

Remember, you do not need to be a wordsmith to write a good essay.

5:B. The Word Count Is of Little Importance

Several students ask me how important the word limit is. Some tend to go the extra mile and disregard it altogether, writing a 700-word essay where a 500-word one was asked for.

I cannot stress this enough: Do NOT flout the word limit the school has set. Doing so shows a disregard for rules set by the AdCom. Further, it could reflect poorly on your writing as the word limit is a challenge to condense your experience in a set amount of words. Exceeding this count showcases your inability to do so.

Lastly, but importantly, remember that the AdCom has hundreds of applications to process. If you go 200 words over the word limit, you increase the amount of attention they have to give to one application. This can severely affect your chances of being viewed favorably.

Most online applications will not allow you to upload a document that is longer than the prescribed word limit. If you are working on a Word.docx document and simply copy and paste your essay on to the online form, if your essay exceeds the word limit, the system will automatically truncate it, thus rendering the ending abrupt.

6. Real People, Unique Skills, Common Errors: Analysis and Fixes

6:A. Kartik Played Down His Strengths

K: But VK, I do not want to brag about my work.
VK: I appreciate the humility. However, drawing attention to your accomplishments is not bragging.

Kartik's profile was strong. He had secured regular promotions and had recently led a project in his organization to streamline very complex operations. However, his essay barely scratched the surface of these accomplishments. He only spoke about his achievement briefly and missed out important facts. He did not even mention that he was the youngest in his company to have spearheaded such a massive operations overhaul.

When he spoke about the positive outcomes, he emphasized a lot on his team's work, crediting himself with little of the stellar work. This inhibition caused the reader to question Kartik's role and efficacy.

To fix Kartik's essay, I began by marking out places where he could write more about his contributions. We retained his exposition on teamwork, but cut down the length by more than half. Over several drafts, we slowly but surely ensured that he was not playing humble but was actively stating his role in the project.

My Take

In an attempt to be humble about their accomplishments, students tend to play down their roles.

A common error is over-emphasizing the teamwork. While business schools want to see the team player in you, they also want to know how you added to the team:

- What did you do to help the project?
- How did you manage or motivate the team?

Talking about these points is not bragging. It merely informs the reader about your role.

6:B. Ramish Had a Lot to Say, but His Essay Asked for Very Little

R: Shouldn't I focus on adding more experiences to my essay, VK? Wasn't that the whole point of brainstorming?

VK: Yes, experiences are key. However, they must be picked in relation to the specific essay topic!

Ramish had an impressive profile for a 26-year-old. He had worked with top marketing firms and was a Marketing Associate at a leading startup in India. He also managed a small animal shelter on the side with friends. Business school was the next logical step for him to advance his career.

However, Ramish said very little in his essays. One asked him to explain why he wanted an MBA. Here, in his zeal to showcase the breadth of his work experience, he had added four varied stories, which, while impressive, made the essay look very disjointed.

To fix his essay, we had a brainstorming session with him. We began structuring his thoughts to answer the question.

First, we eliminated all the stories except the most relevant one. While working as a Marketing Associate, he had failed to complete a project. This was mainly because he was unable to manage the team and delegate tasks and do his own work simultaneously. He realized that if he were to ever lead a team, he would have to improve in this area. Five years into his career, Ramish believed the best way to learn this would be at business school.

We helped position this experience through Ramish's essay and tied it to his post-MBA goal of wanting to work in management positions in marketing. This experience accurately pointed out where Ramish was lacking, and how business school would help him fill this gap.

That year, Ramish was accepted at Johns Hopkins Carey Business School.

My Take

Ramish was unable to structure his thoughts optimally and build a compelling case for why he needed an MBA. He was trying to use the essay to showcase the depth of his work experience. However, the essay demanded that he identify a gap in his profile. It is crucial to answer the specific question asked.

6:C. Esha Thought Her Accomplishments Only Had to Relate to Work

E: But VK, I'm applying for an MBA. I do not think a personal experience will be as impactful.

VK: It's not only through your work that you display your skills. They can definitely come through in other areas of your life.

Esha had a strong professional profile. She was a financial analyst at one of the Big Four firms in Mumbai, and was handling many multi-million-dollar clients. She had four years of work experience and was ambitious. At the time of our first counseling session, she was working closely with her company's top management on a project.

However, Esha had one worry. She did not have a lot of extracurricular activities on her profile to boast of. While her peers were out investing time in these activities, she had personal matters to attend to. Her sister, who was battling certain mental health issues, required her care and support. To help her sister, Esha had spent much of her college and professional life between her responsibilities at home, her education and work.

An essay topic required Esha to talk about her greatest accomplishment in life. During our brainstorming session, we recommended that she use her personal experience of supporting her sister. Esha was reluctant. She believed that since an MBA is a professional degree, the AdCom would only be interested in professional experiences.

We had to explain that this is not the case. Qualities like empathy and compassion are highly valued, and they are exhibited through personal stories. Esha had a compelling story and this experience had shaped her personality.

Over five drafts, we worked to capture her experience in the essay. Her ability to maintain a balance between her work and personal life and still excel at both were emphasized. Her journey with her sister to help her overcome her condition and become stable was brought to the fore. When it was completed, it had all the markers of a compelling essay which accurately captured Esha's experience and was relatable.

That year, Esha was accepted at her dream school.

My Take

Some candidates believe personal accounts are irrelevant in an essay for a professional program. However, nothing is farther from the truth. As long as your personal story directly addresses the essay topic and portrays a skill you possess, the AdCom will be receptive to it. Furthermore, personal stories work better to showcase key life skills such as empathy, compassion and resilience. They also connect better with the reader.

6:D. Naman Tried to Use Complex Language to Impress the AdCom (and Failed)

N: VK, I've been told B-schools want the essays to be of a very high standard.

VK: Yes, that is correct. However, they want to get to know you as an individual. Your motivations, drive, and ambition will set the standard, not just the language used.

When Naman began working on his essays with us, the first draft he sent overshot the word count. Since this was the first draft, it was not a big problem. However, this arose from another mistake he was making. Take, for instance, this line from his essay:

"I had led the Logistics at the conglomerate's event, which had several Eminent, Strong personalities present, talking about their Experiences in the Publishing field, showcasing their results from research work."

Here are the common errors prevalent throughout his essay:

1. Long sentences.
2. Random capitalization.
3. Mashing up of two ideas in one sentence. He speaks about who the speakers were as well as what their topics were in the same sentence. This makes it long and unnecessarily verbose.
4. Repetition of an adjective, noun or verb over five times in a 250-word essay.
5. Unnecessarily complex word choices.

We had to explain to Naman that application essays require articulation of experiences, not overly complex language. He failed to address the topic effectively as the reader was lost in trying to decipher his writing. Impeccable grammar is recommended, flowery language is not.

I tracked comments on this first draft and sent the essay back to Naman. He took a week to rework it, but his second draft marked a step in the right direction. Long sentences were cut down, he began using words that were apt. This made his essay far more readable and the reader was immediately able to glean the information he needed.

He was accepted that year to SDA Bocconi Business School.

My Take

Naman's misconception is a fairly common one among candidates. They believe they will impress the AdCom with longwinded sentences, big words, and ad-hoc stylistic choices. More often than not, these tactics do not work.

Remember, you are applying for a master's degree in business administration, not fine arts. Your essay will be judged largely on the basis of its content and articulation. It is important to talk about your experiences clearly and address the topic. Here are a few simple tips to help you out in this regard:

1. Avoid longwinded sentences. If a sentence is over 18 words, rephrase it or break it down unless it is absolutely necessary.

2. If it does not come naturally to you, do not use flowery vocabulary. You are likely to use words out of context and raise a red flag.

3. Avoid using bullet points in your essay; express everything in paragraphs.

4. Do not omit commas or full-stops, capitalize randomly, or use other stylistic effects in your essay. Keep it simple.

5. Whatever dictionary you follow, UK or US, it is important that you stick with the same throughout the application process. For instance, be careful to not spell it as 'colour' in one place and 'color' in another.

If you are worried about the language of your essay, I recommend using ReachIvy.com's Essay Editor tool, which will flag errors and help you fix them. Finally, remember the rule of thumb we spoke about in Chapter 4: substance over fluff.

6:E. Satish Wanted to Write a 'One-Size-Fits-All' Essay

S: VK, why should I waste time writing so many different essays? I could just write one and send them to all schools!

VK: Tempting thought. However, doing so will severely hurt your chances of being accepted at any top business school.

Satish, a Senior Systems Analyst at a leading data startup in Gurgaon, wanted to quickly finish the essay, which he mistakenly believed to be a 'formality' in the application process.

During a brainstorming session, I informed him that we would be working on three essays; one for each school he was applying to. He was taken aback and resisted the idea. He wanted to write a single essay and ship it to all the schools with minor tweaks.

Seasoned at spotting such generic essays, AdComs will immediately flag any lines that are irrelevant to their schools or essay topics. They show a lack of consideration or interest on the part of the candidate.

This convinced Satish to work on different essays (sometimes maintaining similar experiences) for the schools he was applying to. While this was hard work, it all paid off when Satish was accepted at Cambridge Judge and Chicago Booth, two of the three schools he applied to.

My Take

I often see that students, already exhausted by the application process, just want to be 'done with it'. In this case, the essay bears the brunt of this exhaustion. The result is a generic essay that:

1. Has no specific information.
2. Does not adequately address the topic.

When schools ask you specific questions, they demand specific answers. Generic replies will do you no good.

Often, students forget to change the name of the school when using the same essay for different schools! This immediately results in a rejection.

To avoid these mistakes, no matter how exhausted you are, I recommend persevering and writing a different essay for each of the business schools you apply to.

6:F. *Aryan Was Too Focused on the Wrong Parts of His Application*

A: VK, I want them to know the details of the situation, so they understand why it was such a big deal!

VK: Agreed. The situation is awesome but the AdCom wants to know YOUR contribution therein.

Aryan's first draft came to us in really good shape. As was expected of a sub-editor at a major publishing house, it was free of language errors. However, he had not effectively used the experience we had discussed in the brainstorming session to relate why he wanted an MBA. He was to talk about his own short-lived stint at establishing his publishing house and how the failure led him to realize that he would need business knowledge and a better understanding of operations before he could attempt it again.

However, Aryan spent 40 percent of the essay talking about the state of publishing in India, a recent acquisition in the sector, and the effects of digitization: all fascinating aspects and relevant, too. But he failed to address his own experience and position within the macroeconomic picture of the industry. His aspiration to become an entrepreneur in the field and build a business that adapted to the digital age was barely addressed. This led to the essay being less about why he wanted an MBA and more like an article on the publishing industry.

We began by flagging portions where Aryan delved too much into the details of publishing. The flagged portions were replaced with Aryan's own work in the space and how he wished to address problems. These two fixes helped to adequately answer the essay topic and showcased Aryan's vision for the field.

When he applied that year, Aryan was accepted at IMD Switzerland.

My Take

The focal point of an MBA essay is not the situation but the action, result and learning. Sure, the reader needs to know the context of an experience, but you need not go into minute details. Simply explain the problem and save the word count for YOUR role.

Do not spend your words unnecessarily describing the situation. Limit it to 10 percent of the total experience and spend more time detailing your actions and results.

6:G. Anand Thought Portraying Weaknesses Was Counterintuitive

A: Are you serious, VK? Why would I want to list a failure in my essay? It would weaken my application!

VK: I understand what you are thinking, but that is not how the AdCom thinks.

Anand was an entrepreneur who had had two unsuccessful startups. However, his third jab at cracking the ed-tech space was successful. With help from friends, he was able to build a platform and sustain it, peaking at 15 lakh users before he sold it to another major ed-tech player. He was applying to INSEAD, IESE and Esade after this endeavor, hoping to acquire additional skills before he went back to entrepreneurship.

An essay topic required that he talk about one accomplishment and one failure in 400 words. While writing about his accomplishment was no hurdle for Anand, he struggled with the failure. The first draft that we reviewed did the classic "my strength is my greatest weakness" maneuver. Instead of listing a legitimate failure, Anand spoke about how he worked so hard that maintaining relationships was a problem for him.

This was both untrue and a blatantly obvious disguise for a strength.

The AdCom will not be judging you on the basis of your failure but your takeaways from it and how you persisted thereafter. In Anand's case, he had two failed attempts at entrepreneurship which made for excellent additions to the essay. After six rounds of editing, we arrived at a draft that accurately answered the essay question. It truthfully captured a failure in Anand's career. Further, his self-awareness regarding his failure and ability to learn from it was highlighted.

That year, Anand was accepted at all his three target schools.

My Take

I can understand the reluctance to add a legitimate failure in your essay. You want every possible advantage and do not want your attempts to be thwarted by a negative experience.

However, your self-awareness and ability to learn from rough patches in life are being scrutinized. If you have failed, they want to see if you understand the cause of the failure, and how you could have done better. This showcases maturity. Moreover, it grounds you as an individual with a fair share of failures, not mere accomplishments.

Still don't believe that a failure can make for a good essay experience? Look at how Anand's turned out:

To facilitate informed decision-making in India's fragmented education market, I launched ▪▪▪▪▪, a technology platform that curated information on coaching institutes and private tutors. I needed a diverse team with skillsets ranging from sales to design and technology. Riding high on securing pre-seed funding, I hastily chose co-founders from relatives and close friends to attain first mover advantage. Due to my rush, I fell short of acquiring the right technical talent; I was forced to outsource this key function, leading to a significantly higher payroll and a delayed product launch. For my founding team, I had also divided tasks based on individual interests as opposed to individual strengths; a trained accountant was overseeing sales and a marketing associate was handling finances. Over six months, revenue fell by 80 % and I lost 50 clients. The downward spiral led to the project shut down and an eventual fallout between the co-founders, severely straining my personal relationship with one of my closest friends. Through this experience, I learned that planning strategically, staffing pragmatically, and leading objectively are three key pillars of professional success.

The above says a lot about Anand's character. He is willing to admit his faults and can accurately pinpoint where the venture went wrong. Furthermore, he knows what to take away from the experience and expresses it with distinct maturity. Even though this is an expression of failure, it paints a positive image of the candidate in the reader's minds.

6:H. Clarissa Was in the Habit of Quoting Famous Personalities to Back Her Standpoint

C: Wouldn't what these people say confirm my stance?

VK: In a research essay, maybe. However, this needs to be personal, and their word doesn't show how you practice these values in your own life.

Clarissa was a public-sector professional who was working with us remotely from Kerala. She wanted to start a volunteering platform to help NGOs recruit more effectively. When she had signed up for our services, she wanted a second opinion on her essays.

The first draft she sent us was riddled with quotations and citations from famous authors and stalwarts in the nonprofit/social-impact space. While the writeup did lend credibility to her theory about the volunteer gap in NGOs in India, there was no personal slant. She barely touched upon what drove her to work in the sector and fix the problem.

As a first step, I began by asking her to remove all quotations from her essay. They were general in nature and while she used them to substantiate her stand, they added no personal experience or information. This made the essay impersonal. It could have been written by anybody. We reframed the essay making Clarissa the protagonist, bring out HER perspectives.

That year, Clarissa was accepted at Duke University's Fuqua School of Business.

My Take

I have seen many students quote eminent personalities in their essays as the sole qualifier to their statements about themselves or their goals. Stick to personal stories and experiences to back up your content. Remember, the essay needs to be about YOU.

7. Errors in a Nutshell

7:A. Playing Too Humble

Many candidates (understandably) want to refrain from bragging. However, they confuse "talking about your role in a project" with bragging.

Insider Tips

1. Clearly state your 'action' in any given experience you include. This should comprise 50 percent of your essay.
2. Use active verbs when talking about your role. For instance:
    "I led a team of…"
    "I collaborated with…"
    "I analyzed…"

7:B. Arbitrarily Adding Experiences to an Essay

Every word, every experience you add in your essay must have a reason to be there.

Insider Tips

1. Ensure each experience you talk about, each line in the essay, serves a purpose.
2. Do not go overboard littering the essay with random accomplishments or experiences.

7:C. Giving Language Importance at the Expense of Content

Business schools do not give you brownie points for using big words.

Insider Tips

1. Use short, simple, succinct sentences.
2. Do not use ad-hoc stylistic choices like omission of commas and full-stops, random capitalization, etc.

7:D. *Writing the Same Essay for All Business Schools You Are Applying To*

Do not ship identical essays to all schools without fine-tuning it to suit the requirements of the topic and the school you are applying to.

Insider Tips

1. Spend time on each individual essay you are to write for the application.
2. Ensure you use specific information about the schools in these essays.

7:E. *Thinking Personal Accomplishments Are Irrelevant for an MBA Essay*

Many students avoid personal feats and experiences in their MBA essay on account of them being 'irrelevant'.

Insider Tip

1. Do not shy away from adding personal experiences as long as they adequately addresses the essay topic.

7:F. *Giving 'Situation' All the Attention*

Great essays are often held back by a longwinded description of the problem at hand. Giving the situation the spotlight takes it away from you.

Insider Tips

1. Let the situation be only about 10 percent of the total experience.
2. Use at least 50 percent of the experience to describe action— what did you do? How did you do it?

Insider Tips in a Nutshell

DO:

✓ Ensure you do your research on the schools.

✓ Make sure you read the essay topic multiple times and break it into fragments.

✓ Use the STAR and Learning approach when adding experiences to your essay.

✓ Ensure the information in your essay is consistent with your résumé and LoRs.

✓ Use specific information in your essay.

✓ Write separate essays if applying to multiple schools.

✓ Use the active voice in your essays.

✓ Sleep on your essay before finalizng it.

✓ Get an opinion from a third party.

✓ Proofread multiple times.

DON'T:

Χ Write generic information in your essay.

Χ Use excessive or self-depreciating humor.

Χ Use big words and complex sentences to sound intelligent.

Χ Understate your role in projects/teams.

Χ Arbitrarily add experiences.

Χ Exceed the word limit.

Χ Write points that do not match the essay prompt.

Χ Try to force-fit essays from one school to another.

APPENDIX

SAMPLE ESSAYS:

1. PERSONAL ESSAY

Harvard Business School

Essay Topic:

You're applying to Harvard Business School. We can see your résumé, academic transcripts, extracurricular activities, awards, post-MBA career goals, test scores, and what your recommenders have to say about you. What else would you like us to know as we consider your candidacy?

> The essay clearly states that they want something other than what would be readily available on the submitted documents. Thus, using a personal story will add value to the application. It will give the AdCom what they want: an insight into areas that the mentioned documents don't cover.

Word Limit: None

In caste-and-creed conscious India, where age-old Hindu-Muslim communal tension persists and interreligious marriage is taboo, my Hindu father and Muslim mother raised me in both faiths with the autonomy to shape my own beliefs. During my upbringing we celebrated Hindu and Muslim festivals with equal gusto, always appreciating their significance in relation to other faith-based traditions.

> This is the **situation** and building up of story. Note how the candidate adds a personal element that helps the reader relate to their situation. Such an opening for personal essays effectively gives the reader context to your background.

My flexible religious identity often manifested itself in unorthodox experiences. I remember when my father, dressed in Muslim garb, conducted my Nana's (mother's father) burial rites. Today, fondly recalling this scene, my mother says that it would have pleased Nana – XXXXXX.

This early exposure to religious and cultural tolerance influenced my character development, specifically my open-mindedness and inclination to consider all sides of an argument. Thanks to my duality I overlook differences and focus on similarities, mobilizing me to unite people from disparate backgrounds. My sustained efforts in mediation have been consistently and demonstrably successful: first in high school, then in college and now as a professional.

"An exact re-creation of the UN – Mumbai Model UN meets" -- Indian Express

After months of research, conceptualization and groundwork, we had finally executed India's XXXXXX-agnostic national-scale Model UN: a three-day forum where 250 student delegates from more than 25 schools across 7 states reached resolutions on current global issues.

Representing our high school at Harvard Model UN had inspired my friends and me, including XXXXXX to create a similar platform in India, where schools provide limited exposure to supplementary economic and political systems and fail to promote geopolitical awareness.

Because the MUN concept was little-known in India, we met with more than 75 school principals to explain our vision and request their participation. Moreover, thanks to our persistent efforts, several foreign consulates and corporations XXXXXX sponsored the event, leading to media coverage and increased credibility. We even approached schools in XXXXXX, hoping to foster constructive interaction between students from both sides of an enduring international conflict. Sadly, the associated visa issues proved insurmountable.

250 students transformed into delegates of different countries and fiercely debated on potential solutions to real-world global crises – this was our biggest reward. I felt the full power and potential of collaboration when, while moderating the XXXXXX, I oversaw the diverse delegates pass a resolution to inhibit trafficking of Ukrainian and Thai women. As one newspaper put it, "The second day of MMUN seemed indistinguishable from the real thing – apart from the fact that some delegates were as young as 13."

"Launch party of Global Student Council at XXXXXX" -- multi-colored flyers I'd tacked onto bulletin boards all over campus.

When I arrived at XXXX I hoped to join

an international student organization that would help me assimilate—none existed. I could join the India Student Association, European Society or Asian Student Union but no single integrated club. My roommate XXXXXX and I decided to create an umbrella group for international students modeled on XXXXXX Student Council, a structure which required permissions from various offices including Development, Student Affairs and Admissions. Initially, we encountered resistance because the University "didn't require a second student council." Thankfully, after a year of determined lobbying, we secured the XXXXXX approval by sharing with the Vice President our plans to leverage international students to create XXXXXX and elsewhere. He subsequently rallied other offices and a year later we founded the XXXXXX Student Council XXXXXX. Within months of operation, we created four new international XXXXXX clubs, a video for prospective international students and a buddy program which matched incoming international students with XXXXXX students. Since we graduated, a thriving XXXXXX has more than doubled its membership.

My multicultural roots fuel my curiosity to explore different cultures and ultimately shaped my decision to study in America. I now realize that my biggest achievement at

XXXXXX was building a global network of friends. Today I'm proud to know that incoming students can avail of GSC's resources to initiate similar experiences.

"XXXXXX expands to India with Mumbai office"—headline of an Indian business daily.

Owing to my quantitative toolkit, international work experience, familiarity with cold calling (I raised over $230,000 from alumni at XXXXXX) and ability to speak three regional languages, XXXXXX had just hired me to set up their India operations and build an investment pipeline via directly reaching out to entrepreneurs.

To develop an initial network of diverse investee companies I utilized my ability to easily connect with people from different backgrounds: for example my fluency in XXXXXX helped me communicate on a personal level with a sixty-year-old entrepreneur from rural XXXXXX. He owns a XXXXXX factory and was delighted when I shared a XXXXXX that my family has passed down for generations. Similarly my international education and work experience allowed me to interact comfortably with a savvy, 32-year-old XXXXXX alum who has started a XXXXXX business in India. Additionally, it is my job to communicate these varied entrepreneurs' stories to XXXXXX Committee – a group of XXXXXX based in London, Boston XXXXXX. This means that I must seamlessly switch between languages, attitudes and ages and bridge cultural and geographical gaps in order to consummate a transaction. Consequently, building upon relationships I have sown, XXXXXX has made investment offers to many small-town entrepreneurs who speak limited English.

Living and working in a number of different geographies and socioeconomic silos, I've discovered my aptitude for assimilation and interpersonal communication: volunteering at a church in XXXXXX with my American host family, solving the New York City scavenger hunt with my peers at XXXXXX, savoring pale ales with co-workers at a pub in London and teaching English to slum children in Mumbai. At each stage of my life, I have fervently absorbed and shared new ideas while seeking out opportunities for collaboration. I owe this global identity and extroverted disposition to my background.

Summing up the result of the candidate's work.

The candidate effectively sums up his essay using all the three talking points:

1. The power of diversity afforded to him

2. How he is able to leverage this diversity

3. How he has learned from his varied experience

This concludes his positioning as a global citizen with an aptitude to learn and adapt to new ideas and challenges.

2. EVALUATING AN EXPERIENCE

HEC Paris

Essay Topic:

Leadership and ethics are inevitably intertwined in the business world. Describe a situation in which you have dealt with these issues and how they have influenced you. (250 words)

Learning to say 'No'

The XXXXXX of a corporate-multinational had received approximately XXXXXX in cash and wanted to save taxes on it. I provided them two legitimate options. The promoters' XXXXXX suggested creating a XXXXXX document-trail. We had to sign-off on this strategy.

My task was twofold – since the strategy suggested by the XXXXXX was illegal, I had to refuse signing- off on it, but retain the client at the same time. I consulted XXXXXX, who backed me completely. Thereafter, I conveyed our objection to the illegal strategy, much to the displeasure of the client. Consequently, I had to conceptualize a feasible solution quickly or end up losing the client. I did extensive research on the issue, conceptualized a potential solution, brainstormed with XXXXXX and other seniors, found solutions to their queries and finalized the solution within a week's time, which envisaged routing XXXXXX in a XXXXXX. The client ultimately implemented the advice.

Helming this engagement end-to-end, I established credibility with my client, to the extent that I am now consulted in XXXXXX matters as well. I not only retained the client, but also secured numerous follow-on assignments.

This incident taught me the importance of standing one's ground and selecting long-term ethical solutions and ignoring the unethical short-term distractions. My self-confidence improved enormously as I relentlessly tackled a challenging situation in stressful conditions and in an unfazed manner successfully. It helped me gain credibility and stature within my organization and with the client.

3. WHY THIS SCHOOL AND GOALS ESSAY

University of Pennsylvania, Wharton School of Business

ESSAY TOPIC:

What do you hope to gain professionally from the Wharton MBA?

Word limit: 500

I am passionate about helping businesses navigate political and regulatory challenges as they grow in emerging markets. Post my MBA, I aspire to head the XXXXXX team for emerging markets at a technology firm such as XXXXXX. In the long run, I aim to setup my own XXXXXX focused XXXXXX consultancy. These markets are still marked by tough regulatory challenges, with the constant threat of local governments tampering with operations. My XXXXXX knowledge along with consulting and in-house experience will help me build a world-class, locally-rooted advisory firm to help clients prepare for such risks.

To achieve my goal, I need to build a strong academic base of business fundamentals and hone my political knowledge. Wharton uniquely offers the XXXXXX program which combines international studies and business education. A conversation with

This essay topic specifically asks what one wishes to gain 'professionally' from the Wharton MBA. Thus, it is important to list both your **professional goals** and **how you will leverage the school to achieve this.**

A single opening statement that clearly communicates the candidate's passion and their branding.

This is an excellent example of opening with a bang. Iterates the candidate's passion right at the start.

Immediate **short term goal.**

Long term goal.

Communicates the current landscape of the industry/market.

Communicates what skill they possess that will help them achieve this goal.

Overall, the first paragraph quickly gets to the point. They communicate:

- What the candidate is pasionate about.
- What he wishes to achieve
- What the current scenario is of his industry
- What skillset he possesses.

Communicates what the candidate lacks and needs to gain in order to achieve their goal.

XXXXXX about how Wharton-Lauder gave him the academic grounding to navigate the challenges of running a global business has reaffirmed my passion to pursue this program. As the only interdisciplinary MBA with a core language requirement, it will allow me to learn XXXXXX. This, coupled with my existing language skills, will widen my ability to engage in the XXXXXX, especially in XXXXXX economic powerhouses like XXXXXX and the XXXXXX

To build my XXXXXX consulting firm, I must sharpen my overall leadership skills while also understanding how leaders manage external risks such as unpredictable political shifts or disruptive regulatory changes. Wharton emphasizes this through its XXXXXX and XXXXXX Center. Professors XXXXXX and XXXXXX conduct research on effective leadership and governance practices to prepare for and respond to major external risks; I hope to assist them on their research and publications. I also want to be involved in organizing the Centre's XXXXXX Seminar Series, which would help me interact closely with policy makers and executives grappling with such issues. Furthermore, I aim to enroll in the XXXXXX Program; I wish to improve my interpersonal effectiveness, especially in influencing team members and clients, and will benefit from a strategic leadership development plan and

Notice the highly specific nature of the information included. The candidate talks about specific courses. Additionally, they also talk about their conversation about a similarly-minded alumnus.

Expresses what Wharton offers differently and how this will benefit the candidate.

As with the previous paragraph, opens with what they lack and what they need to gain to achieve their goal.

The rest of the paragraph adds highly specific information such as:

- Specific departments at Wharton
- Specific professors whose research will help the candidate
- Specific events conducted at Wharton
- Specific programs at Wharton that may be beneficial to the candidate.

Additionally, also note that the student talks about how these resources will help them.

one-on-one coaching.

Lastly, I wish to gain a sophisticated understanding of how global XXXXXX firms operate. I intend to apply to participate in Wharton's distinctive XXXXXX Practicum to work with teams from partner universities to consult a technology client entering an emerging market. This will give me a bird's-eye view of the challenges such firms face, and will allow me to learn practical lessons. I also hope to gain further knowledge through my interactions with alumni. Speaking to XXXXXX I learned that nearly XXXXXX of Wharton alumni forge careers in XXXXXX; I would seek to leverage this resource to build strong relationships in the sector.

In conclusion, Wharton will help me achieve my future goals by giving me solid interdisciplinary training, knowledge of XXXXXX and the XXXXXX space, and by developing my leadership skills and networks.

4. OPTIONAL ESSAY

University of Chicago, Booth School of Business

ESSAY TOPIC:

Is there any additional information that you would like the Admissions Committee to know? If so, please address in an optional essay.

Word Limit: 300 words maximum

As part of my undergraduate thesis, XXXXXX I spent several days in XXXXXX, the world's largest slum. I encountered the socioeconomic traps that dwellers were stuck in due to unresolved affordable housing issues. While I came across several small nonprofits working to help residents resolve these, I noticed that these organizations were constantly pulled back due to a lack of proper funding. I decided to work towards bridging this gap.

Interested in finance, I took baby steps and pursued investment banking. I chose real estate to be well versed with the constantly evolving industry dynamics. I worked on deals such as a XXXXXX merger of the two largest XXXXXX Investment Trusts XXXXXX; this helped me contrast the formalized real estate and infrastructure investments of developed markets with the inconsistently regulated

> Again, this essay, owing to the limited real-estate afforded, gets right to the point and introduces the first experience.
>
> This is the **overarching situation** of the essay.
>
> Also, this showcases a sense of purpose in the candidate and sets their vision from the start. This is an excellent example of opening with a bang.

> This is the **task** of the experience.

> This is the **action** of the experience.

> This part encapsulates what the candidate **learnt** in process of the action itself. Furthermore, it positions them as being highly perceptive and understanding of new information.

and incentive lacking real estate sector of an emerging market XXXXXX. Through these experiences, I decided to create the right financial incentives for entrepreneurs and developers in emerging markets for long term value creation.

> Note how this line captures the candidate's **decision making** skills.

I next joined the XXXXXX, the private equity arm of XXXXXX, to bring me closer to my pursuit of impact investment.

> This is another **action statement**.

Every investment project I have executed has strengthened my belief in how impact and profitability can go hand-in-hand. Assisting XXXXXX team in forming the XXXXXX vehicle worth XXXXXX million reaffirmed my decision to work towards

> This is a strong line that communicates the candidate's **learning and the impact** it has had in shaping their beliefs.

fostering housing innovation by leveraging the transformational power of funding. The investment has created more than XXXXXX affordable houses for slum dwelling families working in various industrial zones of India.

> These two lines sum up the result of the candidate's efforts. This is the culmination of their efforts and showcases that they have been successful.

These formative experiences sparked me with a strong desire to solve the socioeconomic housing trap that plagues millions of undeserved communities; I plan to keep working towards this as I evolve.

> These final lines convey the candidate's learning from the experience. Furthermore, the last few words showcase a **commitment to their industry and a genuine sense of purpose.** It also helps solidify their branding.

5. GOALS ESSAY

National University of Singapore

Essay Topic:

Briefly describe your immediate post-MBA career goal including your industry, function and country of choice and how have your prior experiences motivated and prepared you to pursue these goals?

Word Limit: 300 words

Having quantified the 'risk factors' in my career, I intend to leverage a pedigreed MBA to 'claim' the role of Project Manager at a leading XXXXX consulting firm (such as XXXX or XXXX) in Asia, primarily XXXXX. My vision is to fuse technology with strategy in the disruptive XXXX landscape to augment business-offerings to clients.

Due to my father's itinerant job, I travelled across cities and became a natural extrovert. My peripatetic upbringing made me innately adaptable and resilient. Forging deep-rooted friendships with new people instilled in me a strong sense of empathy and honed my interpersonal skills. Carrying this trait into every endeavour, I successfully managed a four-member team during the formative stages of my career and won several awards for my leadership.

Having capitalized on different avenues

available to me, I have inculcated a deep understanding of formulating strategies for formidable problems. Working extensively with three XXXXXX insurance companies, I utilized XXXX XX paradigms to analyse premiums and reserves, enabling clients to make complex decisions faster. Further, authoring papers on XXXXX and completing an industry certification in XXXXXX, I elevated my functional acuity.

Observing government machinery operate at closer quarters has given me a sense of respect for 'structure', 'order' and 'efficiency'. I have strong technical skills in my arsenal such as XXXXX, XXXXX and XXXX. Through my undergraduate and work experience, I have striven to accelerate processes to save time and costs in business processes. Owing to this strong technical base, I built a front end application that saved 50 percent man-hours by automating the resolution of production issues and pioneered 'XXXXX XXX XXX' to automate and optimize daily consulting processes.

'With insurable interest' and 'utmost good faith', I believe I am perfectly positioned to carve my niche in XXXX consulting.

7

Recommendation Letters: How to Enable Your Recommenders to Enable You

Hi VK,

With your team's guidance, the essays have been a breeze. Now I am very confused when it comes to the 'recommenders'. My target schools ask for between one and three recommenders each, and I simply don't know whom to pick. I looked online, but the advice is vague. They ask me to pick someone who 'will be able to describe my skills and personality', but that's a lot of people! Please help me zero in on the right person(s).

The letter of recommendation (LoR) is a critical document. All the other documents you submit to the AdCom are written by you and subject to your biases. But the recommendation letter is written by an external entity (with his/her biases) who can provide a third-party perspective to the AdCom. The AdCom can learn a lot about your personality, character and work ethic from what your LoRs say. These should not be taken lightly at all.

A recommender is the equivalent of a brand endorser who knows and understands your positioning statement. While picking a recommender sounds easy, many students use the wrong parameters to do so.

Take Suyash, who wrote the above email. In his four-year career with a top consulting firm, he had worked under several managers. When the time came to apply to an MBA program, he was unable to pick one person to write the recommendation. When he came to me to brainstorm on his recommenders, I began with a three-step process. First, we would identify the recommendation questions sent by the school; second, we would list and zero in on the recommenders; third, we would brainstorm the content (highlights of his profile and primary talking points) for the recommenders.

Finding the recommendation questions was fairly straightforward. Many schools list these upfront on their website. Others will email the list of questions to your recommender once you enter an email address on your application form. You can request your recommender to forward to you the email which contains JUST the questions. There is nothing unethical or illegal about being privy to the questions asked by the school. It is alright to know what the recommenders have been asked, not what they answered. In fact, I believe that knowing the questions helps you to understand the school better and judge what it values in its applicants. This will help you gauge the kind of recommenders you will require.

Every school has different stipulations for who can be your recommender. There is no set format or requirement, so be certain to review this for each school you apply to. For most schools, you will need one recommendation from a current direct supervisor and another from a colleague or supervisor.

Listing Suyash's potential recommenders was a challenge because he was working on multiple projects simultaneously and reporting to at least three different supervisors at one time. Moreover, he had an amicable relationship with many of his co-workers and was unsure whom to pick among them to write his recommendation. To narrow his list down, I asked him to take his time and think of his relationships with everyone on his list, asking himself these questions:

1. Who was the most supportive of his goals?
2. Whom had he worked most closely with?
3. Who knew him for the longest duration?
4. Which supervisor understood Suyash's skills, personality and ambition?

Please note that there is no formula to apply to the above four parameters; you have to find a fine balance among them. Finally, Suyash arrived at his potential recommenders and reached out to them. Both enthusiastically agreed. However, this was only half the job done. Now, he had to help the recommenders with talking points.

This demanded brainstorming (yes, again!) and listing experiences specific to his recommenders. His experiences were broken down in the STAR and Learning format (covered in Chapter 6) to make them specific and have maximum impact on the reader.

These experiences ranged from office projects to in-office extracurricular events which Suyash would help organize. These experiences would then become talking points for the recommenders.

We told Suyash not to write the recommendation letters himself. This is the ethical route and allows for an authentic recommendation. I asked him to send the talking points to his recommenders in an email and inform them of the deadline by which they needed to upload the recommendations online. Then came the time to wait.

Thankfully, Suyash's recommenders were very responsive and required little to no follow-up. Beyond sending the talking points, Suyash had no further input in the recommendations. Neither did he ever see or read what had been written by the recommenders; this would remain a mystery for him.

That year, Suyash was accepted at the Yale School of Management and the Haas School of Business at Berkeley. Can we attribute his admits entirely to his recommendations being stellar? Absolutely not.

Did they play a major role in his being accepted? Absolutely, yes.

Let's revisit a point I made at the start of the chapter:

"A recommender is the equivalent of a brand endorser."

The recommender's word can confirm your conviction about yourself or contradict it. To the AdCom, the recommendation letter is a confirmation of your statements from a peer or superior who has known you for a considerable period. In the world of business, you work with several people from diverse backgrounds. What do they think of you? This is an important question to ponder over. It is your equation with your peers and superiors that will make or break your career. This equation often trickles down to how well you have nurtured your relationships.

Year after year, I work with some students who are unable to identify any recommenders. When it is time to apply for an MBA, they have a compelling profile but no reliable endorsers. They fail to build bonds with people at their workplace and outside of it and then feel at a loss.

I will cover a few points to help you make positive change in your inter-personal relationships right now. This will hold you in good stead when you are applying for an MBA later in life.

1. Relationship Building on the Road to an MBA

As early as their high-school years, students partake in activities they are interested in, at school and outside. This is when many revelations are made and you learn a lot about your personality. However, I have seen that most people fail to keep in touch with the people they work with after a project or activity is completed. I have been guilty of doing the same. I met some wonderful mentors and teachers in my early years who made a significant impact on my life. However, for no particular reason, I took the task of keeping in touch lightly. In hindsight, the loss is entirely mine. I would recommend that my readers take this insight from my experience.

Mentors who have known you over many years can provide immense professional and emotional support in the years to come. I strongly recommend keeping in touch with anyone you really enjoyed working with, had a positive experience with, and learned a lot from. This creates a base of people you know early on. Keep building from here. How do you do this?

1:A. Four Simple Networking Tips

1. Check in on these relationships at a regular frequency (avoid long lags in communication)

Checking in does not have to be an elaborate dinner plan or meeting (it doesn't hurt to have those going, though!). We live in a connected world. Touching base is as simple as a few button taps. Ask them how they are doing, tell them how you are doing, and keep the conversation on.

2. Keep tabs on their achievements and congratulate them

Did you find out that your ex-boss won an award, achieved a milestone or got promoted? Go ahead and congratulate him. However, do this over a personal message or an email. Open forums like the comments section of LinkedIn, Facebook and Twitter are not recommended for this purpose. Moreover, add a line or two about how this achievement is significant and express your admiration. This will elevate their spirits and showcase that you are actively following their journeys.

3. Attend events that they invite you to

If one of your contacts invites you to an event (be it personal or professional), try to attend it. This could be their book launch, a party, a company event or something similar. This is an opportunity to connect face-to-face with them and will definitely go a long way in solidifying the relationship.

4. *If you can, help them*

While networking has become a textbook term for knowing people who can help you when needed, it is important that you also 'nurture' the network and genuinely care about them. Do not build networks for purely selfish reasons. It is your personal responsibility to contribute to society and help in the growth and advancement of a fellow human being.

You need not wait for a contact to ask you for help. Taking the initiative to help them out can go a long way. If you know someone in need of services that you or your contact can offer, refer your services or your contact to them. This will create goodwill and help you to maintain a strong bond with them.

These tips I have mentioned are applicable to anyone, no matter the age or purpose. However, the ball game changes once you have decided to apply for an MBA. Hereafter, you must take active steps to ensure that you get stellar recommendations. Here is how you can do it:

1:B. How to Reinforce Your Network AFTER You Decide to Apply to Business School

1. *Contact Your Immediate Manager*

Set up a meeting with your manager to request him to write a recommendation letter for you. Be direct when telling him about your MBA plans, including your planned dates. If he seems eager to support you, ask if you can take on some additional responsibilities in line with your post-MBA goals. This will help you to learn more about a new function potentially and also help you to improve your work profile.

Additionally, ensure that you tell your supervisor that you wish to hand over your work before you leave and are willing to invest the time and energy to train the next person. Giving them this heads-up will prepare them so that when the time comes for you to quit, they will have a new hire ready. Do NOT put this conversation off until the last minute. This would come off as unprofessional and might catch him off guard. Ideally, a year to six months is considered sufficient heads-up.

2. *Revive Old Contacts*

If your manager agrees, you still need one or two more recommenders, depending on which college you are applying to. This is a good time to start reviving old contacts. Set up an in-person meeting, if possible, to discuss your plans. Tell them why you chose them over other people so that they know where they stand in your eyes.

Please note that not all contacts wish to be revived. Nor can you appear out of the blue and hope for them to welcome you with open arms. You will have to rebuild a rapport with them first. Let them in on recent developments in your life. You cannot expect them to magically know what you have been up to since you last spoke with them.

For instance, I had a student who had worked at a top consulting firm for a year after college. After this, he worked with Teach for India for two years and then started his own ed-tech startup. In his case, when reviving the contact with his manager at the consulting firm, it would have been ideal on his part to tell him all that he had done in the two years after he had left.

Tell them the following to bring them up to speed with your current profile:

1. Places you worked at since you left the organization.
2. Projects you undertook in the meanwhile.
3. New courses, certifications and diplomas you completed.
4. How your goals have changed or developed since you last worked together.

You may also give the contacts your current résumé.

If this process takes time, delay your application. Many students I have worked with had to delay their application by a round or a year because they did not have strong recommenders. This is perfectly fine. You should apply when every component of your application is strong.

3. Connect in All Directions, Not Just Upward

The common tendency is to only keep a good rapport with your supervisors and CEOs. However, I advise you to keep a congenial rapport with everyone you work with, be it your superiors, the people you manage, or those below you. If you are an entrepreneur, engage actively with clients, vendors and suppliers. If you are a professional, ensure that you build a good rapport with your superiors and peers. Keep in touch and sustain the network using the four tips I gave you earlier. Some schools may also ask for an LoR from a peer. In such a case, prior horizontal networking will come to your aid.

2. What the AdCom Wants

It is important to know what the Admissions Committee expects from a recommender or referee. With this information, you can formulate your next steps with more clarity.

2:A. Pick a Recommender as per the Specifications of the Business School

I cannot stress the importance of getting recommendations written by exactly the kind of people the AdCom has asked for.

These are different people that the schools may seek a recommendation from:
- Your current supervisor at work
- A previous supervisor at work
- A peer at work
- A peer or a supervisor from a non-work-related activity

However, each school will have its own policy for the recommendation letters. Let us look at the policies of three top schools:

1. *London Business School:*

1. Your current employer (if you don't want to ask your employer to be a referee, a colleague is acceptable).
2. Someone else who knows you well in a work context, like a former employer or a long-standing client.

2. *Wharton:*

They require two letters of recommendations from individuals who are well acquainted with your performance in a work setting, preferably from a current or former supervisor.

3. *National University of Singapore:*

Two referee reports are required to complete your application. The two referees can be your current employer, previous employer or corporate client.

The people who have been specified by the school will be in a much better position than anyone else to answer the questions they put forth.

Some schools may allow you to get a recommendation from a different person as long as you can provide a compelling reason for doing so. For example, one of my students was a professional national-level badminton player. He got a recommendation letter from the coach of the Indian team. This was done because the coach had known him in a personal capacity for over five years and thus was an ideal recommender.

2:B. A Recommendation Letter That Endorses You with Examples

The LoR is very similar to the essay when it comes to the amount of specificity required. Your recommender cannot merely state:

"XYZ is a fast learner and very skilled when it comes to UI/ UX design."

The above is a vague statement with no example backing it up. WHAT incident demonstrates the said skill? HOW is XYZ a fast learner? HOW did this impact the organization? These are the questions that must be answered. Such specificity will allow the AdCom to accurately gauge your skills and traits since it is not a mere abstract statement.

Here is how the above statement can be made more specific:

"When faced with a major overhaul in the designing software we used, the workplace had come to a standstill. Despite XYZ's expertise being in business analytics, he took the initiative to learn the new software. He spent an afternoon learning how to design software on YouTube. By the end of the day, he was able to pitch in and provide valuable feedback even in an area which he did not have expertise in. Furthermore, he was able to help the team figure out the new software and use it effectively. Not only did he learn fast in this situation, but was also crucial in helping the rest of the team figure out the new software."

2:C. A Recommendation Letter by Someone Who has Worked Closely with You

"VK, I have managed to get my CEO to write my letter. Isn't that awesome?" Yes, this is "awesome" if you work directly and closely with your CEO.

Recommendation letters need to be personal. This is possible only when someone who has worked with you closely or for a significant period writes them. I have seen that students have a tendency to approach high-ranking people from their organization to write recommendations. Oftentimes, this high-ranking and influential person barely knows their name or what work they do. Recommendation letters written by extremely senior people, even when they agree to write them, are going to be generic, providing no personal information about you unless you had a strong working relationship with them.

Instead, pick the peer you have been closely collaborating with, the manager whom you worked under for two years, or the client you have been servicing for two years. They will all be able to write infinitely better recommendation letters even if they don't have fancy titles. This is because they know your characteristics, strengths and weaknesses, having witnessed them personally.

3. How to Pick Your Recommenders

3:A. How to Shortlist Potential Recommenders

Begin with a tentative list of people who can recommend you. You can do this brainstorming with a friend, family member or admissions expert. List at least five people.

I understand that there might be more, or even less, that come to mind. However, take into consideration the following factors about your recommender before adding them to the list:

1. Relationship and Period You Worked Together

As already mentioned, the relationship and context of your connection with this person has to be in accordance with what the school has specified. Additionally, the depth of the relationship should come through. For example, if you had a daily reporting relationship with someone versus a quarterly review, the former may be preferred since he has deeper insight into your work patterns and behavior.

Here are two questions that business schools ask your recommenders to understand their equation with you.

    a) **INSEAD:** *"How long have you known the candidate? Define your relationship with the candidate and the circumstances whereby you met."*

    b) **LBS:** *"How long have you known the applicant and in what connection?"*

These questions establish your recommender's credibility at the outset by assessing his relationship with you. If this credibility is not built adequately, the validity of the recommendation becomes questionable.

I always recommend picking at least one person from the professional sphere when applying for an MBA—it is a business degree, after all. If you do not have full-time work experience, you can ask your supervisor from your summer internship to write you a recommendation.

2. *Understanding of Your Goals*

Your recommender must be privy to your long-term goals and support and endorse them. Ideally, he should know your career journey and believe in your potential.

Schools may ask the following questions of your recommenders about your goals:

    a) **INSEAD:** *Comment on the candidate's career progress to date and his/her career focus.*

    b) **LBS:** *What will this individual be doing in 10 years? Why?*

Questions like these are a means of cross-checking your goals and career trajectory with your recommenders. This is why we urge you to ensure your recommenders are armed with this crucial bit of information beforehand.

3. First-Hand Experience of Working with You

Consider how many incidents the recommenders are armed with to discuss when they write your recommendation. What professional experiences have you shared with them? When and where did these occur? Were you successful at solving the issues on hand? What kind of skills and traits do these experiences exhibit about you? You will earn plus points if these experiences showcase leadership and managerial potential!

Here are a few ways the school may try to dig for specific experiences from your recommenders:

a) **INSEAD:** *Describe the candidate as a person. Comment on his/her ability to establish and maintain relationships, sensitivity to others, self-confidence, attitude, etc. Specifically comment on the candidate's behavior or skills in a group setting/team environment.*

b) **LBS:** *In what developmental areas has the applicant changed most over time?*

Such questions demand specific information that only someone who has a close relationship with you will know. A CEO, minister or celebrity who knows of you but does not know your work or your goals will not be able to add such specific examples.

When brainstorming on potential recommenders, I suggest that you rate them on a scale of 1–5, where 1 indicates unsatisfactory and 5 indicates excellent, in the above three areas. Put these down in the table given overleaf:

Name	Relationship	Period Worked With	Understand-ing of Your Goals	Content for the LoR (Experiences Shared)

3:B. Narrow Down the List of Recommenders

Once you have made this list, narrow it down to the number of people required by the school. Pick those who scored the highest in the above table. Based on the factors discussed above, **make a strong distinction between friends and associates and a good recommender.**

Next, contact your recommenders using the tips I gave in section 1:B.

Have you heard the saying, "There is a time and place for every-thing"? It applies even in case of approaching your recommenders.

4. When to Approach Your Recommenders

First, please respect your recommenders' schedules. Inform them that you will be needing a recommendation from them the moment you decide you want to apply to business school. For instance, if your deadline is in January, you cannot expect the recommender, who might be on a Christmas holiday, to write you a recommendation at short notice.

LoRs are lengthy; each school may ask your recommenders

anywhere from two to five questions. Moreover, the schools ask for a lot of detail, and such detailing may take long to formulate. Please bear this in mind and always give your recommenders enough notice. Rushed recommendations are as shabby as rushed essays, and I urge you to avoid them.

If you approach your recommenders and they agree to write you a recommendation, congratulations! You have got your recommenders pinned down. Now comes the time to help them add content to the letter of recommendation.

5. How to Help Your Recommenders

Remember, you cannot expect your recommenders to write stellar recommendations without your help. Their statements should ultimately reaffirm your positioning statement and endorse your positive traits. However, I have seen that many students falter in giving the recommenders enough information to work with. The result ends up being a generic LoR that could have been written by anyone.

You can avoid this by helping your recommenders with talking points. Here are a few ways you can do this:

5:A. Give Them Your Positioning Statement and Communicate Your Goals

By this time, you would have created a strong positioning statement that captures your personal brand. I recommend that you provide this statement to your recommenders. This will give them some food for thought and help them to deremine what to include in your recommendation.

Please note that sharing your résumé, positioning statement, goals, talking points, etc., is an absolutely critical step and completely ethical. Ultimately, the recommender will decide what to write.

5:B. Remember a Compliment They Gave You?

It is likely that your recommender complimented you during the period you worked with him. If you remember any such compliment, flag it and ask them to use it as a talking point. Remember to break this experience down in the STAR and Learning format.

5:C. Begin Listing Experiences You Have Had with Them

To ensure that your recommenders have a wide range of talking points, you should begin brainstorming experiences that they can add. Here is a questionnaire to help you brainstorm on your experiences:

Talking Points Brainstormer

1. What significant project(s) did I work with them on?
2. What was my contribution to these projects? How were my recommenders related to these projects?
3. What was the STAR and Learning of this experience?
4. Were there any hiccups we had to deal with? How did the two of us collaborate?
5. What trait or skill of mine does this experience shine a light on?
6. Does this reaffirm my positioning statement?

List anywhere from two to 15 of such experiences using the above method. You can include different instances within the same project that place the spotlight on different areas.

5:D. Share Your Résumé

I would also recommend informing your recommenders about your recent achievements (both professional and nonprofessional) via your MBA résumé. Tell them how these achievements tie in with your long-term and short-term goals so that they understand the big picture as well.

6. What Problems Could You Face (And How to Overcome Them)

Since you are dependent on another person for writing your LoR, it is likely that you might run into a few hurdles. However, there is nothing that you cannot get past with a bit of time and effort!

Let us cover some of the more common hurdles and fears students face with their recommenders:

1. *My Recommender Is Going to Miss the Deadline!*

This is a common panic message I encounter every admissions season. The recommenders either go missing in action owing to their own commitments or delay the letter indefinitely.

To avoid such a scenario, set a mutually agreed date with your recommenders at the outset and then follow up regularly. Keep a dialogue going and keep checking in periodically. Remember, this is a delicate task: your recommender should not feel harassed or pressured.

More importantly, ensure that they are aware of the recommendation deadline. It is more likely that they will be proactive about writing you an LoR if you give them a definite date.

Please remember that your recommenders are busy as well. The more workload you place on their shoulders, the more likely they are to take time and delay your application.

Also, it is for such situations that I asked you to pick five potential recommenders at the start. If one suddenly goes missing, you can contact the next best from your list to help out.

2. *The People I Approach Are Refusing*

I have seen instances of students being turned down by a recommender. In this case, you might want to ask him why and if there is anything you can do to fix the situation. However, I am not a fan of this approach. While you might be able to fix things temporarily, a letter from such a recommender is likely to be underwhelming.

This situation is indicative of a weak network and I suggest tackling it at the root.

3. *Will My Recommenders Sabotage My Application?*

I have heard variations of this question from students. I believe there are two forms of sabotage. One is when your recommender writes a negative LoR. This scenario can be avoided by meticulously following my tips on how to pick the right recommenders. Use your judgement. Do not pick recommenders you think may sabotage your application. People you have a good relationship with and those who are invested in your success will never attempt to set you back.

A second form of sabotage is that of a recommender who does not know the candidate well enough. Such recommenders are likely to misunderstand your profile and positioning and (unintentionally) deliver a very different view to the AdCom. Using such 'forced recommenders' is a common form of disservice candidates do to themselves.

4. *Will My Recommenders Focus More on the Project or My Contribution to It?*

Sometimes, supervisors or colleagues lose focus and go into detailing how well a project performed, how well the company is doing, and what their role in the project was. They may forget that they are writing your LoR. Consequently, their letter focuses more on the success of the project than on the work you put in. Therefore, always inform your recommenders that the recommendation must focus on YOUR contribution.

7. Reality Check: Busting Common Recommendation Letter Myths

7:A. My Recommenders HAVE to be Influential People

A quick quiz: who do you think is a better brand endorser for you?

a) The global CEO of the Fortune 500 company you work for

b) An influential minister or celebrity you or your family 'knows'

c) Your immediate manager in your home office whom you report to

If you picked C, congratulations! You have absorbed the main points covered in this chapter.

Just because a person is a celebrity or influential figure does not mean he makes a good recommender. Winning LoRs are written by people who know you well, can vouch for your profile, your skills and your goals.

A recommendation from an influential person may work if you have had intensive experience with them. For instance, one of my students, Harsh, proposed that Shah Rukh Khan, a prominent film star, write an LoR for him. My immediate reaction was, "Most definitely not!" since I thought he did not have substantial work experience with SRK, as Khan is known. However, as he explained his story and family background, things began to make sense.

Harsh ran one of the largest media companies in the country. It was a second-generation family business and SRK had known his now-deceased father closely. SRK had mentored Harsh for over a decade after his father's death. Harsh had also spent six months working full-time for Red Chillies Entertainment, SRK's production company.

Further, Harsh's goals were to build a media conglomerate in India and worldwide and SRK was a key proponent and supporter of his growth strategy. His name wasn't being used just to bring a 'glam quotient' to the application. In addition to being an influential personality, SRK understood Harsh's profile and goals. This checked off all the boxes to create an effective LoR.

Therefore, if you can establish strong context with a celebrity, you can most definitely request him to write you a recommendation.

7:B. I Can Write the Recommendations Myself and Submit Them

We have heard of instances when a student has tried to fake a recommendation by creating a dummy email ID and persona. Do we advise doing this? NEVER!

It should be common sense to be ethical during the application process.

"VK, will they really check up on the recommenders? How will they know if I have written it?"

Let me explain. The most obvious giveaway will come from the content. If you have doctored an LoR, it is likely that you will be caught, as it will reflect your language and writing style, a sample of which is readily available in your essays.

Secondly, business schools already deploy several measures to avoid such possibilities. Often, recommenders are directly mailed the link to the portal where they can submit their letters. Moreover, the IP address from which the LoR is submitted may be tracked by the schools. If you are caught submitting a fake recommendation, you will be blacklisted.

7:C. Colleges Want Recommendation Letters from Their Alumni

While getting an LoR from an alumnus is definitely a plus, this should not be a 'namesake recommendation'. Only include a recommendation from the alumnus if you have worked with him, or if he fits the school's specification for accepted recommenders. Other than that, this offers the same downsides of a recommendation written by a CXO who doesn't know you.

7:D. Length of Relationship Is Always More Important Than Quality of Experience

Sometimes, the duration of your relationship with your recommender might have been short, but the interaction itself may have been of high quality. This allows the individual in question to speak of you in detail. Longevity of relationship does not always supersede the depth of a relationship.

For instance, Nandita had been working at a top Indian bank for two years. The bank's Managing Director (MD) had been part of her final-round interview, but her interaction with him thereafter was limited to the quarterly review meetings. Technically, she 'knew' him for the three years she worked there.

In contrast to this, her newly assigned reporting manager had only had eight months of experience with her, but he had worked with her closely for the duration. They had collaborated as a team, managing workflows, assigning tasks, etc. In this case, I asked Nandita to pick her reporting manager over the MD as a recommender.

As illustrated by this case, the depth of your relationship with the recommender may be a better marker of a good recommendation. However, there is no right answer to the question of length versus depth of relationship. It is up to you to pick the person who will best represent you and your strengths to the AdCom.

8. Real People, Unique Skills, Common Errors: Analysis and Fixes

8:A. Lisa Thought Her Older Sister Could Write Her LoR

L: But VK, I come from a family business background, she IS my direct superior.

VK: I understand, but please avoid sending an LoR written by a relative. It doesn't have adequate credibility.

Lisa's family owned a small chain of hotels in India. When she graduated, Lisa joined the family business. She began in the business development department and soon climbed her way to head national sales. She had achieved some truly wonderful feats. The most striking was that Lisa had been successful in getting five out of their seven hotels a four-star rating within six years of joining. Now, she was working directly under her older sister and father.

Lisa was applying to London Business School and Cambridge Judge. That year, London Business School required one letter from a direct supervisor and one from a professional colleague. Cambridge Judge required just one, from a supervisor. During our brainstorming, we asked Lisa whom she would contact for the supervisor reference. She immediately said it would be her sister since she was working directly under her. She was General Manager of the group and knew her best.

I explained that this was a bad idea. Schools do not accept LoRs written by direct relatives. According to Lisa, that rule only applied to people working for companies, not to family business candidates. Wrong again.

The rules are uniform across candidates, regardless of their profiles. A school will not accept a recommendation by a relative as it is likely to be biased. Furthermore, there was no dearth of excellent recommenders for Lisa.

I recommended that she ask the Vice President of the chain to write her LoR. She had worked with him when acquiring the ratings and, with a little nudge, I was sure he could write Lisa a shining recommendation.

Though resistant initially, she agreed and approached the VP, an industry veteran with over 25 years of experience in the hospitality industry. Lisa had worked directly with him for over five years now and they shared an amicable relationship. This made him an ideal recommender. He agreed to be Lisa's recommender and we began brainstorming the content and experiences that he could use to answer the college's questions.

That year, Lisa entered London Business School's MBA program. She continues to have a strong bond with both the VP and her sister.

My Take

I encounter this commonly, especially from candidates who come from a family business background. Since their 'direct superior' in the organization's hierarchy is usually a relative, they tend to gravitate towards relatives as recommenders. I strongly urge you not to do this. Even if you are in a family business, there are several other people who are eligible to write you a recommendation as a superior. Take, for instance, the following:

   i.   Investors
   ii.   Clients
   iii. Vendors or suppliers
   iv.   Distributors
   v.   Joint-venture partners
   vi.   Senior managers in the business

8:B. Aditya Had Written and Submitted the Recommendations Himself

A: VK, there is no way they would know!

VK: Even if they did not, it is unethical. We don't support getting into school by being dishonest. This will hurt you in the long run.

Aditya, a marketing entrepreneur, had signed up with me for a rejection analysis for two schools. His profile was stellar. In just five years of founding his firm, he had completed one round of funding and employed over 20 people. Furthermore, his company was very active in social sustainability initiatives and he was at the helm of such activities. When I read his essays, I saw some room for improvement but was unsure that would have been the only reason he was rejected.

Then I chanced upon the recommendations during a counseling session. Aditya admitted doctoring one letter. The other he had submitted for his referee through his personal laptop since his recommender had emailed him the final version.

The reason Aditya was rejected by the schools was evident now.

My Take

It is unfortunate that Aditya had to learn the hard way that doctoring applications is not the best route to take if you want to be accepted at a top school. As I have mentioned before, schools employ several measures against such actions. Additionally, even if you are accepted, they may do a 'recommender check' via email or call. This is done as part of the background check, and if your recommenders are found to be bogus or unaware of what is in the LoR, the schools reserve the right to withdraw your admission.

8:C. A Month Away from Deadline, Satish Had No Recommenders

S: VK, you are an HBS alum and have worked with me for six months now. Can you please write my LoRs? It will really help!
VK: Not really. The AdCom wants people you have worked with in a professional capacity. I am your counselor.

Satish was a dynamic professional from the insurance and banking sector. However, he was at odds with his immediate supervisors. They had had some disagreement over the last project they had collaborated on, and since then their interactions were curt. Moreover, Satish had been at this workplace for over three years and finding other supervisors seemed tough. Needless to say, he was one recommender short for his application with no relief in sight.

At first, he wanted me to write an LoR for him since we had been working on his profile for six months. I was against this. Firstly, as his admissions counselor there would be a conflict of interest. Secondly, though I am an HBS alumna, I was not an ideal recommender for Satish. Alumni recommenders, like celebrity recommenders, are only good if they know you personally and deeply.

Instead, I recommended he wait a year to apply to business schools, change jobs, and find a new recommender over the year. This would help him add to his already strong profile and act as a lesson in networking.

Satish was resistant to this advice; he did not want to delay his MBA plans by a whole year. However, having tried all avenues to find a recommender from his current firm, he reluctantly agreed. We sidelined the MBA for the time being.

The first course of action was to get Satish placed at a top insurance firm. After a month of applying at several different places, he was accepted in a senior role in Mumbai. Over the next year, Satish doubled the efforts he put in at work and strove to cultivate amicable relationships with his superiors. He exceeded their expectations and took on many tasks over and above his work profile.

When the time came to apply to business school that year, the process was a breeze, since we had already done 75 percent of the work the year before.

Satish was accepted at Rotman School of Management in Canada that year.

My Take

Let me reiterate: there is no gap in your profile that time and effort cannot fix. Satish's case and many others in this book are testament to this. Recommenders are a crucial aspect of the MBA application. If, in the final few weeks before your application, you do not have the right recommenders, I suggest you wait it out. Rushing an application with 'namesake' recommenders is unlikely to yield the desired result. Take a year to build a network; change jobs to do so if necessary. These activities will also add to your profile, reinforcing it.

8:D. Samiksha Could Only Get an LoR from Her Previous Supervisor

S: Are you sure, VK? Didn't you tell me that I should stick to the kind of person the school has asked to get a recommendation from?

VK: Yes, but yours is a unique case, and most business schools are accommodating of such anomalies.

Three months before she was applying to a top MBA program, Samiksha had moved to a different workplace. While her essays were shaping up well in our editing sessions, the LoRs seemed to be the roadblock. This stemmed from the fact that in the three months she had been at the firm, she did not have a stable supervisor. The company had just found a new manager, who would join a week before Samiksha's deadlines. The school had specifically asked for a "current supervisor" to write the recommendation.

When she approached me with this problem, I had some unconventional advice for her. Instead of asking Samiksha to put her application on hold, I asked her to seek a recommendation from her previous supervisor. She was hesitant, because she would be flouting the school's instructions in doing so. But I explained that in certain cases, the schools are accommodative and will accept a recommendation from a previous manager, provided the candidate gives a good reason.

In Samiksha's case, this reason was her recent job shift, which meant that she did not have a strong rapport with her current immediate supervisor. Thus, she had to rely on a past supervisor's recommendation. We underlined this rationale in the optional essay, explaining her situation.

That year, Samiksha was accepted at the Indian School of Business.

My Take

While I am a strong advocate of sticking to the school's instructions, exceptions do apply. Business schools are willing to accommodate changes provided you have a strong rationale for them. Samiksha's case is testament to this fact.

9. The Errors in a Nutshell

9:A. Getting a Relative to Be Your Recommender

This is best avoided since your family will be seen as biased towards your performance.

Insider Tip

1. Find someone who impacts your business and with whom you have interacted extensively.

9:B. Getting a Person in an Influential Position to Write a 'Namesake' LoR

Students tend to think that the more influential the recommender, the better their chances of being accepted. This is untrue.

Insider Tip

1. Unless you have a professional track record with such a person, pick someone else.

9:C. Doctoring a Recommendation

Though uncommon, students end up doing this when they do not have recommenders. I strongly discourage this.

Insider Tip

1. Instead of doctoring recommendations, take your time, build strong relationships, and find a good recommender.

Insider Tips at a Glance

DO:

✓ Spend the years before your MBA cultivating a strong network.

✓ Try to revive old contacts if you don't have recommenders or a network to fish in.

✓ Take a year to build a network and find recommenders if the above fail.

✓ Ensure that the recommenders fulfill the school's specifications.

✓ Ensure that you give your recommenders concrete talking points.

✓ Brainstorm and provide talking points to your recommenders.

✓ Ensure your recommenders know the ins and outs of your profile, your goals, and your positioning statement.

✓ Look for people other than relatives if you are in a family-run business. Investors, clients, vendors or partners can also write your LoR.

DON'T:

Χ Get recommendations from people who barely know you ('namesake recommenders').

Χ Doctor a recommendation.

Χ Get recommendations written by relatives.

APPENDIX

1. Sample Recommender Questions

We have compiled a few questions from two top schools that may be asked of your referees. This will give you an idea of what is required of your recommenders.

INSEAD:

1. How long have you known the candidate? Define your relationship with the candidate and the circumstances whereby you met.
2. Comment on the candidate's career progress to date and his/her career focus.
3. What do you consider the candidate's major strengths? Comment on the factors that distinguish the candidate from other individuals at his/her level.
4. What do you consider the candidate's major weaknesses?
5. Comment on the candidate's potential for senior management. Do you see him/her as a future leader?
6. Describe the candidate as a person. Comment on his/her ability to establish and maintain relationships, sensitivity to others, self-confidence, attitude, etc. Specifically comment on the candidate's behavior or skills in a group setting or team environment.

LBS:

1. How long have you known the applicant and in what connection?
2. What do you consider to be the applicant's major talents and strengths?
3. What do you consider to be the applicant's major weaknesses or areas for improvement?

4. In what developmental areas has the applicant changed most over time?
5. What will this individual be doing in 10 years? Why?

2. Document Recap

The recommendation letter marks the last 'admissions document' you will need to submit before being invited for an interview.

Before we move on to our interview strategies, here is a list of all the documents you need to submit:

1. Application Form
2. Official College Transcripts
3. Official Test Score Reports
4. Résumé
5. Essay(s)
6. Recommendation Letter(s)

Once you have submitted the complete application, the waiting game begins. If the AdCom finds your profile worthy of acceptance, they will send you an email inviting you for an interview. A big step forward and the last bridge to cross.

8

The Interview:
How to Make Your Mark Verbally

You have come a long way in your application journey at this point. The AdCom considers your profile strong and is intrigued by your résumé and essays. Things are moving in the right direction!

Now it is time for one of the most competitive phases of the MBA application process: the interview, a face-to-face interaction where your profile will be validated, cross-referenced and dissected. You will narrate your story, in person.

The interview is not a battle of wits between the interviewer and you. It is a conversation that focuses on getting to know you, the candidate. How you answer questions, your mannerisms, your tone, how you dress and even how you shake hands can make a difference.

Rochelle, who wrote me the above email, was a Financial Analyst who had been working for the Big Four in the United States. Though she was not new to being interviewed, the MBA interview was still an unnerving prospect. Rochelle had a promising profile and many experiences to share. However, to impress the AdCom and cement her candidacy, she would have to prepare.

We revisited her essays, statement of purpose, transcripts and résumé. All these documents could be referenced by the interviewer during the interview. I then began mock interview sessions with her, scrutinizing Rochelle's experiences. We dug deep into her profile across academics, professional and extracurricular activities. Her rationale for wanting an MBA and getting it from Tuck and/or Yale were also put to question.

Over three rigorous sessions, I dissected every part of her profile and asked second-line questions based on them. By the end of our preparation sessions, Rochelle had mastered how to structure a variety of answers. More importantly, she was able to articulate her experiences clearly. Our efforts attained fruition when Rochelle was accepted at both schools.

Rochelle's interview success was due to many different factors working together, which we will cover in this chapter.

However, before we dive in, I would like to discuss a commonly asked question:

1. How Is the MBA Admissions Interview Different from a Job Interview

Over my career, I have noticed that some students tend to conflate the job interview process with the admissions interview. However, there is one MAJOR differentiating factor in an MBA admissions interview: content and scope of questioning.

In a job interview, the scope of questions may be limited to your professional accomplishments. But the MBA admissions interview is different. You have already laid many aspects of your life and profile bare to the school through your essays, résumé and recommendation letters. All these documents can be used as reference points to cross-question and validate your profile.

Let's assume that the AdCom refers to your essay while interviewing you. They could ask you to elaborate on the experiences therein, ask you for your learnings, or why you failed in that entrepreneurial venture, why you need an MBA, why now, why the school, and so on. These questions arise from what you have written in your essay.

You could also be questioned on the basis of your LoRs, your résumé, and transcripts. Sometimes, they may even ask what you think of an important global economic, political or social event, your favorite personalities, and crucial moments in life, among other questions.

The MBA interview aims to dissect and understand your 'holistic profile'. All aspects of your life will be considered by schools to gauge whether you are an ideal candidate.

2. What Admissions Officers Want

2:A. Maturity

Maturity is an important skill to display while you are being interviewed. It could come through subtly in your manner of speaking, your interactions with the interviewer and how you handle difficult questions.

Not being flustered when faced with a difficult question and providing an honest answer is a great way to demonstrate poise and maturity. If you panic and try to dodge questions it will send a negative message.

2:B. Self-Awareness

Please note that I said self-aware, not self-conscious. The latter often leads to very nervous candidates who second-guess every line they utter.

Self-awareness denotes being able to accurately capture your thoughts and feelings and communicate them to the interviewer. It also captures how well you understand yourself. Reflect and be aware of both, your strengths and shortcomings.

2:C. Good Communication Skills

For the interviews, you do not have to be an orator like Martin Luther King, Jr., or Jawaharlal Nehru. All you need is the ability to communicate clearly and concisely. This is important because:

1. Speaking slowly and effectively will ensure that the AdCom is able to comprehend, process and absorb what you are trying to say. A good story communicated poorly is rendered futile.
2. Business schools love future leaders. Communicating effectively signals to the school that you are well positioned and have one of the core ingredients of being an effective leader or manager.

2:D. Answers That Are to the Point

MBA admissions interviews can last anywhere from 30 to 60 minutes. Typically, they are half-hour interviews. In this time, it is important that you enable the AdCom to question you on a wide range of questions. Doing so will ensure that they leave the interview with as much information as possible about your candidacy. Be mindful of the length of your answers to allow the interviewer time to ask you sufficient questions.

Avoid going off on tangents and structure your answers beforehand. I will discuss this strategy in detail later in the chapter.

2:E. *An Interviewee Who Asks Questions*

It is an interview, not an interrogation. While the AdCom will be probing, drilling and dissecting your profile, you must realize that this is also a chance to have a conversation with the AdCom. Asking questions informs the AdCom that the candidate is focused and genuinely interested in what the school has to offer.

Prepare questions specifically for the interview. However, ensure that your questions are specific to your profile and personal requirements. Avoid asking for generic information that is available on the school's website.

Do not open the interview with your questions. Save them for the end, when the interviewer will ask if you have any questions.

I have noticed that as soon as the interviewer stops asking questions, students slip into 'casual mode'. They think the interview has come to a formal end and the interviewer is just trying to build an informal rapport with them. This is not the case. Remember, you are being scrutinized even at this point. Stay professional and treat this part of the interview seriously.

Interview formats vary vastly from one school to another. Additionally, the location, style and medium of the interview may also vary. Before you go into your interview, it is important to know what to expect.

3. What Should You Know about MBA Interviews?

3:A. *Know Who Will Conduct Your Interview*

It is commonly thought that admissions interviews are conducted exclusively by members of the AdCom. This is not true. Interviews may be conducted by:

    a) A member of the AdCom.
    b) An alumnus of the school.

c) A current MBA student who has been trained to interview you.

Please note that the student or alumnus interviewer may be just as rigorous as the AdCom, if not more. Furthermore, evaluations made by students and alumni are given just as much importance as those made by members of the AdCom.

Whoever your interviewer is, it is recommended that you take him seriously and act professional. An interview should not be perceived as 'easy' or 'not so serious' just because your interviewer is someone other than an AdCom member.

3:B. Know Where the Interview Will Be Conducted

It is important to know where your interview will be conducted so you can plan your schedule, how you dress, transportation and other logistical factors accordingly.

In my case, I was sent an email by HBS inviting me to come to Boston for an on-campus interview in the middle of February. Like most of you, I did not want to take any chances with my admission to a top business school. When I saw the interview letter, I did not think about negotiating terms or my mode of interview with the school. I booked my flights instantly and left the 30° weather in Bombay and landed in snowy Boston one day before my interview.

While the trip was hectic and costly, it gave me a chance to revisit the campus and meet with an Admissions Director face-to-face. After my admission, the same Admissions Director ended up mentoring me for the two-year duration of my program.

In hindsight, I could have requested an online interview, but in that moment of excitement, all logic was lost. At the very least, I should have been better prepared for the freezing Boston winter!

Doing a face-to-face, on-campus interview was helpful for me. However, there are many other modes of interview. I recommend that you pick one that works best for you based on personal preferences and constraints. If invited to an on-campus interview, please note that it will not hurt your chances of being admitted if you request for any of the following alternatives:

1. **Online Interview:** This is a very popular format of interview and typically uses a video-calling platform of the school's choice. The important thing here is to ensure that your internet connection is strong so as to avoid delays or other issues that could arise. Also, it is likely that you will be required to use a webcam for this interview. In this case, I recommend that you:

   - Dress appropriately.
   - Ensure there is no clutter on your desk.
   - Ensure there is no background noise and all phones are put on silent mode.
   - Sit at an appropriate distance from the screen so the interviewer can see you clearly.

2. **Central Location in Your City or Country:** This is the next most popular format of conducting interviews for international students. Schools may pick a central location in a major city in your country of residence to conduct the admission interviews. These interviews may be conducted by alumni of the school or members of the AdCom. It is important to be on time to the interview in person.

   I had applied to Wharton Business School in Round 1 and was called for an interview at the office of a tier-1 consulting firm at Nariman Point. I reached well in advance of my time slot and still had two people ahead of me and had to wait an hour for my turn to be interviewed. However, this allowed me to speak with the other prospective candidates who had gathered in the waiting room (one of whom eventually got into HBS as well and is now a dear friend!).

   Needless to say, having the interview in your own city or

a nearby location is a great option. It comes with the added benefit of meeting with an Admissions Officer without having to travel. Typically in India, the AdCom conduct interviews in hub cities such as Bombay, Delhi and Bangalore. They will invite students from neighboring cities to come to these hubs. Ensure that you are dressed appropriately and reach the venue on time.

3. **Phone Call:** Your MBA interview may also be conducted over a phone call. Here, it is extremely important to be aware of your tone and manner of speaking. Since the interviewer cannot see you, his judgement of your enthusiasm, passion and focus will be based only on how you sound. Ensure that there is no background noise and all phones (landlines and mobile phones) in the house are placed on silent. Additionally, ensure that your phone line is free at the time you are expecting the call.

3:C. Know How Your Interview Will Be Conducted

MBA interviews mainly fall in two categories:

1. **Blind Interviews:** As the name suggests, the interviewer walks into these interviews with no prior knowledge of your candidacy. He will not have reviewed your application and the only reference point will be your résumé, which he will be seeing for the first time. The most common opening question in a blind interview is "Walk me through your résumé". I will cover how you can answer this question in Section 5 of this chapter.

2. **Non-Blind Interviews:** In these, the AdCom will have reviewed your entire application or at least your résumé beforehand. These interviews may entail detailed questions and/or push back on what you have written in your application. Since your complete application is likely to have

been scrutinized before the interview, the questions asked may be very specific to the experiences you shared in your essays, or those that a recommender may have shared.

Needless to say, both interviews carry their own challenges. In the blind interviews, you need to tell the AdCom your trajectory, your stories and your experiences in a concise manner. This is because they have no idea what your essays or recommendations hold. You are required to narrate your overarching story to the interviewer and convince him of your candidacy.

In non-blind interviews, you must be well acquainted with everything you have shared or will share with the AdCom. Since your profile has been reviewed beforehand, deeper second-line questions may be asked.

For maximum success, I suggest that you prepare well, regardless of the type of interview you are to face. Practice, practice and practice again. Answer each potential question and time your answers.

3:D. Know Whether the Interview Is Invitation-Only or Open

Interviews may be invitation-only (as in the case of HBS and Stanford) or open (as in the case of Tuck and Fuqua):

1. **Invitation Only:** This is the more common type. Here, the AdCom will review your application first. After that, if the AdCom is interested in your candidacy, they will inform you so, and invite you to the interview.

2. **Applicant-Initiated Interview:** These are offered by very few schools and you may complete your interview even before you submit an application. As the name suggests, any applicant can self-register for this interview and schedule it via the school's website. However, open interviews are mostly conducted only on campus. Thus, international students may not be able to benefit from these owing to the cost of travel.

Nevertheless, if you feel ready and have the financial means I recommend this interview highly. It is a great opportunity to learn more about the school and showcase your interest to a particular school.

However, if you are not ready or able to travel, I would urge you against scheduling an open interview. After you have submitted your application, the school will still call you for an invite-only interview if they are interested in your candidacy.

With the essentials covered, let us now dive into my key interview strategies.

4. Key Interview Strategies

4:A. Keep Practicing

While you cannot accurately predict the interviewer's questions, practice will ensure you are prepared. Think through the answers, write them down and time your responses.

Once you have been through multiple rounds of preparation and refined your structure and content, rehearse your answers repeatedly to build fluency in your speech.

4:B. Practice With the Right People

To rehearse for the interviews, you can ask a friend or family member to prompt you with a question, review your answer and time your response. While this will give you repetitive practice to ensure that you have the content and structure in place, it is preferable to get advice from a seasoned MBA admissions consultant.

Please note that even if a friend works as a human resources professional or hires employees regularly, he may not be the best person to help you practice for the MBA interview since business schools evaluate candidates very differently from companies (see

Section 1 of this chapter).

I also recommend using the free Interview Prep Tool available on ReachIvy.com, which will allow you to record an audio and visual form of your response and time it. These clippings can then be played back so that you can self-assess, catch errors and fix them.

4:C. Stay on Course

I strongly recommend not diverging from the topic when answering the interviewer's question. A common reason for students diverging or going on a tangent is lack of preparation. Thus, they tend to ramble as a last-ditch effort when a difficult question is asked. Rambling gives the impression that the candidate is trying to dodge the question or is underprepared. Do not make this mistake as this will hurt your candidacy.

A good way to keep yourself from rambling is to keep track of time. No response should be more than five minutes long for any question posed by the AdCom. Naturally, this may not be easy at first. With practice, however, you will be able to provide short, succinct answers.

4:D. Remember That the Interviewer Is Human

The interviewer shares common human instincts. Hence, the general tips used to engage an audience in a professional setting apply to your interview as well.

1. Greet cordially but not too informally. Avoid informalities such as "How's it going" or "Hey, what's up?" with your interviewer.
2. Maintain eye contact. This showcases confidence in your speech.
3. Be relaxed but professional. When answering, do not use too many hand gestures. You can use mild gestures; just speak naturally.

4. Speak in an engaging manner. Showcase enthusiasm in your speech. Maintaining a stoic expression when talking about the greatest achievement of your life is not ideal. Bring energy and vitality to the conversation.

5. Watch your tone and be humble. Speak firmly and assertively about your accomplishments, but don't come across as a narcissist; showcase some humility.

6. Make the interview a conversation. The interview is meant to be a two-way conversation. Go prepared with questions for the interviewer.

7. Avoid filling pauses with 'umms' and 'aahs'. If you are thinking, it is better to ask for a moment and be silent.

8. Avoid talking negatively about others. Do not speak poorly of any colleageus, bosses, professors, peers, etc. An interview should be focused on positive talk, unless specifically asked otherwise.

4:E. Dress Well

Regardless of whether the interview is being conducted virtually or in person, it is important to dress well. Yes, even for online interviews. Wearing formal business clothing will reflect positively showing your professional attitude towards the interview. My recommendation is to wear business attire as follows:

- Men: Suit, with formal shirt and tie.
- Women: Skirt- or pant-suit with formal shirt/blouse.
- Wear closed-toed shoes; no sandals or slippers.

4:F. Foreseeing a Second Line of Questioning

MBA interviews are not a series of straightforward questions. Your profile will be dissected and second-line questions are more than likely.

Before we dive into how to 'foresee' questions, let us clear one thing: there is no way to predict what the AdCom is going to ask you.

What you can do, however, is dissect your profile yourself. Go back to your essays, the brainstorming sheet, and your résumé. These documents contain all the information that you will need. Further, begin asking yourself the STAR and Learning (covered in depth in Chapter 6) of each experience.

If there is a gap in your profile, have an honest answer ready to address it. If you are changing careers, ensure your rationale is airtight. Think through any perceived red flags in your profile.

Moreover, ensure you review your résumé line by line and are able to defend and validate anything mentioned there.

This is the only reliable method to ensure that you are ready to respond clearly and effectively to second-line questions.

For instance, I once had a student with a primary background in the entertainment industry who had also done some nonprofit work. Given his diverse background, we worked extensively on his profile and positioning statement. He walked into his Stanford GSB interview hoping that his professional background in films would be the focal point of the interview. However, the alum interviewing him did not focus on his entertainment background and spent 90 percent of the time on a small nonprofit weekend project that had nothing to do with his future plans. Despite my advice, the student had not thought through the nonprofit aspect of his life in depth. Unfortunately, he was rejected from Stanford GSB that year.

The takeaway from this experience is valuable. Do not brush off any part of your profile as unimportant. You never know what might catch the interviewer's eye. All experiences mentioned anywhere in your application (the form, the résumé, all essays and the letters of recommendation) are within the scope of questioning for the interview.

4:G. After the Interview, Send a 'Thank You' Email to the AdCom

As small a gesture as this may seem, it is an important step that I suggest all my clients follow. The email does not have to be fancy. Thank the AdCom for taking the time to interview you, and tell them you will be happy to provide any further information that they may require. Doing so will help you stand out among other candidates. It also reflects good etiquette.

With my interview strategies covered, let's now get to the meat of this chapter.

5. How to Answer Key Interview Questions

For easy reference, I have classified the questions asked in MBA admissions interviews into six buckets. Additionally, I have picked one question from each bucket and explained in detail how to approach it.

Types of Interview Questions:

1) Academics

1. What was your favorite class in college or high school?

2. How did your college or high school influence you?

3. Explain any shortcomings on your transcript.

4. Why are you applying to this degree or program?

5. Why have you chosen this college or university?

2) Professional Life

1. Walk me through your résumé.

2. Explain your career path to date; why did you choose the jobs you have had?

3. Discuss a decision you made in your career that you wish you could change.

4. Tell me about a time when you had an innovative idea and implemented it.

5. Tell me about a challenging team situation and how you dealt with it.

6. What is your elevator pitch?

3) Goals

1. What are your short-term and long-term goals?

2. If these goals don't work out, what will you do?

3. Tell me about the industry you want to enter. What are its key challenges?

4. If you could do anything with your life, what would you do?

4) Profile/Personality Based

1. What do you bring to the classroom versus the many others who come from a similar professional or academic background?

2. What do you think will be your biggest challenge in our program?

3. What are your areas of weakness?

4. What is your leadership style?

5. Tell me about a time you helped someone else succeed.

5) Personal

1. How do you define success?

2. Tell us about a time when you wanted to give up and how you motivated yourself to keep going.

3. What do you do for fun?

4. Tell me about a recent disappointment that you faced and your reaction to it.

5. Is there anything you wished I had asked you in this interview?

5:A. Walk Me through Your Résumé

This is a very common and deceptively simple question. Many students believe this question merely requires them to regurgitate the information on the résumé. It is not so. You are not displaying your reading skills to the AdCom. Do not directly read lines from your résumé. Discuss your chronological journey, highlighting and elaborating the most significant experiences.

How to Structure This Answer

1. Open strongly. Give the interviewer some context of your early years, what kind of family you come from or your upbringing.
2. When talking about your academics, tell the AdCom why you picked your college major and why you chose to attend the college you did.
3. Discuss key accomplishments and skills built from each work experience.
4. Do not gloss over leadership experience or community work. If you have worked for a cause, tell the AdCom why you picked that cause.
5. Throughout, ensure there is a single, coherent narrative. How does one story connect to the other? Did you transition smoothly from academics to professional life? From one job to another? From one role to another?
6. Your decision-making process should shine through as you discuss the turning points in your journey.
7. Close with a statement that sums up your life to this point and ties up the response.

Suggested Length: 4–7 minutes.

5:B. Why Are You Applying to This Program?

This question is a reiteration of the "Why this school?" essay. Similar to the essay, ensure that you not only answer WHY you want to attend the school, but HOW you are a good fit for the institution.

How to Structure This Answer

1. Open with a strong emotional or personal connect with the school.
2. If you have visited the school, mention this fact.
3. What was your decision-making process? How and why did you zero in on this school?
4. Talk about a value or passion you hold dear. Connect this value or passion with the school.
5. Mention specific factors that led you to pick the school. Doing so will show that you have researched the school thoroughly.
6. Use three or four core points that establish why you want to attend the school.
7. Close your answer by restating the value or passion you mentioned earlier and tell the AdCom why and how you connect to the school.

Suggested Length: 2–3 minutes.

5:C. What Are Your Short-Term and Long-Term Professional Goals?

Students often make the mistake of simply mentioning their goals briefly. Such an answer lacks detail. Talk instead about how you arrived at your goals, how you plan to achieve them, why they are important to you, and more. Here are some tips.

How to Structure This Answer

1. Discuss your journey so far. Why did you take or leave the jobs you have had? What did you learn at each company? What led you to your goals? Join these dots for the AdCom.

2. What is happening in your industry or field at present? What is its future, according to you? How do your goals tie in to these?

3. Bring out a sense of purpose behind your goals. Tell the AdCom WHY you want to achieve them; why they are important to you.

4. Make sure you define your short-term and long-term goals clearly.

5. Sum up with an overarching statement that captures the essence of your answer.

Suggested Length: 2–3 minutes.

5:D. *Tell Me about a Time You Helped Someone Else Succeed*

This question falls into the category of "talk about an experience". As mentioned before, use the STAR and Learning method (covered in depth in Chapter 6) for the answer. The focus in this answer will be your actions, which should comprise 70 percent of your answer.

How to Structure This Answer

1. Set the context for the experience. What was the situation, the task at hand? The AdCom needs to know what area you helped the other person succeed in.

2. Use the STAR and Learning structure for the rest of your answer.

3. Focus on your action. How did you determine what area he or she needed help in? What did you do to help the other individual succeed? How did you circumvent any challenges that arose?

4. Discuss the outcome of your actions.

5. Close your answer by talking about your learnings from the experience. How did helping the other person help you to grow?

Suggested Length: 2–3 minutes.

5:E. What Is Your Biggest Weakness?

When answering this question, my number one tip is to use a real weakness and not a disguised strength such as: "My biggest weakness is that I work too hard" or "I am a perfectionist". Students tend to use such answers because they think their weakness will work against them. This is not true. The interviewer only wants to gauge your drive to improve upon your weak areas.

How to Structure This Answer

1. Open with your weakness.
2. Tell the AdCom how you discovered this weakness.
3. Talk about HOW you have worked on this weakness.
4. How successful have you been in addressing your weakness? (Be truthful!)

Suggested Length: 1–2 minutes.

6. Reality Check: Busting Common Interview Myths

6:A. I Should Not Practice Too Much; My Answers Will Sound Rehearsed

Sure, your answers should not sound mechanical. However, I am a big advocate of practice. In fact, rehearsing your answers to the point where they flow naturally is a skill. Try to master it.

6:B. The Interview Is Just a Formality; I Have Already Been Admitted

Interviews are highly competitive and schools may reject over 50 percent of the candidates they interview. Being invited for an interview is NOT a definite yes. It only indicates that the school is interested in your candidacy. They want to know more about you before they make a decision. Your candidacy is still under scrutiny and it is imperative that you take the interview very seriously.

6:C. My Interview Went Great! I Will Certainly Be Admitted

I agree, having a great interview is a definite plus. However, I would urge you to go back to my advice from previous chapters. No single part of the application is a silver bullet. The AdCom will definitely revisit your application after your interview before making a final decision. Thus, there is still a chance that they may reject your application.

7. Real People, Unique Skills, Common Errors: Analysis and Fixes

7:A. Abhishek Was Very Different in Person Than on His Application

A: VK, but that is how I become in front of strangers. It takes me time to warm up.

VK: I understand. But your personality is a key factor in the interview. You will have to work on getting over 'stranger anxiety' and learn to strike a chord with people you do not know. This will help you crack the interview and ensure that you thrive at business school.

I was working with Abhishek, a banker, for his Columbia Business School interview. Before our first interview practice session, I had asked him to give me copies of his essays and résumé. Upon reading his essays, the word 'passionate' stood out in many places. His essays showcased a deep understanding of and zeal for his field of work and his résumé was full of amazing feats.

However, as our first interview session progressed, I felt something was off. Abhishek did not come across as the passionate banker his essays and recommendations projected him to be. When asked questions like "Why do you want to start a fin-tech company?", "How does Columbia align with your mission?" or "Tell me a difficult situation you faced personally", Abhishek had curt, lackluster responses, each of them under 15 seconds. No details. No emotions. This was a major red flag.

Naturally, after our first session, I sent him my feedback and set up another call with him. I urged him to reflect on his journey and explain why he envisioned the future he had mapped out.

I also helped him to pick experiences and brainstorm his answers. Instead of them being quick and short, I helped him to pack as much impact as possible in them. He had to begin emoting, be enthusiastic about his answer and tell the AdCom a story when the question so demanded. To explain this better, I drew a parallel between a storytelling session and the interview. You hold the power to get a reader involved in the story you are telling him. I asked him to imagine watching a potboiler drama:

- What is the situation, the crisis the hero (you) is facing?
- Who else (the stakeholders) is in the scene?
- What action does the hero (you) take to solve the crisis?
- What or who does the hero (you) save?

More importantly, I asked him to narrate a story instead of just listing facts. We worked on factors such as:

- Narration
- Voice modulation

- Body language

These are all storytelling fundamentals. After a few practice sessions, we were able to arrive at answers that were far stronger than his original ones. They had begun including a great beginning, a build-up of action, and a conclusion. Within two weeks of preparation, Abhishek was ready for the interview.

He was accepted that year at Columbia Business School.

My Take

You must be able to verbally communicate your story. Simply penning down beautiful essays is not enough.

Moreover, treat your answers as you would a story. You should be able to grip the listener with a well-thought-out, structured narration and help them to connect with you. This will draw the interviewer in and make a compelling case for your candidacy.

7:B. Aditya Was Terrified of the Interview

A: VK, I really dislike being interviewed. It makes me very nervous! VK: I know just the right way to get rid of your nervousness—practice.

Aditya was a successful web developer from Mumbai. He worked with a small group of friends and mainly developed software for large companies. In his spare time, Aditya was an active member of a Rotary Club and had grown to a prominent position with it. His profile was very strong and he was invited to be interviewed by both Cornell Johnson and UCLA Anderson. While fairly social in person, Aditya was "terrified" (his words) of the interview process. He disliked being "put on the spot" and made to answer questions.

My first and only order of business with Aditya was practice. Over the two weeks that we worked on interview preparation, I did not give him a magic pill to relieve him of his fright. All I did was conduct five practice sessions with him, dissecting each and every part of his profile and the experiences he had mentioned.

Aditya began as a nervous candidate, taking up to 10 minutes to answer each question with many "umms" and long pauses. We worked slowly, discussing every response and detailing the stories he would discuss. Each question was rehearsed so that his responses had an overall structure. As we neared the end of our practice sessions, I saw his confidence grow. He began answering the questions concisely, assertively and with ease.

A week later, Aditya emailed me saying he had had a flawless interview, did not stumble at all, and was able to answer every question without hesitation or nervousness. He had surprised himself. Honestly, the only thing I had changed from our starting point to now was the amount of rigorous practice he did.

Eventually, Aditya was accepted at both schools.

My Take

Being nervous before an interview is normal. However, there is no quick fix to this affliction. No coach, consultant or friend can instantly make you less nervous. The only tool that can help you is practice. However, it is not just the hours of practice you put in. You must get the right feedback with every iteration and improve your delivery and response progressively. Practice without the right guidance is an exercise in futility.

7:C. Sandeep Meandered Before Getting to the Point

S: VK, but shouldn't they know everything about the story? How can they understand what I am saying without any context?
VK: Context is good, but only where necessary. Make efficient use of your limited interview time.

When I asked Sandeep to talk about his goals during an interview preparation session, he began by detailing out his résumé. Then he added why he wanted to go to that particular school, before concluding the answer with his goals. He took nine minutes to answer a question that should have taken no more than three.

Why did he take three times the recommended duration to answer the question? It was partly because he had no structured answer ready for the question and partly because he believed in 'giving context'. Consequently, Sandeep ended up covering content for the "Walk me through your résumé", "Why this school" as well as the goals questions.

I explained why this was sub-optimal. To ensure that this was not repeated, I began by helping Sandeep to structure his answers. I also began timing his answers and would cut him off as soon as the clock ran out. This nudged Sandeep to make his answers concise and to the point. By the fourth interview preparation session, Sandeep was ready. In his 60-minute interview preparation sessions (including 30 minutes of feedback time), we were able to cover between eight and 12 questions, which was ideal. Moreover, he had compelling, well-structured answers for each type of question.

Sandeep was accepted that year at the Darden School of Business.

My Take

While context is essential in storytelling, an excess is not good. First, you spend too much time. Secondly, you are likely to end up answering other still-to-be-asked questions instead of just the one you have been asked. If you need to provide context, do so quickly and get back to the point. Avoid merging answers to other questions at all costs.

7:D. Ritu Had No Questions for the AdCom

R: But VK, I genuinely have no questions for them. I'm sure they would not mind this!

VK: You are going to spend two years of your life at that school. How can you have no questions for the AdCom, Ritu?

Ritu was a strong candidate. With over five years of entrepreneurial experience in the apparel industry, she had a solid profile.

At the end of an otherwise solid interview preparation session, when I asked if she had any questions for the AdCom, her reply was "No, that's it."

When I asked her to think again, she persisted. There was nothing she could think of to ask the AdCom. Upon much insistence, she asked why this was important at all.

I explained to her that it was unlikely that an applicant has no question at all for the school they are interviewing with. You are investing a large amount of time, effort and money. Surely you want to learn something about them?

Ritu was surprisingly proactive in taking this feedback and asked me to help her frame these questions. I gave her some ideas. For instance, she wanted to go back to her apparel business after the MBA. She had heard that HEC Paris was an excellent school for entrepreneurs. However, she was not sure how exactly the school could help. To this end, she prepared questions about certain electives, whether they would help her goals, what other resources on campus she could use, how she could gain assistance for her venture at the program, and so on.

This made a major difference in our interview sessions. The interview became a two-way affair where both the interviewer and Ritu were able to learn more about each other. Furthermore, her questions made Ritu seem just as enthusiastic and calculated in her approach as she really was.

That year, Ritu was accepted at HEC Paris.

My Take

You are still being judged when you ask the AdCom a question. It is good to have questions ready for the AdCom from a personal standpoint as well. Would you really want to dive into a 12- or 24-month program without having all your questions about it cleared? Getting your questions answered would also help greatly if you are accepted at multiple colleges and have to pick between them.

8. Errors in a Nutshell

8:A. Not Emoting or Playing Stoic Before the AdCom

I have often noticed that students neglect how they deliver their responses to the AdCom's question. Thus, their answers fail to engage the listener.

Insider Tips

1. Look at the interview as an opportunity to tell the AdCom a compelling (authentic) story about your profile.
2. Emote your experiences, narrate a well-structured, gripping story, and show enthusiasm during your interaction with the AdCom.

8:B. Being Nervous (Often a Result of Underpreparing)

Being nervous is normal. However, do not let this cloud your performance.

Insider Tips

1. Practice, practice and practice again using our suggested method.
2. Go through the interview questions I have listed in this chapter for practice.

3. Use ReachIvy.com's Interview Prep Tool to prepare yourself optimally.

8:C. Getting Flustered at Second-Line Questions

Second-line questions are used by the AdCom to probe deeper into your profile and get a better sense of it.

Insider Tips

1. Ensure you read through your complete application in detail.
2. Have complete mastery over your stories and experiences.

8:D. Not Preparing Questions for the AdCom

The interviewers will almost always give you a window to ask questions. They want to give you an opportunity to learn more about the school. Take it.

Insider Tip

1. Prepare specific questions for the AdCom before the interview.

8:E. Taking Too Long to Answer Questions

The MBA interview typically lasts 30 minutes. It is important to ensure that you use this time effectively.

Insider Tips

1. In your practice sessions, ensure you have a structured response to all potential questions.
2. Ensure that you time yourself on each question and do not exceed more than one to five minutes, depending on the question.

Insider Tips in a Nutshell

DO:

- ✓ Answer clearly and concisely. No answer except elaborate ones should take more than two minutes.
- ✓ Study our list of 150 potential questions available on ReachIvy.com.
- ✓ Review your profile inside out, break experiences into the STAR and Learning format before the interview.
- ✓ Dress well.
- ✓ Maintain eye contact.
- ✓ Practice, practice, and practice again! (Use our practice tool).
- ✓ Speak about your accomplishments firmly and assertively.
- ✓ Keep questions handy to ask the AdCom at the end of the interview.

DON'T:

- X Be too modest; you are expected to shout out your strengths in an interview.
- X Stray from the suggested time frames I have provided in Section 5.
- X Take the interview casually just because it is being conducted by an alumnus or current student.
- X Go off on a tangent when answering a question.
- X Try to cozy up to the interviewer.
- X Portray a diametrically opposite persona to the AdCom than your essays and LORs showcase.
- X Go without preparing questions for the interviewer.
- X Undermine yourself or your accomplishments.

9

Admissions Outcomes: What Are the Possibilities and How Can You Manage Them?

Hi VK,

I have been waitlisted by my dream school. While I have been accepted at another program, I have always wanted to go here. What are my chances of getting in? Do waitlisted students like me ever get accepted? I'm feeling very anxious right now. Not sure what to do!

Business schools may take up to three months from the date of submission to inform you of your outcome. The decision the AdCom makes is not a binary choice between 'accepted' and 'rejected'. Schools also waitlist you. It is important to know about all the possible outcomes beforehand so you can prepare yourself accordingly.

If you have been accepted, there are still many formalities to complete. If you have been rejected, you should introspect and try to understand where you faltered. If, like Jai who wrote us this email, you have been waitlisted, you must try your best to convert that waitlist into an admit letter.

Jai was a junior analyst at a top Indian consulting firm and had applied to Cornell Johnson and McCombs School of Business. He was accepted at McCombs while Cornell had waitlisted him.

Our first order of business was to understand why he had been waitlisted. This could be gleaned from the areas Cornell Johnson had asked him to improve on in their waitlist email. His GMAT score, at 690, needed improvement as did his leadership and work profile.

Jai took the AdCom's advice and retook the GMAT, scoring 710. Incidentally, he was also at the cusp of earning a promotion at work, which he pushed for, and took on a leadership role at a local Rotary Club. I suggested that Jai also inform Cornell Johnson that he had competing offers from other business schools to which he would have to respond soon.

As we strengthened his profile, I asked Jai to send the AdCom updates about his profile only when a significant milestone was achieved and not to inundate them with emails.

Almost three months after being waitlisted, Jai was granted admission.

If, like Jai, you too apply to multiple programs, you may be faced with different admissions outcomes. Over the rest of this chapter, I will cover how you can handle each type of outcome.

First, let us have a look at the most desirable outcome: being accepted.

1. I Have Been Accepted at My Target School! What Should I Do Next?

Being accepted at a top MBA program is no mean feat. However, there is still some work to be done.

1:A. Start With a Note of Gratitude

Write thank you emails to your recommenders, the people who helped you edit your essays, your mentors, peers and family members who supported you through the journey. Remember, all these people invested in your success and at the very least deserve to know about your admissions outcome. Express gratitude to them for their role in your admissions process.

1:B. *Explore All Possible Financing Options*

Your cost of attendance may go into hundreds of thousands of dollars. To avoid any last-minute anxiety, start looking for financing avenues as soon as you receive your admit letter. You should first explore personal avenues (savings, family and friends). Additionally, you may look for a scholarship or grant from external sources. For any additional funding you may consider bank, NBFC or international loans, which come at a cost. I will cover financing in detail in the next chapter.

1:C. *Complete the Necessary Formalities*

Once you have been admitted, you cannot sit back until classes begin. The school will send a slew of information your way regarding the formalities you need to complete. A few examples are:

- Housing
- Pre-MBA coursework
- Course selection
- Registration for orientation
- Vaccinations
- Financing
- Compulsory health insurance
- Visa

Each of these usually has a deadline attached. It is recommended that you act fast and keep an eye out for every email the school sends you.

1:D. Discharge Your Duties at the Workplace

You may have to leave your current job if you have enrolled in a full-time program. Once you receive your admit letter, it is imperative that you inform your supervisor at work about it. You may have to serve a notice period and hand over your responsibilities. Remember to handle this situation delicately. Perform your duties diligently until the last day.

Here is a checklist to help you navigate the post-admit process:

1. Send thank you emails to everyone who helped you during the application process.

2. Keep an eye out for all emails that the school sends.

3. Most schools have an orientation session for incoming students: make sure you register for this.

4. Begin looking for financing opportunities.

5. Take a few pre-MBA courses on core subjects (economics, operations, strategy, finance) so you can hit the ground running and gain knowledge in areas you may be unfamiliar with. There are several pre-MBA courses available online.

6. Begin your visa proceedings.

7. Inform your manager about your MBA admit and begin proceedings to discharge your duties at work.

8. Ensure your housing arrangements have been made (on-campus dormitory or flat, or off-campus hostel or flat).

9. Once you know when classes commence, book your flight tickets (it is ideal to arrive a few days in advance).

10. Begin connecting with other students who have been admitted to your MBA program. If there are a few from your city or state, you could take the initiative and arrange a meeting with them.

11. Join the Facebook and LinkedIn groups of the incoming class to connect with your classmates.

> 12. If you have been admitted to multiple schools, send the others an email politely declining their offer.
>
> 13. Check if your program requires you to arrive early to take pre-MBA courses offered at the school itself. This may push back your travel dates by almost two months.

2. What Should I Do If I Have Been Waitlisted?

The waitlist is a difficult spot to be in. Once you are on the waitlist, a decision about your candidacy can take anywhere between two and 16 weeks. Here, there are only two possible outcomes:

1. Rejected after being waitlisted
2. Accepted after being waitlisted

The AdCom waitlists students whose candidacies they are interested in, but given the limited class sizes, they are unable to accommodate within a given batch. If waitlisted, you stand a good chance of being accepted provided you can demonstrate a good fit, and/or provide information that strengthens your candidacy.

To move up the waitlist, you also have to hope that someone who got admitted to the program decides not to accept the offer, thus opening up space for another applicant. There is nothing you can do to change these odds.

Over the years, I have developed a waitlist strategy for candidates who wish to convert the waitlist to an acceptance, which I will share with you now:

2:A. Respond to the AdCom's Email

After you receive information about your waitlist status, first reach out to the AdCom. Communicate your gratitude to them for updating you on your status. Additionally, inform them that you wish to stay on the waitlist and reiterate why you think you are a good fit with the school's program.

Please note that schools' waitlist policies differ. For instance, Yale SOM may automatically place you on the waitlist and continue to review your application until the final round of the same admissions cycle. On the other hand, INSEAD asks you to reach out to it and accept your position on the waitlist before a deadline. If you do not accept your position on the waitlist before this time, your name will be taken off it.

I would also recommend asking the school if it is open to receiving additional information that may bolster your candidacy. Some business schools may not accept additional information after you have been waitlisted; you cannot send any updates to the school after the final application deadline. If you have been waitlisted by such a school, unfortunately, there is not a lot you can do apart from waiting.

However, if the school is open to accepting additional information, you can send an email to the AdCom. Ask what the weak parts of your candidacy are and how you can address them. At many business schools, the AdCom is open to giving students insights into their applications.

An interesting and common case: you are waitlisted by School 1 and accepted by School 2. In this situation, first evaluate your preferences. If you are content with School 2 and would rather go there in any case, simply go ahead and accept that offer. There is no point staying on the waitlist for School 1 just to see if that gets converted to an admit. Instead, I recommend that you ask the AdCom of School 1 to remove your name from the waitlist. It is unethical to block a seat on the waitlist when you are not planning to attend the school. Let another deserving candidate take your spot.

2:B. *Work on Your Weaknesses and Update Them*

If the AdCom sends you specific reasons explaining shortcomings in your profile that led to you being waitlisted, I recommend you work on the advice right away. They may point out specific areas for improvement, which could be your GMAT/GRE score, a lack of demonstrated leadership experience, lack of international experience, not enough professional experience, and so on. Work on these shortcomings and update the AdCom as you start fixing these. Sending them an email two to four weeks after receiving their decision is perfectly fine.

A good waitlist letter usually includes:

* Strong statement of purpose which explains WHY you would choose that school.
* HOW the school specifically contributes to your long-term goals.
* HOW you can enrich the student body and classroom experience at the school.
* WHAT efforts you have made since you received the waitlist decision.

You can use this excerpt from a student's Waitlist Letter to guide you own efforts in this direction:

Waitlist Letter Sample

Dear XXXXXXX,

The combination of the location, the academics and the opportunities for professional enhancement at XXXXX makes it the best choice for me to pursue my MBA, and if accepted, I will definitely take up the chance to attend.

As I aim to develop skills required to start an XXXXX organization. I believe the city of XXXX is the perfect stepping stone to get there. The Indian education system directly supports over 400

---

million students making India's student population the largest in the world. As I aim to bring a change by making this system more efficient, I would have to learn to innovate. XXXXX has always led the race on innovation in XXXX, evident by the fact that it has been ranked number one on the "Innovation that matters (ITM) report" twice in a row.

The best way I could take advantage of all the opportunities presented by this city is by becoming a part of the XXXXX community. The spirit of the XXXXX startup culture and innovation is well represented by the MBA program at XXXXXX through its well-founded curriculum and extracurricular opportunities. For example, XXXXX and the resources presented by it like the XXXXX would prove to be the ideal platform to start building my startup. Similarly the knowledge and exposure I would gain from the professors at XXXXX would truly be unique considering their vast experience in various fields of management and their success in those. I am particularly keen on learning from Mr XXXXXX, XXXX professor and serial entrepreneur, who recognizes the potential of the XXXXX industry. He has not just co-founded the XXXXXX accelerator but through it he has funded over 30 XXXXX startups.

Also, since I received my 'waitlist' decision, I have…

2:C. If the AdCom Is Unwilling to Share Information, Reflect upon Your Profile

Sometimes, schools may accept additional information from waitlisted candidates but will not give specific feedback on areas for improvement. While such a situation is puzzling and perhaps frustrating, I recommend you revisit your profile to identify and plug any glaring gaps. For this purpose, I urge you to go back to Chapter 2 on Profile Building and Positioning.

Additionally, please note that excellence is always valued. If you have received an award, earned a promotion, or achieved a significant milestone, inform the AdCom of the same if they are accepting additional information.

2:D. Fill out the Missing Links for the AdCom

Students may sometimes apply for an MBA when they are on the brink of achieving a milestone. If you have been waitlisted and one of your targets has manifested itself, I recommend that you update the AdCom about the same.

Please remember to make every email you send the AdCom count. You do not want to bother the AdCom by sending them an email every day, as this will come off as extremely unprofessional. ONLY send them emails if you have a notable achievement they might want to consider.

With the above points covered, I will iterate that getting off the waitlist is not easy and is sometimes beyond the applicant's control.

Also, if an admitted student decides to drop out at the last moment, the school may take you off the waitlist just days before classes commence, or even a few days after classes begin. Have patience and hang in there. Parallelly, begin working to strengthen your application for the next season. My best students don't waste a minute!

3. How to Understand Rejections (And Come Back Stronger!)

While being rejected is not pleasant, it is important to keep a level head and understand what went wrong. Let's see how you can interpret and analyse your rejection:

3:A. How to Analyse the Rejection

If you have been rejected by multiple schools, chances are that a part of your profile or your application documents (essays/LoRs) is weak. Also check your GMAT/GRE score. If it was lower than the school's average, this could be another factor that can be fixed with some focused effort. In essence, revisit all the different profile buckets I have discussed in Chapter 2 on Profile Building to identify a potential cause for the rejection.

Next, I want you to revisit your essays and pick them apart.

- Were the experiences you incorporated impactful?
- Did they accurately address the essay topic?
- Did they distinguish you from the rest of your applicant peer group?
- Was the 'wow' factor missing from your essays?

Here are a few common reasons why applicants are rejected every year:

1. Lack of a strong rationale to do an MBA.

2. Lack of a strong positioning statement.

3. Lack of substantial work experience (2–3 years of impactful experience is the bare minimum).

4. Lack of demonstrable leadership or managerial skills.

5. Low GMAT/GRE score in comparison to the rest of the pool.

6. Weak GPA and no demonstrable improvement either through GMAT/GRE or additional courses.

7. No demonstrated 'fit' with the program.

8. Lackluster recommendations or LoRs that did not match the applicant's view about himself.

9. Compelling profile, but outshone by the remaining applicants.

You may also contact the school to ask if it could help you figure out what led to your rejection. While school policies differ in this matter, the AdCom may get back to you and offer some insights. Additionally, schools may offer a feedback session for promising candidates to highlight the shortcomings of their applications. Once you are able to assess why you were rejected, it is time to plan your reapplication.

3:B. How to Come Back Stronger

Schools are always open to reapplicants. As long as you are willing to put in the work, you have a good shot at being accepted when you reapply!

Reapplication criteria differ from school to school. HBS asks reapplicants to follow the same process as first-time applicants. Additionally, it will review your reapplication the same way that it would review a first-time application. CBS follows a very different process. CBS asks you only to update your profile details, including any additional courses you may have taken, if your last application was submitted less than 12 months ago. Reapplicants only need to submit one essay: a reapplication essay that details how the applicant has grown or advanced his profile since the last attempt.

Therefore, I recommend that you check the specific reapplicant requirements on the school's website. These may be updated every year, so look for the most current data.

For your reapplicant essay, look over the strategy outlined in Chapter 6: Essay Writing. Draw the spotlight upon NEW additions to your candidacy. You need to showcase how you reflected upon your rejection and improved.

Needless to say, leading up to your reapplication, continue to build your profile and work diligently to produce tangible, impactful results. A purposeful strengthening of your profile will make a compelling case for your reapplicant candidacy.

Wondering whether you should reapply at all if you have offers from schools other than your top choices? Let's find out.

4. Should You Reapply If You Have Been Rejected by Your Dream School but Accepted at Other Reputed Schools?

The decision to reapply or not is very personal. It varies from case to case. Here is a list of questions I suggest you consider as you are making this decision:

- Why do you want to attend your dream school (where you got rejected)?
- How does it compare with other reputed schools to which you have been accepted?
- Can you arrive at a compelling (and truthful) reason to NOT attend the other schools?
- Given your profile, are you being realistic about getting admitted to your dream school?
- If you want to reapply, do your current professional and personal conditions allow you to delay your plans by another year?

I have often seen students in a situation where their dream school has rejected them but other reputed schools have offered them admission. Take, for instance, Juhi, who came to us with a rejection from HBS but an admit letter from other top-tier business schools. Since she was determined to go to HBS, Juhi rejected all her other offers. Instead, she took the year to work on her profile so that she would be accepted into HBS. When she reapplied the next year, she did get accepted.

On the flip side, I have also heard of candidates who have let go of admits from top-tier schools in pursuit of getting into their dream school, but could not make it. There is, therefore, no right or wrong answer to whether to let go of your admits and chase your dream school. Consider your personal factors and judge if it is worth reapplying. While greed is good, too much of it can land you in a position with no recourse.

5. Reality Check: Busting Common Admission Outcomes Myths

5:A. I Have Been Rejected; I Am Not Cut out for Business School

Business schools are always open to re-applicants! Do not let one rejection determine the course of your life. If you have been rejected, it is time to engage in purposeful self-reflection. Additionally, speak to a variety of people who can offer fresh perspective on your candidacy. These could be your ex-bosses, colleagues or an expert counselor. You can work with them to determine the areas of your application that need to be improved.

Most importantly, make sure you are not just shooting arrows in the dark. The application process is not cracked by brute force but by taking measured steps.

5:B. The Waitlist Is a Limbo I Cannot Get Out Of

I won't lie; a very small number of students are usually accepted from the waitlist. Nevertheless, it is important that you keep striving to get into the program and express your interest in doing so to the AdCom. Even if the percentage of waitlisted students who are granted admits is low, you could be among those that do get in. Follow the steps provided in this chapter and make a determined effort to improve your shortcomings.

6. Real People, Unique Skills, Common Errors: Analysis and Fixes

6:A. Srinivas Was Able to Successfully Convert His Waitlisted Status

S: But VK, I have a 700 GMAT. That is the 90th percentile! Why would I retake it?

VK: Sure, 700 is a fairly strong score. In your context, however, it falls short.

Srinivas had approached us for waitlist strategy. He was a Teach for India fellow who had recently begun an events and talent management company to sponsor artists from underserved sections of India. At the time of his application, he was raising the first round of funding for his company. A month after applying, he was informed that his application had been waitlisted. In his mind, Srinivas was sure he would have to reapply next year, as he had read online that it was rare for candidates to get off the waitlist.

Thus, he had not communicated with the AdCom since he was sent the waitlist email. I explained to him that while converting waitlists is a rare feat, it is still possible. I know because I have helped many students get off waitlists.

I suspected that his waitlist status was due to his entrepreneurial experience being at a nascent stage (just four months since launch) and a GMAT score of 700 as opposed to UCLA Anderson's 712 average. When he wrote to the AdCom asking for information about the same, their reply affirmed my hypothesis.

Additionally, we needed his startup to show potential. It would help if he closed the first round of funding (which was already in an advanced stage) for his venture. Thus, I asked him to direct his focus towards that one aspect in the coming weeks.

Furthermore, Srinivas needed to retake the GMAT. He was initially resistant, as he believed 700 was a strong score. He wasn't wrong. But I explained that his context was different. Srinivas was a nontraditional candidate with a Bachelor of Arts degree. This meant that he would have to demonstrate his quantitative skills through his GMAT score at the very least. His score being lower than the school's average did not help.

Srinivas agreed, retook his GMAT, and was able to make a significant 30-point improvement. Additionally, his term sheet with a leading early-stage investor, which was under serious negotiation for five months, finally came through.

Srinivas sent the AdCom an update and also reiterated his interest in the school. It took about four weeks to hear back from the AdCom, but he was accepted at UCLA Anderson that year.

My Take

Srinivas's case demonstrates two things:

- The importance of following the AdCom's advice.
- How profile building is beneficial even AFTER you have applied.

While Srinivas was hesitant to retake the GMAT, I'm sure his eventual decision to do so and the 30-point improvement had significant impact on his candidacy. Also, had he not continued to work on his startup and raised that crucial funding, he may not have converted his waitlist status.

6:B. Nikhil Was a Re-Applicant Who Got Accepted at CBS

A: VK, I have no idea why I was rejected. I'm a senior business development associate and have a strong sports background as well!

VK: Yes, but there are some glaring gaps too: no international experience, no brands on your résumé and a GMAT score that could be improved.

Nikhil had applied to five business schools and was rejected by all without an interview. When he came to us, he was restless. He was sure he had a strong profile and could not figure out where he had gone wrong.

In our first counseling session, I helped him pinpoint his areas of weakness. First, Nikhil was working in a small enterprise which had limited resources. His role did not afford him any international experience, and the impact he made was limited.

I recommended that he seek out opportunities in large multinational corporations as soon as possible. Once there, he could try to climb his way up to a cross-border international project. This would help him strengthen his branding and provide him strong international exposure.

Within two months, Nikhil was able to land a position at a leading technology firm. Fast forward to four months and he was working on his first on-site project abroad as the firm looked to expand operations in Africa. In the meantime, Nikhil retook the GMAT twice, and was able to improve his score to 750.

When the time came to apply, Nikhil had a much stronger profile than he did the last time. That year, he was accepted at CBS.

My Take

The major takeaway from Nikhil's case are the calculated attempts we made at strengthening his profile. I recommend all re-applicants improve upon their individual profile using the profile-building fundamentals discussed in Chapter 2. Look for gaps across your professional, academic, leadership and extracurricular profiles and plug them before you reapply.

7. Errors in a Nutshell

7:A. Thinking That Communicating With the AdCom When on the Waitlist Is a Waste of Time

As frustrating as being on the waitlist can be, do not give up. Continue to communicate with the AdCom.

Insider Tips

1. Write the AdCom an email asking why you were waitlisted. Also, clarify if they accept additional information from waitlisted candidates.
2. If the school accepts additional information, send the AdCom a waitlist letter.

7:B. Thinking That the Only Reason You Were Rejected Is 'Bad Luck'

If rejected, do not pin it solely on bad luck. Take a step back and reassess your profile.

Insider Tips

1. Reflect upon your profile, pick out glaring gaps and fix them (refer to Chapter 2).
2. If the school provides an information session for rejected applicants, register for it and speak with them.

Insider Tips in a Nutshell

DO:

✓ Continue working on your profile until you receive a final admit.

✓ Send thank you letters to the AdCom and all your well-wishers if you have been admitted.

✓ Ensure that you complete all formalities (housing, insurance, course selection, etc.) on time.

✓ Discharge your duties at work gracefully and maintain a cordial connection with your ex-colleagues and superiors.

✓ Send an email to the AdCom expressing your desire to stay on, or be removed from, the waitlist if you have been waitlisted.

✓ Find out if your target school accepts additional information and send it a waitlist letter, additional recommendation letters and information about significant achievements since you submitted your application.

✓ Revisit Chapter 2 and reflect on your profile and plug gaps if you have been rejected.

DON'T:

X Send additional information to schools that don't accept it from students on the waitlist.

X Cease communication with the AdCom after being waitlisted.

X Pin your rejection on 'bad luck'.

X Lose heart over a rejection. You can always improve your profile and reapply.

Financing Your MBA: How to Make Money the Least of Your Concerns

Hi VK,

I've been successfully admitted to my dream school.

Now, I'm beginning to figure out how to pay for my degree. I've been pooling my resources and have realized that I only have about $70,000 as opposed to the $140,000 I will have to pay.

There is a lot of pressure from my family to let go of my MBA plans. I'm currently very stressed about this, VK. I'm very close to fulfilling my dream and do not want to throw it all away due to my financial situation.

Please suggest a way out!

Congratulations on your admit! You have been selected from a highly competitive pool of candidates. This is a feat in itself.

Now, you will need to begin accumulating funds to pay for your MBA degree. You may have to pay anywhere between ₹30,50,000 on the low end of the fee-spectrum (ISB) to $250,000 on the high end (Stanford GSB) to cover your cost of attendance. Nevertheless, with resources such as scholarships, grants, loans and crowdfunding, the modern world makes financing your MBA easy.

I have seen that the amount of financial assistance that students may require varies vastly. Some may require cent percent funding from external sources, while others may be able to cover a part of their fees through personal resources.

For instance, Avi, a business analyst, who sent us the above email, could cover only about 50 percent ($70,000) of his $140,000 cost of attendance at Kellogg School of Management. The remaining 50 percent was the missing piece of the puzzle. He had exhausted all personal options, and had applied to external scholarships. Unfortunately, his scholarship applications had also been rejected.

I advised him to take a loan. He was initially apprehensive owing to the collateral he might have to provide. However, I explained to him that not all student/study-abroad loans require collateral. Some International Lenders allow students to take a loan for their cost of attendance without having to provide a collateral. Provided with a range of such options, Avi picked one that fit his personal needs. He had to submit his proof of admission, and a bank statement that showcased his current financial assets, among other documents. Within three weeks, his loan was approved and Avi was able to acquire the remaining sum.

When Avi would graduate, as per the 2018 statistics on Kellogg's website, he was set to earn anywhere between $45,000 to $126,000. Within three to five years, he would be able to repay his entire loan (assuming he kept a stable job and lived within his means!).

Like Avi, every year, many students go through funding anxiety for their MBA. At events, I constantly meet parents who are stressed and feel that they might have to compromise on their child's education just because they do not have the financial means. However, there are several ways to finance your MBA. I will cover all financing possibilities in this chapter and discuss the various options you can consider.

Before we dive into the various financing options, let's first understand how you can plan your finances to fund your MBA.

1. How to Ready Yourself Financially for an MBA

I have noticed that students begin thinking about financing their MBA only a few months before they apply. However, I do not recommend this approach. Planning how you will finance your MBA and listing all possible sources early on will always be helpful. I recommend you begin financial planning from the moment you decided to get an MBA. Allow me to list a few prudent steps you could take:

1. Build a savings/reserve fund: Often students begin splurging as soon as they begin earning. Thus, when it comes time to make a major financial investment such as an MBA, they are left with little to no savings. This is why I suggest you save periodically keeping your long-term goal in mind. Ensuring that you systematically put aside a portion of your monthly income towards your MBA funds is a terrific practice.

2. Invest your savings: While it is fine to have your savings stored in a bank account, it is not the smartest choice to make. There are several avenues for investment that can yield secure and steady returns. Some notable options are mutual funds (moderately risky) and fixed deposits (very safe), among many others. I had moved my investments from stocks to fixed deposits in 2007–2008, just before the financial crisis. I managed to avoid a massive loss on my investments and paid a large amount of my college tuition by breaking my fixed deposits that yielded me a fair interest rate in addition to keeping my principal amont safe.

3. Maintain a good credit score: If you have to take a loan to finance your MBA, your credit history and score will be considered by some lenders. Banks are usually apprehensive

of borrowers who have poor credit history or unpaid dues. Make your credit card payments on time; ensure you don't default on any outstanding debt.

4. Keep a cosigner handy: Most bank loans require a cosigner in order to get a loan approved. Your cosigner is akin to a financial recommendation letter. Except, in this case, the cosigner is not only endorsing you but agreeing to step in and pay back the loan, in case you are unable to. He is giving a personal guarantee that the lender will get his money back. A cosigner could be a family member or one of your friends who, at the very least, has a good credit history and assets worth your loan amount. Plan well in advance who your cosigner will be if you plan on taking a loan.

All in all, plan ahead and take prudent financial decisions on your road to an MBA.

2. What Additional Costs May You Incur?

I have noticed that many students I work with tend to forget that the cost of getting an MBA also includes several pre-MBA fees. I will cover a few of these here:

1. GMAT/GRE Preparation (if you join a tutoring program): ₹15,000–1,00,000

2. GMAT/GRE Test Cost: $250 for GMAT and $205 for GRE

3. School Application Fees: 100–$250 per school depending on the school and program type.

4. Visiting School for an Interview or Campus Tour: Over ₹3,00,000*

5.   Assistance from Guidance Counsellors: ₹10,000–5,00,000*

Do remember to factor in these costs before you apply. Now, let us look at how you can fund your MBA:

3. How to Make the MBA Free: Scholarships/Loan-Forgiveness/Free Grants/Company Assistance

This is the low-hanging fruit. Secure as much funding as possible from these sources since these are free (they may have caveats associated with them).

Scholarships can be made available either by the school (let's call these internal) or by a third-party organization/foundation (let's call these internal). Internal scholarship decisions are sent by the school with the admit letter. In some cases, after admission, the school may ask you to apply for specific internal scholarships, the result of which will be revealed well before the program starts, enabling you to plan ahead. External scholarships typically have their own selection criteria and process. Some will require you to apply by completing a formal application process followed by rigorous interview rounds. It is ideal to do your research and make a list of external scholarships beforehand.

Based on the amount of scholarship you receive from these sources, you can plan your finances. Once you start college, scholarships are rare.

Here are some of the scholarship options available at top schools:

INSEAD

1.   INSEAD Andreas Lehmann MBA'83J Scholarship for talented students with financial need

---

*   Optional

2. INSEAD Deepak and Sunita Gupta Endowed Scholarship for candidates from emerging/developing countries with financial need
3. INSEAD Forte Scholarship for Women
4. INSEAD Henriette and Norbert Albin Endowed MBA Scholarship Fund based on financial need
5. INSEAD Padma and Rashmi Shah Social Enterprise Scholarship

Kellogg

1. Forte Foundation Scholarship for Women
2. Fredrick C Austin Scholarship for students who demonstrate academic excellence, leadership and community impact
3. Kellogg Scholarship awarded on the basis of overall merit
4. PepsiCo Scholarship for students interested in marketing careers
5. Donald P. Jacobs International Scholarships for strong international students in two-year programs

National University of Singapore

1. NUS MBA Study Awards
2. NUS MBA ASEAN Scholarships for students from ASEAN countries
3. NUS MBA Women in Business Scholarship
4. Lam See Chiew Memorial Scholarship in Social Entrepreneurship and Philanthropy

Rotman School of Management

1. Joseph L. Rotman Scholarship which covers full tuition and is awarded to two exceptional students
2. Forte Fellowship for Women
3. Entrance Awards based on merit that range from CAD 10,000 to CAD 90,000
4. Creative Destruction Lab Fellows Program for candidates

committed to careers in entrepreneurship and the startup space

Indian School of Business

1. Full and partial merit-based tuition fee waivers
2. ISB Merit by Diversity scholarships of up to ₹10 lakhs
3. Citi Scholarships of ₹7.5 lakhs
4. Bajaj Auto Scholarship
5. Lakshya Scholarship for women

Please note that the schools may change the scope and eligibility criteria (gender, nationality, industry, academic performance, etc.) of these scholarships.

Let us now explore the various kinds of scholarships available to aspirants.

3:A. Scholarships/Loan-Forgiveness Programs Provided by Schools

Internal scholarships can be broken down into: need-based and merit-based scholarships.

1. Need-Based Scholarships

A need-based scholarship extends aid on the basis of your or your family's current financial status (need). Assistance could be in the form of scholarships, grants or even assistantships. To establish your 'need', the school may ask for a detailed income tax returns (yours and your family's), savings statements, and balance sheet with details of all your assets and liabilities among other documents.

Most top MBA programs offer students need-based funding. For example, at Columbia Business School, almost half of the incoming class receives funding ranging from $7,500 to $30,000. Similarly, HBS Fellowships and Stanford Fellowships are need-based financial assistance programs where nearly 50 percent of the class receives some form of aid. Indian School of Business also offers need-based waivers in the form of D'décor Scholarship and Shapoorji Pallonji Scholarship among many others. Review your target schools' websites to see what need-based scholarships they offer and their requirements.

2. *Merit-Based Scholarships*

Merit-based scholarships, as the name suggests, are given to outstanding students. The application process for these scholarships varies by school. For instance, INSEAD requires you to submit an application for merit-based scholarships at the interview stage. On the other hand, Yale SOM automatically considers you for a merit-based scholarship when you apply to their MBA program. Some scholarships may also require you to write essays or a statement of purpose and/or go through a complete application process. Thus, I recommend that you check the method of applying for merit-based scholarships with your school.

3. *Loan-Forgiveness Programs*

You may sometimes receive assistance in paying back your student loan or even have your loan forgiven. At many top MBA programs, loan-forgiveness or assistance is available to students who specifically work in the public or nonprofit sectors. Please note that the loan-forgiveness program kicks in after you have graduated, once you begin your payback period for the student loan. Typically, this program is applicable globally. Even if you decide to come back to India and choose to work in the social enterprise sector post-graduation, you will be eligible for the program. You need not have any past experience in the public or nonprofit sectors. As long as you are working in these fields post-MBA, the school can deem you eligible for this program.

Each school has its own rules and processes. For instance, such forgiveness programs are available at Yale SOM, Wharton, INSEAD, Stanford GSB and HBS to name a few. If your job/role/organization makes you eligible to receive assistance, the school will pay either:

- The full amount of your annual loan payments
- A partial amount of your annual loan payments
- One-time lump sum amount

However, if you transition out of the nonprofit or public sector before your loan is paid back, you will stop receiving this aid. Such programs are designed to encourage MBA graduates to work in the public sector over other lucrative corporate offers.

3:B. Scholarships by Foundations and Fellowships

Apart from the school you will attend, several other foundations/trusts offer scholarships to students who wish to pursue an MBA abroad. These may cover all or a portion of your cost of attendance, depending upon the scholarship. External funding or scholarships are usually granted on merit, after the student has received an admit letter from the school. You may be required to furnish proof of admission, a statement of purpose, a letter of recommendation as well as your transcripts. Please note that these scholarships are highly competitive, and you will be required to build a case for why you should be selected from the pool.

Here are a few notable foundations, trusts and institutions that offer scholarships to Indian students who wish to earn an MBA abroad:

- The JN Tata Endowment offers a loan scholarship of up to ₹1,00,000.
- The Aga Khan Foundation offers a scholarship which is awarded as 50 percent loan and 50 percent grant to outstanding students who (as quoted on their website):
    - Have an excellent academic background.
    - Have gained admission to a reputed university or course in

an area relevant to the Aga Khan Foundation's focus areas (education, agriculture, culture, health, media, music, etc.)

- Have genuine financial need.

- The KC Mahindra Educational Trust offers a scholarship of up to ₹8,00,000.

- The Stanford Reliance Dhirubhai Fellowship covers up to 80 percent of an Indian student's cost of attendance. The condition here is that the student has to work in India for two years after he graduates from Stanford.

- India4Eu II Scholarships provide assistance for up to 12 months for students who wish to pursue education in Europe.

- GREAT Scholarships offered by the British Council for students that wish to pursue their education at select UK colleges.

- The Prodigy Finance Global Scholarship is open to all admitted international students at postgraduate degree schools. One recipient will be chosen to receive the equivalent of the full cost of one year's tuition (up to $100,000). Applicants need not be borrowers of Prodigy Finance.

3:C. *Company Assistance*

Some multinational corporations want to reward employees who are high performers. They may offer such employees some form of mentorship, coaching or financial assistance towards their MBA. Some global consulting companies that provide this assistance are:

- Bain
- McKinsey
- BCG
- Deloitte

For instance, Deloitte's Graduate School Assistance Program helps to send outstanding performers to top business schools. However, in some cases, students are only paid the full reimbursement AFTER two years of employment with Deloitte post-MBA. So, candidates might have to take on a loan initially if they wish to opt for this route.

The catch here is that you will have to come back post-MBA and work with the company for a stipulated period of time. While this is lucrative to students who wish to stay and grow in their existing companies, those who wish to begin an entrepreneurial venture or change their jobs or industry after an MBA may not find this appealing.

Also, please note that the Indian offices of these companies may not offer an MBA sponsorship. I recommend that you check with your supervisor or HR about the opportunities available to you for company sponsorship.

These were the scholarship options available to business school applicants. Let us now look at the nuances of earning scholarships and deciding on them.

4. What Should You Know About Scholarships?

4:A. How to Write a Winning Scholarship Essay

Some scholarships may require you to write an essay and/or a statement of purpose. Please note that the following essay-writing tips also apply to MBA application essays:

- Be authentic
- Be specific
- Share personal experiences
- Ensure flawless grammar

In addition to the above, I want to emphasis one factor here:

Tell a Unique Story

Scholarships are awarded to 'outstanding' students. However, an outstanding student doesn't merely boast of strong academic qualifications. Your live experiences and your personal story are a major part of what make you unique. While writing your scholarship essay, let the reader know HOW you are different from the rest of the applicants. Additionally, it is important to address why you need the scholarship. Can you demonstrate genuine financial need?

A sense of purpose and passion should run through the essay. Let the reader know what you believe in and validate your beliefs thorough anecdotes. Here's an example of how you can demonstrate your unique skills as well as needs on a scholarship essay:

Student Submission:

"An important aspect for me to come to XXXXXX is getting a scholarship that covers part of the tuition.

While I am leading a division within my family enterprise, I work at a moderate salary that I draw from the business and do not have access to any large funds.

My family has paid through my schooling as well as undergrad, and I don't want to burden them more and will be funding the MBA without their help as much as possible.

My father is currently working on expanding the business, and a lot of the money is tied up in the expansion process. Over and above that, I have saved some amount through my own work at the organization and will be using that to cover my staying and travelling expenses in XXXXX. My organization will be funding the tuition and the aid is for the part of the tuition I cannot cover and is what I am seeking today."

In the above snippet, the candidate only details why he would need a scholarship for the first three paragraphs. The essay does not make much impact as the AdCom is not explicitly told why the student is deserving of such a scholarship.

Final Version after ReachIvy.com's Edits:

"A commensurate scholarship will enable me to actualize my dream of pursuing the XXXX MBA.

Having funded my entire education thus far, my father is currently working on expanding the business, and most of our assets are tied up in the expansion process.

The company is already highly leveraged and cannot take up any further loans. Presently, I draw a moderate salary from the business and plan to cover my living expenses amounting to XXXXX with my meager savings.

My endeavors over the years demonstrate my ability to take impactful initiatives, effectuate business growth, and formulate and implement sustainable solutions to diverse challenges. My diverse pursuits encompass starting a business vertical, liaising with diverse stakeholders in a hugely competitive industry, and managing multiple departments. Such pertinent formative exposure will allow me to contribute to the intellectual capital at XXXX and enhance the peer-to-peer learning process."

In the final version, notice how a balanced view is brought forth. It mixes both financial need, the student's unique skills and explains why the student will benefit from such a scholarship.

4:B. How to Pick a School: Money vs Brand?

Throughout the book, I have advocated that students pick a school by looking at multiple factors; one does not supersede the other. For instance, my student, Adarsh Roy, earned a cent percent scholarship into University of Washington, Michael G. Foster School of Business. However, he chose to attend Northwestern Kellogg, which offered him no funding at all. He was keen on getting an MBA from a top-tier school and wished to be a part of the strong alumni network that Kellogg offers. Despite having to take on a large financial burden, he was confident of being able to pay back his loans in a short span of time and hence let go of the scholarship. He was willing to take a financial hit in the short term for what he believed would set him up for the long term.

5. How to Make the MBA Accessible

Even if you have been unsuccessful at attaining a scholarship, you can still find a way to finance your MBA—you don't have to drop your dream. However, I recommend taking this route ONLY after you have exhausted your personal resources (savings, family, friends, etc.) and scholarship avenues. Your next best option: **Take a Loan.**

While it may be tempting to keep your savings intact and just take a loan, remember that loans come at a cost. You will have to make regular interest payments on the loans you take. The interest you pay on your loan is typically higher than the interest you earn on your savings, making it costlier. Also, having to pay back a loan could eat into a significant portion of your income in the early years of your career. However, there are some benefits to taking on an education loan as well.

To confirm your admission, schools may ask you for a solvency letter which declares yours or your family's assets. This acts as proof of your ability to bear the cost of attendance. For many students, this may be a hurdle, as not everyone has such large amounts of liquid funds available. The advantage of taking on an education loan is that you can pre-approve your loan from some lenders and get a loan sanction letter. Thus, when asked for proof of funding upon admission, you can furnish this letter and confirm your enrolment to the program with ease.

Tackling a large amount of debt early in your life may also be an exercise in financial management. You will learn how to handle monthly installments while also paying for your own rent, food and lifestyle. Furthermore, if you successfully pay back such a large amount early in your life, you are likely to build a good credit score. This will help you avail other loans in the future at lower interest rates.

Assess your personal situation and determine what amount (if any) you want to take on as loan. Also, I would like you to note that all loans and grants are sanctioned before you begin your program, so you have a clear idea of your financial outlay a priori.

Let us do a brief preparatory course on some common jargon you will encounter while determining how to finance your education. Understanding these terms will allow you to make an educated decision.

MBA Loan Terms to Know

1. **Cost of Attendance:** The total amount of money you will have to pay for your MBA. This includes the tuition fees, living costs (dormitory, rent, food), mandatory insurance, books, transport among other additional costs.

2. **Repayment Period:** The duration within which you are required to repay the loan. The repayment period usually starts shortly after or immediately after you graduate from the program. This varies from lender to lender.

3. **Fixed Margin (Spread):** A fixed rate of interest that is levied at the time of loan approval and does not fluctuate during the period of the loan.

4. **Base Rate:** Variable interest rate charged against the amount yet to be repaid, that fluctuates as per market factors.

5. **Marginal Cost of Funds-Based Lending Rate (MCLR):** The minimum variable rate of interest prescribed to a bank by Reserve Bank of India, below which it cannot lend.

6. **Annual Percentage Rate (APR):** APR can be simply understood as the annual cost of borrowing. The basic (and most commonly understood) cost here is the interest you pay against the loan. However, there would be one or more

additional hidden costs such as:

- Processing fees
- Origination fees
- Paperwork-related fees
- Servicing fees
- Foreign exchange conversion fees

   All of the above factors add to the total amount you will pay to the lender against your loan. Given the hidden costs, the APR will be higher than the interest rate, and is intended as a tool to compare loan offers from different companies.

7. **Cosigner:** A person (usually close family or friends) who signs the loan agreement alongside you, and is equally liable to pay the amount back.

8. **Collateral:** An asset which you (the borrower) or the cosigner on your loan pledges to the lender as a means of securing the loan. For large sums of money, this is usually a fixed asset such as property. Collaterals are the lender's way of ensuring that the borrower does not default on the loan, and in case he does, the lender can sell the collateral to recover the loan amount.

Note: The credit score of your cosigner is also affected once he agrees to share the liability of your loan with you. Additionally, if you have pledged your or your parents' property for a student loan, you or they will neither be able to draw any other loans against the same property for the repayment duration nor sell the property as it will be hypothecated to the lender for the repayment duration.

   Now, that you are familiar with the key terms involved with student loans, let's dive into the various loan options at hand.

5:A. Bank Loans (Public Sector Banks)

Banks are the most popular loan providers among students. Here, we will cover public sector banks to give you a brief overview of what a bank loan entails.

Examples of Public Sector Banks Offering Loans: State Bank of India, Central Bank of India, Punjab National Bank, Bank of India, among several others.

Maximum Cost of Attendance Covered: Up to 90 percent.

Requirements: Will require a cosigner and collateral asset in order for the loan to be approved and forwarded.

Schools They Will Lend Against: No restrictions on school or program type, as long as the student has been admitted to the program.

Interest Rates: Public sector banks charge a rate of interest on student loans which is a combination of the spread (2 – 2.5 percent) and MCLR (8.55 percent as of March 2019) and any additional costs associated with taking on the loan. Please note that the MCLR may change as per the Reserve Bank of India's decision. Even if you apply for the loan today and get it approved, the effective rate of interest you may have to pay could vary.

Additionally, the bank may also consider if you are attending business school in India or abroad. Since loans for students studying abroad are usually of a greater amount, the banks may also charge a greater margin against the loan. For example, Central Bank of India will levy margins as per the following criteria:

1. Loan amount up to ₹4,00,000: No margin

2. Loan amount above ₹4,00,000 in India: 5 percent margin

3. Loan amount above ₹4,00,000 abroad: 15 percent margin

Repayment Period: The repayment period begins 6-12 months after you graduate, for up to 15 years.

Note: The bank may also provide subsidies on interest rates as per government guidelines. For instance, I was working with Neha, an investment banker who required an additional ₹15,00,000 to fully finance her MBA. She applied for a student loan and was notified that she would receive an interest rate subsidy available to female candidates. Instead of the 2 percent spread +MCLR for male candidates, she could avail the loan at 1.5 percent spread +MCLR. Thus, she was able to shave 0.5 percent off her effective interest rate. I recommend that you keep an eye out for such subsidies across lenders.

5:B. Non-Banking Financial Company (NBFC) Loans

An NBFC does not hold a formal banking license. While you cannot deposit money in these institutions, they are still allowed to grant loans and other facilities. Since they are not restricted by RBI regulations like traditional banks, they loan money in varied formats.

Example of NBFCs: HDFC Credila, Avanse, Auxilo, InCred.

Maximum Cost of Attendance Covered: Up to 100 percent.

Requirements: A cosigner (parents, close family, friends) will be required in most cases. Additionally, you may be asked to provide a collateral if the loan value is high. For loans below a certain amount threshold, you may not require a collateral. For example, HDFC Credila offers loans without collateral security up to ₹35,00,000.

Schools They Will Lend Against: This varies from one lender to another. Typically, they look for universities that are accredited, well established and known to produce well-performing graduates. The loan provider assumes these students will have a lower default rate since the probability of them getting high-paying jobs is relatively higher, making their loan more secure from their perspective.

Interest Rates: Unlike at public sector banks, interest rates are not regulated by the RBI for NBFCs. Thus, they may vary from one lender to another.

Margin: Additionally, NBFCs may not charge you a margin against the amount they lend.

Repayment Period: The repayment period for NBFC lenders begins around 6-12 months after you graduate and can go up to 10-12 years.

5:C. Loans from International Lenders

International lenders are usually NBFCs that are based outside India. They usually lend in a foreign currency.

Examples of International Lenders: MPower Financing, Prodigy Finance, etc.

Maximum Cost of Attendance Covered: Up to 100 percent.

Requirements: Since international lenders are private organizations, their requirements vary. For instance, some international lenders do not require a cosigner or collateral or credit history to sanction your loan. This flexibility and access makes loans from international lenders extremely tempting for students.

Schools Accepted: The schools that are accepted by international lenders for loan approval may vary. Usually, this is a select list of colleges, and could be limited to universities in certain geographies. For instance, Mpower Financing only gives loans against admission to univerisities in USA and Canada. Some providers will provide a list of colleges on their webiste that qualify for their loans.

Interest Rates: As with NBFCs, the interest rates with international lenders may vary vastly. Furthermore, the interest rates may fluctuate as per your profile and credit history or the school at which you have been accepted.

Repayment Period: The repayment period for international lenders begins from 6-12 months after you graduate to up to 7-20 years.

5:D. Loan Grants

Loan grants are similar to scholarships. However, students are required to pay back the amount that was awarded to them at a nominal rate of interest after they graduate. Grant organizations typically factor in both need and merit when evaluating candidates.

Examples of Loan Grants: The Aga Khan Foundation Scholarship, JN Tata Endowment for the Higher Education of Indians, RD Sethna Scholarships, Narotam Sekhsaria Scholarship Program.

Maximum Cost of Attendance: This varies from one organization to another. Mostly, loan grants only cover a part of your fees, on the condition that you can show that you have the remaining amount arranged for.

Requirements: Loan grants usually do not need a cosigner or collateral.

Schools Accepted: Grant organizations are open to a variety of schools and not very restrictive in their approach.

Interest Rates: The interest rates vary from one loan grant lender to another. For instance, the Aga Khan Foundation requires you to pay back 50 percent of the awarded grant at an annual service charge of 5 percent. For instance, if you are granted a scholarship of $50,000, you will have to pay back $25,000 back to the Aga Khan Foundation within five years of earning your MBA. In addition to this amount, you will have to pay an additional 5 percent ($1,250 per year) per annum until you fully repay it. On the other hand, the Narotam Sekhsaria Scholarship Program does not require you to pay any interest on the grant amount when you pay it back.

Repayment Period: The repayment period may begin a few months after you earn your MBA and last for five years (as with the Aga Khan Foundation Scholarship), or within seven years since the approval of the grant or loan (as with the JN Tata Endowment for the Higher Education of Indians).

5:E. How to Compare the Various Loan Options

As you research the various loan options available, you may get confused. Almost all lenders "guarantee" low interest rates and myriad benefits. I urge you to read through the fine print. Similar to my recommendation in the college selection chapter, I urge you to view your choices through the lens of your personal requirements.

For instance, some students may not have an asset to provide as collateral to the bank. In this case, international lenders may come in handy.

However, note that international players lend in a foreign currency. Thus, if you plan on returning to India after your MBA, you will have to pay them back in USD/EUR/GBP/SGD depending on the currency in which your loan was granted. After your MBA, if you choose to return to India and earn in INR, you expose yourself to foreign exchange (forex) risk since you have to pay your debt back in a foreign currency and the exchange rates keep fluctuating. For example, if the rupee depreciates (weakens) against the dollar, you will end up paying more than you initially expected to pay.

Let me illustrate with an example: If you have taken a $100,000 loan, you will have to pay back ₹70,00,000 when $1 = ₹70. However, if this changes to $1 = ₹80, you will have to pay back a total of ₹80,00,000. This is a significant difference of over ₹10,00,000. On the other hand, if you earn money in the same currency as your loan, you eliminate this risk.

Another factor to consider is that the interest paid towards education loans helps you get tax benefits in India under Section 80E of the Income Tax Act, 1961. However, the loan has to be from any scheduled bank in India or gazette-notified financial institution as per the Income Tax Act. There is no upper limit to claiming the tax exemption and the loan has to be in the name of the person claiming the tax break. Thus, if you plan to return to India after your MBA, loans from institutions that qualify for tax benefits will help you save money.

You must also take into consideration how much of the total funding you will require in the form of a loan. Most lenders do not provide 100 percent funding to their borrowers.

As with all financial decisions, factor in your personal requirements, current financial status, and future plans when you take on a student loan. Of all the options above, loan grants usually come at the lowest rate of interest, but are conversely the toughest to obtain.

NOTE: Some lenders may allow you to refinance your loan and change the terms of payback. This may be done while you are at college or even once you have graduated. You may also take this into consideration when comparing loans.

Here's a table explaining the difference between loan types so that you can make an informed decision:

Loan Type	Pros	Cons
Bank Loans (Public Sector Banks)	1. Subsidies may be available on the Annual Percentage Rate as per government policy 2. Bank loans are usually available for all schools and programs as long as you can provide proof of admittance	1. MCLR may change arbitrarily; thus, APR cannot be accurately predicted 2. Candidate has to arrange for 20 percent of the cost of attendance from a different source 3. Requires both a cosigner and collateral (above a threshold)

Loan Type	Pros	Cons
NBFC Loans	1. Can fund up to 100 percent of the cost of attendance 2. Loan amount is greater than what banks usually provide	1. NBFCs require a cosigner and collateral (above a threshold) 2. Loan may be granted only for select programs at select schools 3. Interest rates may vary by school
International Lender Loans	1. May be able to fund up to 100 percent of the cost of attendance 2. May not require a cosigner or collateral 3. Loans are processed in the currency of your country of study, thus foreign exchange conversion fees are not applicable	1. Since the loan is processed in a foreign currency, you are exposed to currency fluctuation risk when repaying 2. Loan may be granted only for select programs at select schools
Loan Grants	1. May fund up to $100,000 towards cost of attendance 2. Rate of interest for repayment is nominal	1. Highly selective process based on merit and need, hence difficult to obtain

6. The New Way to Fund Your MBA: Crowdfunding

Crowdfunding is the new-age way to raise funds online. Here, the community works together to raise funds for causes or people or products they believe in. This is an interesting avenue to explore if you have a strong and reliable network or a compelling personal story. However, this is a fairly recent phenomenon, and the waters are largely untested on success rates of funding. Some popular crowdfunding platforms are GoFundMe, Indiegogo and Ketto.

Moreover, remember: "There's no such thing as free money."

If you begin a crowdfunding project, you will have to market and publicize it. You are required to tell your audience why they should fund your MBA dream. After all, they are investors in your future. You cannot expect them to invest in it until they have good reason to do so and are assured of some reward (personal or societal).

7. Reality Check: Busting Common MBA Myths

7:A. I did not save enough money. I can't get my MBA!

While it would have certainly helped if you had ready funds in your savings account, this is not the end of the world. Most top business schools offer a range of scholarship opportunities for incoming students. In addition to these, external scholarship opportunities are also present. Chances are high that you would be eligible for at least a few of these opportunities. In the scenario that you are not, there are several lenders who specifically help students finance their study-abroad post-graduate dreams via loans.

Explore your financing options before giving up on a life-changing experience like the MBA.

7:B. Only university toppers will get a scholarship; it's not for me

It is true that grades are considered by a school/foundation/trust to determine who gets merit-based scholarships. However, your holistic profile is given more importance.

Moreover, several need-based scholarship programs provide assistance as per your current financial status. The only requirement is that you have been admitted to the program. Thus, even if you are not a university topper, as long as you get admitted to a top school, you will definitely be considered for a scholarship. Your admission to that college in itself signals that you meet their standards.

7:C. International students are not offered scholarships

It is true that many scholarships at top business schools are limited to citizens of the country the institution is based in. Nevertheless, there are several scholarships available to international students as well. The schools typically want to attract top international talent to their campuses to maintain about 30–80 percent (depending on the school and the country) international population on campus to build diversity. To enable this goal, they have to provide scholarships to international students who are unable to afford the high costs.

Here's what AdComs of top business schools have to say about scholarship and funding opportunities for international students:

> **Chicago Booth School of Business:**
>
> "We recognize that an MBA represents a significant investment in yourself and your future. Financial aid opportunities are open to all of our admitted students, including merit-based scholarships, as well as multiple loan options for international students without US cosigners."

Johns Hopkins Carey Business School:

"We offer merit-based scholarships which are based on work experience, GMAT (or GRE) scores, and grade point average in other degree programs. Scholarships range from $10,000 to full tuition (for a few, truly exceptional candidates)."

Yale School of Management:

"We have financial aid available to all students, both domestic and international. In fact, this past year we announced new scholarships specifically for students from India. We automatically consider all applicants for scholarships; there is no need to submit a separate application."

8. Understanding Your Cost of Attendance

Your cost of attendance may include fees for several different facilities alongside the core which comprises:

- Tuition Fees
- Room and Boarding
- Living Expenses

These fees make up for anywhere between 80 and 90 percent of your cost of attendance at business school. Furthermore, there are additional costs which make up the remaining 10-20 percent of your cost of attendance. These may be incurred in the form of:

- Health Insurance
- Books/Program Material Fees
- Transport (includes travel to and from your country to the country of the program)
- Students Body Memberships

While tuition, room and board and living expenses are constant, different business schools have varying additional costs which the students may have to cover. Furthermore, the living expenses also change as per your location. To illustrate the differing costs of attendance, let us look at a breakdown of the same for HBS and CEIBS:

Harvard Business School (For 9 Months)

Item	Cost (Single Candidate)	Cost (Married Candidate)	Cost (Married with one child)
Tuition	$73,440	$73,440	$73,440
Health Fee	$1,206	$1,206	$1,206
Health Insurance Plan	$3,700	$3,700	$3,700
Harvard University Student Health Program for Spouses/ Dependents	NA	$7,178	$13,880
Course/Program Materials Fee	$2,550	$2,550	$2,550
Room and Utilities	$13,940	$20,700	$27,188
Living Expenses	$15,904	$19,588	$32,846
Total	$110,740	$128,902	$154,810

CEIBS (For 18 Months)

Items Covered
Tuition fees which covers: 1) Tuition 2) Teaching materials (excluding textbooks) 3) Use of internet through campus network 4) Access to school's databases which is open to MBA students
Total (considering 18 months of housing expense)   RMB 438,000

*All information in the tables is sourced from the official college websites.

Many international MBA programs offer a detailed cost-breakdown on their respective websites. I urge you to visit your target school's website to get an estimate of the expenses you will incur.

9. How to Pay Back Your Student Loans

Once you have graduated, you will have to begin paying back the student loan (principal + interest) you took on. There are two common approaches to this:

- **Aggressive:** Some students pay back their loans aggressively to become debt-free as soon as possible. This removes the burden of debt from their heads and allows them to take on incremental financial risk as needed. While this is a great approach if your personal financial conditions allow, not everyone is able to approach his student loan in this manner.
- **Calculated:** Here students make the bare minimum payment every month against the loan. In this case, students often invest their savings in other areas (funding their business, paying rent, mutual funds, etc.) to maintain a sustainable cash flow and save on tax payments annually. The tax breaks I discussed above serve as an incentive for students to delay or prolong their payback period.
- **Balanced:** Here students adopt the middle ground between being too aggressive and being too calculated.

My advice is to take stock of your circumstances post-MBA. Not everyone graduates with the same personal financial situation. For instance, let's say that by the time you graduate, you are married and have a child. Then, you may not have as much disposable income to tackle your debt aggressively. Life is unpredictable; I suggest you conduct a regular half-yearly review of your situation and plan your repayment accordingly.

To illustrate how students may tackle their loans, let's review how some of ReachIvy.com's students are handling their own student loans:

9:A. Case 1: Calculated Approach

- **Pre-MBA Career:** Advertising
- **Experience:** 5 years
- **School Admitted To:** Cambridge Judge School of Business
- **Cost of Attendance:** ₹60,00,000
- **Personal Savings:** ₹20,00,000
- **Total Amount Needed:** ₹40,00,000
- **Sources of Funding:** Public sector bank
- **Rationale behind Picking This Particular Source of Funding:** The candidate had a high trust level with the bank manager, owing to a family connection.
- **Payback:** The repayment period was initially planned to be five years. However, post-MBA, the student's income increased substantially and his tax payments also increased commensurately since he was now within a higher tax bracket. Now, he felt that bank loans are "fantastic" to get tax rebates. Thus, the student extended the loan repayment period to 10 years, and is currently paying it back out of the salary he earns while investing his earnings in another venture.

9:B. Case 2: Aggressive Initially and Calculated Later

- **Pre-MBA Career:** Consulting
- **Experience:** 4 years
- **School Admitted To:** Harvard Business School
- **Cost of Attendance (CoA):** $200,000 over a period of two years. Add a discretionary amount, which includes expenditure on personal activities and food at the program.
- **Personal Savings:** 5 percent ($10,000)

- **Total Amount Needed:** $190,000
- **Sources of Funding:** Multiple sources
  - Harvard Business School Fellowship (40 percent of the CoA)
  - Student loan through Harvard Credit Union (40 percent of the CoA)
  - Multiple loan grants from Indian foundations such as JN Tata Endowment, KC Mahindra Educational Trust and RD Sethna Among other (15 percent of the CoA)
- **Rationale behind Picking the Sources of Funding:**
  - **Harvard Credit Union:** Cheaper in terms of interest rates, and gave access to an international loan without an international cosigner. The student wished to work in the USA post-MBA, thus forex risk was absent. Moreover, the interest rates, at six percent (albeit variable), were lower than at the Indian lenders.
  - **Indian Foundation Scholarships & Loan Grants:** The sum they award may seem like a small amount in the grand scheme of $200,000. However, the student could acquire four or five of these, amounting to almost 15 percent of the CoA. Moreover, these loan grants from Indian foundations come at a very low interest rate (2–5 percent as opposed to 8–15 percent from banks).
- **Repayment:** The student has a 15 year repayment period on his loans from multiple sources. He is paying this out of his monthly salary. However, the interest rates in the US have increased in the past two years. He now pays 8.5 percent as opposed to the 6 percent which he started with (on his Harvard Credit Union Loan). Since the student was aggressive about paying off his student loans in the first year and a half after graduating, he was able to pay off 50 percent of his debt in that period. Now, as he has switched locations and is working in India, he is paying the loans off with a more calculated approach.

- **Approach to Repayment:** Aggressive for the first year and a half, and calculated afterwards.

10. Real People, Unique Skills, Common Errors: Analysis and Fixes

10:A. Radhika Secured Funding from Multiple Source

R: I am still falling short by 30 percent of my financial needs—what shall I do?

VK: You are going to have to taken on some liability—get a loan!

Radhika was a business developer from Mumbai who was accepted at Michigan's Ross School of Business.

She could cover only about 20 percent of her cost of attendance with her savings. Even with a 50 percent scholarship from Ross, she only had 70 percent of the total funds needed. She was under the impression that owing to her scholarship funding, nobody else would lend to her. However, this was not the case. I explained to her that students often secure funding from multiple different sources; schools and lenders alike are privy to this fact.

Radhika also wanted to pursue a career abroad. Thus, I recommended that she borrow the remaining amount from Prodigy Finance or a similar international lender. Soon enough, she was able to acquire this funding and pay for her MBA.

My Take

In Radhika's case, the funding for her MBA came from the following sources:

- Twenty percent personal savings
- Fifty percent in-house scholarship form the MBA program
- Thirty percent loan

However, Radhika's case is not uncommon. The funding for your MBA will usually come from many different sources. It could be a combination of a scholarship, your savings, a loan or a grant. MBA programs tend to demand a high price, and it is understandable that you may not be able to acquire it all from a single source.

10:B. Kartik Secured a Full Scholarship to Oxford Said

Kartik was a global citizen in every sense of the word. He hailed from South Africa and had worked in over four countries during his career. Before he decided to apply to Oxford Said, he was working in the social enterprise sector in Africa. This made him eligible for Oxford Said's Dean's Africa Scholarship, which we came across on the school's website. Considering that Kartik had extensive experience in the continent, we highlighted his global strengths with an emphasis on his work in Africa. Additionally, we ensured that he could accurately capture his passion and purpose in his essays.

When he heard back from Oxford, they informed Kartik that he was awarded the Dean's Scholarship, covering 100 percent of his cost of attendance. Oxford loved his profile and wanted him at all costs!

Given the amount of funding he would receive, his preference to study in the UK and his personal situation, Kartik chose to go with the offer from Oxford.

My Take

What I wish to showcase through Kartik's story is that some schools have special scholarships for specific backgrounds, ethnicities and industries. Therefore, I recommend that you check the school's website to determine if you fall within the scope and eligibility of a scholarship. If you are meritorious, there is definitely a scholarship opportunity at your target school that you can avail of. This will greatly help you offset the cost of an MBA.

Insider Tips in a Nutshell

DO:

✓ Begin financial planning as soon as you decide to get an MBA.

✓ Explore all other options (personal savings, family/friend assistance/scholarship/grants) before you decide to take a loan.

✓ If you decide to take a loan, ensure that you compare all factors and make an informed, cost-effective choice.

✓ Ask your manager/supervisor/HR if the company sponsors an MBA degree.

✓ Explore the funding and financing opportunities available at your target schools. They will have a web page dedicated to this purpose.

DON'T:

✗ Refrain from applying to scholarships because you think you aren't worthy enough.

✗ Give up on all scholarship options just because you were rejected once.

✗ Think of loans as the only option to fund your MBA.

A Sneak Peek into the Minds of Admission Officers

Columbia Business School

Name: Nicole Shay
Function/Role: Associate Director of Admissions

1. Students want to earn an MBA for multiple reasons. What do you consider to be strong reasons for doing an MBA? Why should one get an MBA?

Many of Columbia Business School's successful candidates are seeking an MBA to either make a function or industry pivot in their career, or to take a deeper dive in order to gain expertise in their current sector. MBA coursework is valuable for anyone who is looking to be a business leader. This might mean a leader in healthcare or consulting, but we also have many students who are seeking leadership in sectors like nonprofit and the arts. Columbia Business School's core curriculum, paired with our over 300 electives, allows each student to design her academic experience to best suit her goals, and shape her into a leader regardless of her past academic or professional experiences.

2. *What are some of the key features/highlights of your MBA program that make it unique?*

Students often cite their proximity and access to the New York City business ecosystem as a powerful resource in helping to achieve their post-MBA goals. Some of Columbia Business School's most popular electives are our Immersion Seminars which allow students to engage with industry practitioners through downtown site visits to multiple organizations each term. Many students also to participate in part-time, in-semester internships because of the school's proximity to the offices of organizations across all industries. These part-time in-semester internships may be counted for course credit, if students are able to secure a faculty sponsor. Additionally, Columbia Business School has over 16,000 alumni in New York City alone, and this network is available to students to leverage for coffee chats, mentorship, and to carve their own paths for internship opportunities.

3. *What defines a strong candidate for your school? What do you look for when admitting students?*

The Admissions Team at Columbia Business School works hard to make sure our class is as diverse as possible because we believe diversity of thought is extremely beneficial to our academic environment. We are looking for students with varying personal and professional backgrounds who have well-defined goals and understand how Columbia Business School is going to help them achieve these goals. Most importantly, we are looking for candidates who will be kind to their peers and contribute to the school's community in a positive way.

4. *How do you help international students chalk their career paths?*

Columbia Business School has numerous resources for international students, including expert advisement by our Career Management Center members who have extensive experience with international student placement post-MBA. Students also work with our Executives in Residence, industry-specific alumni coaches, and professional clubs (including the South Asian Business Association!) to understand the marketplace and industry into which they are recruiting.

5. *Is there any financial aid available to international students? If yes, who is an ideal candidate for this?*

Both domestic and international applicants are eligible for merit fellowships, need-based scholarships and loans. Merit-based fellowships are awarded based on a variety of criteria, including academic excellence, personal background and professional experience. To be considered for a merit fellowship, an applicant must check the "merit fellowship" box on their application, and submit the application by our merit fellowship deadline, which is early January each year. Once an applicant is admitted she is also eligible to apply for need-based aid regardless of her domestic or international student status. Of course, there are a variety of loan programs that incoming students might consider to help fund the cost of their MBA experience.

6. *What are some of the common mistakes you see frequently on applications?*

Sometimes candidates will use their essays to tell us what they think we want to hear rather than allowing us to get to know them better through the essay questions. We encourage applicants to use this space to help us understand what their goals are, and how they see Columbia Business School helping to achieve them. We also encourage applicants to apply as soon as they are ready rather than waiting until the day of the deadline. Because Columbia Business School operates on a rolling admissions cycle, we read candidates in the order in which their applications are received and are continually rendering decisions and building a class. Applying before the deadline allows candidates to be reviewed and rendered a decision earlier.

7. *Your final word of advice for students.*

Be yourself when applying! There are no molds to fit or quotas to fill at Columbia Business School. We are looking for talented candidates from every walk of life, with diverse experiences to bring to the table, and who will succeed academically and professionally, while also contributing positively to the Columbia Business School community.

Kellogg School of Management

Name: Kate Smith

Designation: Assistant Dean, Admissions & Financial Aid

1. *Students want to earn an MBA for multiple reasons. What do you consider to be strong reasons for doing an MBA? Why should one get an MBA?*

An MBA is a transformative experience for your personal and professional goals. It empowers you to make a lasting impact in the world, while providing you with an amazing alumni network that will help you for the rest of your life.

A top-tier business education gives you strong foundational management skills, and then evolves and challenges those skills through rigorous experiential learning, global coursework, and highly customized electives. Furthermore, the MBA experience allows you to pursue intensive 1:1 career coaching with deep industry specialists, experiment with an internship in your ideal company or industry, and build relationships with an intensely loyal global alumni network. The end result is to develop you into a dynamic leader and, ultimately, launch you into the career of your dreams.

2. What are some of the key features/highlights of your MBA program that make it unique?

We've intentionally designed the Kellogg learning experience to grow you personally and professionally—both in the specific ways you seek, but also in ways that will surprise you. Between extensive global opportunities, challenging experiential learning projects, and a deeply customizable set of electives, a Kellogg education is shaped by real-world experiences that meaningfully evolve your capabilities as a business leader.

At Kellogg, we develop dynamic leaders who see possibilities others can't, and we equip you to stand out—for the rest of your career. It means that in Kellogg's innovative curriculum, you'll learn how to identify new opportunities, catalyze teams to drive breakthrough results, and engage with world-class faculty—whether that is being closely mentored by a venture capitalist while designing a startup business plan, being led on a small-group trek to speak with policy leaders in Brazil, or having a fireside chat about board governance with a professor who formerly served as a Fortune 500 CEO. This experience is grounded in what we're known for: our collaborative culture and distinctive community.

Furthermore, you can have this experience in one of several full-time degree programs that is best tailored to your unique situation. Kellogg offers four distinct options for pursuing your full-time MBA— all of which have been intentionally designed to fit your personal and professional interests. Regardless of which program you choose, you will have exposure to our star faculty, career management coaching, global opportunities, and a world-class network. Our full-time MBA degree portfolio includes:

- 2Y MBA: This is our traditional degree program offering the flexibility to explore a variety of interests and disciplines while developing strong management and leadership skills.
- 1Y MBA: This is an accelerated program for candidates who have completed a business degree before enrolling. Students bypass several core courses and begin taking electives that support their professional objectives.
- MMM: This is a dual-degree program with Northwestern's McCormick School of Engineering, delivering a solid grounding in business, design innovation and technology.
- JD-MBA: This is a three-year program with Northwestern's Pritzker School of Law, awarding both MBA and JD degrees.

Finally, I must emphasize the incredible strength and responsiveness of our alumni network, which includes more than 60,000 business executives across the world. Alumni have a deep sense of pride for their Kellogg experience and a strong sense of loyalty to the school, which creates a wonderful pay-it-forward culture for our students. Whether you are seeking insights about a particular industry, advice about interviewing at a certain company, or ideas for switching careers, you can expect to have access to incredible alumni support that will fuel career success for the rest of your life.

3. What defines a strong candidate for your school? What do you look for when admitting students?

When we evaluate our applicants, a few qualities really stand out to us. These qualities help us understand if an applicant is ready to seize all of the incredible opportunities that come with joining the Kellogg community. We look for people who:

- Can motivate a team to drive impact.
- Are not afraid to question the status quo and seek non-obvious solutions.
- Possess creativity and talent that is rooted in self-awareness.
- Seek diversity in their networks and teams.
- Are eager to dive in and collaborate with an engaged, ambitious community of peers.

These are some of the traits that we really value. Our holistic application process allows us to understand how each person would bring these traits to Kellogg in his or her own unique way. From there, we teach students how to build on these abilities while they're at Kellogg.

4. *How do you help international students chalk their career paths?*

Kellogg students represent the best of international talent. We are continually building relationships with the US and international employers to maximize opportunities for our students. As an example, this year 230 companies hired Kellogg graduates, up 15 percent from 200 companies last year.

Kellogg provides a variety of resources to international students, including personalized 1:1 career coaching, career workshops, an English language consultant, and an international visa advisor. Our Career Management Center works closely with students and employers to build meaningful relationships that align our students' diverse interests with employment opportunities. We consistently see our international students landing excellent options upon graduation—both in the US and worldwide.

5. *Is there any financial aid available to international students? If yes, who is an ideal candidate for this?*

We know that funding your business school education can be challenging. To help all of our students meet this challenge—whether they are US-based or international—we offer merit-based scholarships, which are awarded at the time of admission. Scholarships opportunities for rising second-year students are also available. Applicants can view our full range of scholarship options on our admissions website.

6. *What are some of the common mistakes you see frequently on applications?*

First, there is nothing that would immediately rule an applicant out unless an incomplete application is submitted. We have a holistic admissions process that looks at the entire person.

One mistake, in general, is coming across as disingenuous. It is easy to spot candidates who write what they think we want to hear in their essays. But we want to learn about you—what are you experiences and values? We want to feel like we thoroughly know an applicant after we've read his or her application.

Another mistake is to over-research Kellogg before applying. For example, in an application or interview, a candidate may try to memorize or repeat information from our website. We want you to do your research—but we want you to reflect on how Kellogg resources will help with your specific career goals, as opposed to stating facts about Kellogg and its offerings more broadly.

7. *Your final word of advice for students.*

As you're preparing to apply and seeking more insight into the Kellogg experience, I would absolutely recommend tapping into the Kellogg alumni network, which includes more than 60,000 business professionals across the world. Contact your closest alumni club or individual alumni by searching for them on LinkedIn, or consider engaging any Kellogg alumni at your company.

Finally, our Kellogg admissions team consistently travels to India to host information sessions. I encourage applicants to attend our future events, which are frequently updated on our admissions website.

The University of Chicago
Booth School of Business

1. Students want to earn an MBA for multiple reasons. What do you consider to be strong reasons for doing an MBA? Why should one get an MBA?

Broadly speaking, we've seen successful applicants convey a diverse array of personal and professional reasons for pursuing an MBA. That being said, one of the most important aspects we look for is that your intentions are well thought-out in terms of what you hope to gain from the two-year experience, and that the motivations are genuinely self-reflective to who you are and where you want to be. Additionally, it's beneficial to consider how you'll leverage the MBA to have an impact—on your peers, in your career, in your community, or even in the world.

When we talk to Booth alumni about the benefits of an MBA, overwhelmingly, they reflect on the MBA experience as an unparalleled use of their time and intellect; transformational with regard to their confidence and leadership development, and one of the best ways to invest in themselves and their future. Furthermore, they encourage applicants to view the MBA as not just a static two-year journey, but as an experience that will continue to pay dividends throughout the entirety of your career, no matter what you set out to do.

2. *What are some of the key features/highlights of your MBA program that make it unique?*

Chicago Booth is unique in that the Chicago Approach serves as the foundation of our educational experience. It is rooted in a multidisciplinary curriculum that leverages business fundamentals, analytical frameworks, and evidence-based thinking. What sets us apart in terms of world-class MBA programs, is that we don't teach you what to think, we teach you how to think. And three key values shape the experience:

First, Booth has always been at the forefront of applying data—both qualitative and quantitative—to diverse fields in the world of business. And we've always encouraged faculty to bring their scholarly work into the classroom in ways that are innovative and useful to students. That's important because it helps students gain confidence, not only in navigating unfamiliar, multifaceted problems, but in having a structured and consistent way to ensure impactful solutions and bring about clarity as a leader.

Second, our institution has a deep appreciation for championing intellectual freedom. Booth gives students unparalleled freedom to choose courses and dive into learning experiences that will build upon their educational and professional background. We only have one required course, which is our Leadership Effectiveness and Development (LEAD) class. Beyond that, every student can utilize the full extent of their two years to pursue learning opportunities aligned with their unique goals.

Lastly, the people we bring into Booth drive our culture—a culture where we invest in one another's success. We foster a supportive environment that allows our students, faculty, and alumni to be persistent risk-takers and confidently step beyond their comfort zone. The collaboration and trust within our community ultimately helps push each individual, and each new idea, to be their best.

3. *What defines a strong candidate for your school? What do you look for when admitting students?*

From an admissions standpoint, Chicago Booth seeks to attract talented future leaders who fundamentally believe in our values and are excited to live them as an active part of Booth's community. As a result, compelling candidates draw genuine connections between their own aspirations and how they plan to interact with our community. The application should paint a coherent story around why you want an MBA, why it's vital at this point in your life, and why Chicago Booth is the ideal place to pursue your goals.

At a high level, each application component offers insight into your academic aptitude, career progression and impact, and demonstrated passions. We find that successful candidates also tend to reflect an intellectual curiosity and a need to be part of something bigger than what any one person can achieve. We seek students who embrace diverse backgrounds and build a collaborative environment where respect for each other's individual viewpoint is key. Each time we admit a new class to Booth, we bring together bright minds from numerous industries and cultures to realize the potential for new solutions, impactful decisions, and breakthrough discoveries every day.

4. *How do you help international students chalk their career paths?*

Just like all of our students, international students have the support of career coaches and resources through our office of Career Services. Our Career Services team is among the largest of any business school and we have more "feet on the street" making inroads with new and existing companies than anyone else. We've built a phenomenal team of experts whose job it is to help our international and domestic students explore professional opportunities and relaunch careers in industries around the globe.

Perhaps our numbers can speak for the success of this support. Within the Class of 2018, 95.2 percent of international students received a job offer within three months of graduation. Booth has dedicated coaches for international students, including staff that manage corporate relationships throughout South America, Europe, MEA and Asia. We also have resources outlining companies that have traditionally hired students who require visa sponsorship; as well as programmatic support geared towards international students and how recruiting processes in the US might differ from that in their home countries. Additionally, second-year students serve as career advisors and help mentor first-year students through the recruiting process.

More broadly, 80 percent of hires for the entire class were credited to Booth-facilitated channels. It's a testament to the strength and value of the Chicago Booth ecosystem, which includes an alumni network of 53,000 spanning 120+ countries.

5. Is there any financial aid available to international students? If yes, who is an ideal candidate for this?

We recognize that an MBA represents a significant investment in yourself and your future. Financial aid opportunities are open to all of our admitted students, including merit-based scholarships, as well as multiple loan options for international students without US cosigners. While the selection process is extremely competitive, all applicants are automatically considered for our merit-based scholarships when they apply. The committee takes into consideration the overall merit of the application factoring in academic performance, work experience, activities and involvement, leadership, and competitiveness within the applicant pool. All incoming students also receive detailed information about the loan application process and various possibilities with lenders.

6. *What are some of the common mistakes you see frequently on applications?*

It would be a missed opportunity if candidates neglect to use the application process to show us their authentic selves and underlying passion behind what drives them, as well as their understanding of Chicago Booth's values and how the environment can propel them forward. They should start thinking now about how they will take advantage of our choice-rich environment to maximize their two years.

Also, choose recommenders based on their unique knowledge of you and your capabilities. Your recommenders should be able to tell us about who you are, the type of impact you've had, and how you interact within your professional life. We ask that at least one recommender be your direct supervisor because they can usually best speak to your abilities in terms of teamwork, leadership potential, problem solving, initiative, etc. Pick people who truly know you and can share that perspective over someone with a prominent title who may gloss over the details that we are hoping to glean from your letters of recommendation.

7. *Your final word of advice for students.*

Preparing an MBA application is really a multi-layered process and can take time and organization to compile, so it's important to start early and give yourself plenty of time to get to know the school community and culture.

Talking directly with Booth alumni, students, and admissions staff offers a perspective that can help connect the dots for your own MBA ambitions. There are many opportunities to engage with the Booth community, including virtual events, such as online live chats and webinars, as well as our "Connect with a Student" tool, which is available on our website and helps potential applicants connect directly with current students representing diverse backgrounds and interests. We also host information sessions, participate in fairs, and have student-hosted events and alumni-hosted pop-ups in locations around the world. Investing time to uncover what makes Booth special will not only help you define your own unique path, but it will prepare you for talking about it in your application.

Babson FW Olin Graduate School of Business, Babson College

Name: Colleen Hynes
Function/Role: Director, Graduate Admission

1. Students want to earn an MBA for multiple reasons. What do you consider to be strong reasons for doing an MBA? Why should one get an MBA?

When students have worked for a few years and are beginning to see that managerial, strategic or quantitative skills gap are impacting their ability to move forward in their careers, an MBA can help to close these skills gaps and prepare them for higher level management and strategy execution at work.

2. What are some of the key features/highlights of your MBA program that make it unique?

Babson is the #1 MBA for Entrepreneurship, and students learn a "make-it-happen" mindset that helps them to drive creativity and innovation in organizations of all kinds. Babson is launching a re-imagined MBA in 2019, where two-thirds of the curriculum is electives, providing our students the opportunity to tailor their classes to their interests and careers.

3. *What defines a strong candidate for your school? What do you look for when admitting students?*

Students who are innovative and collaborative will likely thrive at Babson. We review applications holistically, and while test scores and transcripts are of course important, essays, interview and recommendation letters are closely viewed as they help us to better understand your collaborative spirit and drive towards innovation and creativity.

4. *How do you help international students chalk their career paths?*

Babson's Graduate Center for Career Development begins working with students even before Day 1, and students will benefit from experiential learning within the program through Consulting opportunities, available Graduate Assistantships,, study abroad opportunities, and specialized electives.

5. *Is there any financial aid available to international students? If yes, who is an ideal candidate for this?*

Yes. All candidates' applications for admission are reviewed automatically for scholarships, and full tuition scholarships are available.

6. *What are some of the common mistakes you see frequently on applications?*

Sometimes, students try to use one essay for multiple schools, but it's always evident. Babson's essay is less than 500 words, so take the time to specifically answer that question fully, as it well not only help the admissions committee to learn more about you but will also help you to articulate why Babson's focus on innovation is ideal for your MBA studies.

7. Your final word of advice for students.

Apply whenever your application is ready, even if that means Round 3 for an earlier program instead of Round 1 the following year. The sooner you can get started on your MBA, the better!

Johns Hopkins University
Carey Business School

Name: Michael Cuneo
Designation: Assistant Director of Admissions
Function/Role: International Recruiting & Admissions, Full-Time MBA

1. Students want to earn an MBA for multiple reasons. What do you consider to be strong reasons for doing an MBA? Why should one get an MBA?

Taking one's current career to the next level or making a major industry change in your career path are the two best reasons for pursuing an MBA.

2. What are some of the key features/highlights of your MBA program that make it unique?

Experiential learning; small cohorts and class sizes; Johns Hopkins alumni and professional networks which span business healthcare, engineering, international studies, public health, education, development, and other major industries and organizations around the world. Of course being part of the Johns Hopkins University, we are part of one of the world's top players in education and research in those areas.

3. What defines a strong candidate for your school? What do you look for when admitting students?

We look for students with strong backgrounds and proven abilities in in areas such as leadership, taking initiative, work on organization-critical projects, taking risk,

4. How do you help international students chalk their career paths?

We have an excellent Career Development Ofice which partners with students start with working with their Career Coach before arriving on campus. The CDO experience focus on personal development, networking, and the all-important internship and job search.

Successful MBA students will be as busy with CDO activities outside the classroom as they are with MBA classwork and experiential learning activities. This will launch them in the next step in their career post-MBA and beyond.

5. Is there any financial aid available to international students? If yes, who is an ideal candidate for this?

We offer merit-based scholarships which are based on work experience, GMAT (or GRE) scores, and grade point average in other degree programs. Scholarships range from $10,000 to full tuition (for a few, truly exceptional candidates).

6. What are some of the common mistakes you see frequently on applications?

Trying to fit a Statement of Purpose into our essay topics rather than focusing on the essay topic. Applying "blindly" to our MBA program; you should be working with your admissions oficer every step of the way.

7. *Your final word of advice for students.*

Please be in touch with me as much as possible every step of the way. I am here to help and happy to help.

ESADE Business School

Name: Sara Argudo Valero
Function/Role: Recruitment & Admissions Associate Director

1. *Students want to earn an MBA for multiple reasons. What do you consider to be strong reasons for doing an MBA? Why should one get an MBA?*

There are many reasons, for example: career shift, go a step up in their careers, learn leadership and management skills, shift location, get a strong network, get more international exposure.

2. *What are some of the key features/highlights of your MBA program that make it unique?*

Practical education, flexibility in terms of length (12, 15 or 18 months), program relevance in the job environment, customizable program to the needs of students, diversity and internationality, smaller class than other schools, more personalized service from professors and career services. Strong focus on entrepreneurship and social responsible projects.

3. *What defines a strong candidate for your school? What do you look for when admitting students?*

We look at applications using a holistic approach. This means that we will take every part of the application into consideration. We look at their work experience, how they progressed during their careers.

We also consider their academics, GMAT score, reference letters, soft skills during their interview, extracurricular and leadership activities.

4. How do you help international students chalk their career paths?

We have a strong career team that guides and helps students through their MBA. Students have one to one sessions with a career specialist, career networking events, career fairs, events organized by different professional clubs, career treks, alumni support. etc. Apart from that we have on campus a hub of 60 startups called Creapolis and an incubator for people interested in starting their own companies.

5. Is there any financial aid available to international students? If yes, who is an ideal candidate for this?

Yes, we offer scholarships based on merit and scholarships based on need. All candidates are welcome to apply. In case of the merit scholarships, we look for students with strong academic record, good progression in their careers, strong GMAT results, good soft skills, leadership activities, extracurricular activities, etc.

6. What are some of the common mistakes you see frequently on applications?

Poorly written essays, short reference letters, missing important information in their application and CV, no explanation regarding gaps in their work experience.

7. Your final word of advice for students.

A MBA is a life changing experience. I recommend you to take your time and do a good research of the school/s you are interested in. Go beyond the information you find on the Website and talk to people that have studied or are currently studying the MBA. Talk to alumni and current students to get a better feel about the experience and the school. Attend information sessions if possible and meet the admissions team. At ESADE we organize information sessions worldwide, you can check them on our website.

IESE Business School

Name: Pascal Michels

Function/Role: Director of MBA Admissions

1. Students want to earn an MBA for multiple reasons. What do you consider to be strong reasons for doing an MBA? Why should one get an MBA?

At the heart of most students' motivation to do an MBA lies a desire for change. That change can be vertical (career acceleration), horizontal (carrer change) and personal. The majority of applicants also look for a geographical change, be it for the duration of the program or including beyond. The financial gains post-graduation are generally considerable, but most graduates will tell you that a few years down the road, what really stick is the personal transformation.

2. What are some of the key features/highlights of your MBA program that make it unique?

Our full-time MBA program is flexible in length (19 months vs. 15 months) and focused on the case method of teaching with a general management view of the organization. What is unique about our program is the high workload (three cases per day during the first year) and the camaraderie it generates among the class. Beyond friendship, the feeling is one of the community becoming your family. A lot of schools boast about diversity and for sure there are a lot of very diverse programs out there. Because of our program being so general management focused, we attract a class that is diverse not only in nationalities and backgrounds, but also in aspirations. This is definitely a highlight and lies at the heart of all we do.

3. What defines a strong candidate for your school? What do you look for when admitting students?

Our admissions process is very centered on fit with the school. Because we do neither split admissions from recruitment, nor outsource interviewing to our alumni, it means that candidates will be interacting with members of the admissions committee from day one.

Because all of my team have themselves graduated from IESE, we essentially deal with the fit question in terms of asking ourselves "would we have glad to have the candidate in our team/section/class", more crucially "would we have learned from her?" Think of it as the ultimate airport test. On a more tangible level, we take a close look at academic risk ("Can the candidate deal with the high workload?"), which is where GMAT and transcripts come in, and the career potential of the candidate (see below).

4. How do you help international students chalk their career paths?

Candidates are asked about their post-graduation plans as part of the application. We are very aware of the fact that candidates are very likely to change their minds, but this essay serves the aim of getting a sample of how a candidate thinks about their career. Once on campus, candidates have access to a world of resources, including our heavily staffed and world-class career services team. The expectation clearly is of MBA students owning their job search, but the quantity and quality of support is unparalleled. IESE is one of the very few schools that get targeted by the most prestigious on-campus recruiters and this is complemented by a strong career management offering, teaching you not only how to get a job, but how to manage your career during your lifetime.

5. Is there any financial aid available to international students? If yes, who is an ideal candidate for this?

We offer around a hundred scholarships every year. These are all merit based and can cover up to half of tuition. Now, competition for scholarships is fierce so there is no guarantee.

But overall, we see candidates with rare backgrounds and stellar test scores securing them. As a thumb rule, a GMAT above 700 tends to a long way, but of course overall application quality, interview and assessment performance are main drivers in the award decision.

6. What are some of the common mistakes you see frequently on applications?

The biggest and most common shortcoming of often otherwise strong candidates lies in their inability tell a story. Candidates are obsessed with polishing the details of their application (spotless CVs, high test scores, powerful recommenders) and yet not very articulate when it comes to telling who they are, where they come from and where they want to go. Few people spend enough thinking about why they want an MBA. Fewer yet can clearly articulate why that school should be IESE.

7. Your final word of advice for students.

Ask the hard questions during the application process. Don't get blinded by fancy brochures, wishy washy value statements or unrealistic employment statistics. Understand who you are to a school, but also what the school needs to be to you. Look for the click. If you don't click with the school, then you are probably about to spend a lot of money on something that you don't really want or need. There are many ways to further your education, many ways to transform. Gain a deep understanding of what the schools you consider will give you, and be very clear at articulating what you will give them. Because, of course, the click needs to be mutual.

SDA Bocconi School of Management

Name: Tyler Henderson
Designation: Recruitment & Admissions Team
Function/Role: Recruitment

1. *Students want to earn an MBA for multiple reasons. What do you consider to be strong reasons for doing an MBA? Why should one get an MBA?*

There are many valid and strong reasons to do an MBA and this is unique for each individual. However, at a macro level the reason to do an MBA is to provide potential opportunities that would not exist without an MBA. This could be a industry, function or geographic change but it could also be more grounded in personal development and transformation.

2. *What are some of the key features/highlights of your MBA program that make it unique?*

Of course, some of our key features are logistical such as a one-year program that involves an internship, a small program size (just about 100 students), an extremely diverse class of students, unique areas for concentration, and many more. However, many of our highlights are more esoteric and involve the special atmosphere and culture of SDA Bocconi and Milano. We are truly doing unique work at SDA Bocconi, and when coupling that with the art, culture, food & wine and business center of Milano, there is truly no other MBA like SDA Bocconi in the world.

3. *What defines a strong candidate for your school? What do you look for when admitting students?*

Assuming a candidate is intelligent and motivated with a strong professional and academic background, what is important to us is global proficiency. This involves international experiences where applicants have lived, worked and studied, international projects conducted and languages spoken. Our program attracts a diverse audience of applicants from all over the world who are looking for opportunities after the program throughout the world so we want to see that applicants thrive in diverse situations.

4. *How do you help international students chalk their career paths?*

We invest heavily in Career Services as this is an expectation of students and the market for elite MBA programs. Career Services staff work hard on a 360 degree program for students that not only involves assistance with internship and full-time recruitment and placement but also the more nuanced aspects of career building and development through career counselling and coaching.

5. *Is there any financial aid available to international students? If yes, who is an ideal candidate for this?*

We have a robust program for scholarships and tuition waivers. Of course, this type of financial aid is competitive and are awarded to applicants who stand out in all aspects of the application process (strong interview, recommendations, professional background, academic background and GMAT/GRE result).

6. *What are some of the common mistakes you see frequently on applications?*

Applicants can fall into a trap where they believe the school has all the power in the application and try to accommodate what they expect SDA Bocconi wants to see from an applicant instead of just being themselves. We ask that applicants being fully honest and candid in their application (and we will do the same) so that we can be confident that the applicant is a strong fit for us and vice versa. If honesty is not grounded in the process, then an applicant cannot possibly know if they are making the right decision about joining our program and we try to avoid this scenario altogether.

7. *Your final word of advice for students.*

Be yourself, let your personality and motivation shine through and remember that this is an exciting time of life that does not need to be stressful or anxiety provoking. If you find yourself struggling to enunciate why you want to do an MBA, then it probably is not the moment to do an MBA. If an MBA is the right fit for you, then the reasons why you want to do it will be so obvious that the application process will become exciting and full of possibilities.

Yale School of Management

Name: Bruce DelMonico
Designation: Assistant Dean for Admissions
Function/Role: Admissions/Head of Department

1. Students want to earn an MBA for multiple reasons. What do you consider to be strong reasons for doing an MBA? Why should one get an MBA?

As noted, students get an MBA for multiple reasons. In fact, that's one of the main benefits of an MBA as I see it—it is an incredibly flexible degree that will empower you to do a wide range of things professionally. In some industries, an MBA is necessary to progress in your career beyond a certain point. But even in industries where that is not the case, an MBA will give you the tools you will need—both hard and soft skills—to have the kind of impact you want to have. And these skills are relevant across all sectors and industries, so an MBA really does open the door for you to have the kind of career that is meaningful to you, including the flexibility to move across industries and sectors as your career progresses, which is incredibly powerful.

2. What are some of the key features/highlights of your MBA program that make it unique?

We have a very mission-based MBA program. Our founding mission of educating leaders for business and society is very broad and multi-sector, meaning that we aspire for our graduates to have impact not just in the private sector but in the nonprofit and public sectors as well. In support of this mission, we have three main objectives that distinguish us from other top business schools: 1) to be the most integrated business school with our home university (for example, when you come to Yale SOM you can take as many courses as you want throughout Yale University and they will count towards your MBA), 2) to be the most global US business school (we were the first top school to have a required international component to our curriculum, and our distinctive Global Network for Advanced Management is unique among top US business schools) and 3) to be the best source of elevated leaders across all regions and sectors (our unique integrated curriculum teaches business concepts according to organizational perspectives instead of function, giving our students a much broader and more holistic education than other schools). Overall, we feel that a Yale SOM education uniquely positions our graduates to face today's management challenges and to be leaders for the 21st century.

3. What defines a strong candidate for your school? What do you look for when admitting students?

To some degree, we look for many of the same things our peers do: candidates who have been successful academically and professionally as indicators of future success in our classroom and beyond. In addition to these qualities, we also look for students who are broadminded and intellectually curious, since our academic environment requires interdisciplinary collaborative and collegial, since that is a hallmark of our community and culture; and optimistic (they want to have a positive impact on the world), since that is the guiding principle of our mission. We are also a diverse community, so an openness to interact with and learn from people who are different than you is also an important aspect of what we look for.

4. How do you help international students chalk their career paths?

At Yale SOM, we have a full-service Career Development Office (CDO) that works to prepare all students for their job search and then helps connect them with organizations with which they would like to work.

Most of our graduates (about 85 percent) work in the US immediately after graduation, but we also have dedicated CDO resources to help source opportunities for graduates outside the US, for those who are interested. We also have a Yale-wide Office of International Students and Scholars, which works with students from outside the United States to help them navigate their lives and studies in the States.

5. *Is there any financial aid available to international students? If yes, who is an ideal candidate for this?*

Yes, we have financial aid available to all students, both domestic and international. In fact, this past year we announced new scholarships specifically for students from India. We automatically consider all applicants for scholarships; there is no need to submit a separate application. In doing so, we look at all the same things we look at in evaluating candidates for admission. And for those international students who do not receive a scholarship (and even for those who do), we have loan products for international students that do not require a US cosigner, have competitive interest rates and do not accrue interest while you're in school. So there are lots of options in helping you finance your MBA, which can be a major financial investment.

6. *What are some of the common mistakes you see frequently on applications?*

Perhaps the biggest mistake is telling us what you think we want to hear instead of what's important to you. I think there's the belief that you need to be "different" to be successful in the application process, and that especially if you think you have an academic or professional profile that's similar to other candidates being different in some other way (such as activities or career interests) will make a difference. But being true to yourself is always more compelling than trying to guess what others want to hear, and we are very much guided by how well you've excelled in your work and studies regardless of the field rather than trying to achieve some forced diversity for its own sake. So that is one of the biggest mistakes candidates make. In addition, they will often ignore their weaknesses in their application because they think it makes them look less good as an applicant. But we know that no one is perfect and that people seek an MBA to improve themselves, so acknowledging weaknesses in the application can be helpful and can show a degree of self-awareness and humility that actually can help your application.

7. *Your final word of advice for students.*

My main piece of advice is to try not to get stressed out about the application process. It's high-stakes, to be sure, but don't overthink it. Keep it simple and be true to yourself. I think a lot of people want to over-analyze how we make decisions and what we're looking for, but it's not as complicated as a lot of people make it out to be. So take the process seriously and do a good job, but don't get so caught up in the process that it becomes counterproductive. You'll do fine! There's a program out there for everyone, and now is actually a great time to be thinking about an MBA. Good luck!

Georgetown University
McDonough School of Business

Name: 'Iolani Bullock
Designation: Director, MBA Admissions

1. Students want to earn an MBA for multiple reasons. What do you consider to be strong reasons for doing an MBA? Why should one get an MBA?

An MBA is not just for those in finance and consulting. Georgetown MBA alumni also work in technology, real estate, healthcare, hospitality, government and policy, nonprofits, international development, energy, education, military, manufacturing, transportation, media, entertainment and sports. A specialized master's degree is likely to offer a more narrow skill set, while an MBA provides you with a broad range of skills that will prepare you for any industry or job function. No matter the industry or function which you pursue, you'll likely need skills to manage a budget; manage a team; sell a product, service, or idea; understand your broader economy or industry; and develop innovative ideas. Additionally, an MBA experience is just that, an experience. Unlike other graduate degrees where you might take classes and go home, in an MBA program you are expected to get involved outside of the classroom to improve your leadership ability.

Applicants typically fall into three categories—career enhancers, career switchers (function or industry), or aspiring entrepreneurs who either want to launch a startup or who seek employment at an existing startup, with an angel investor, or at a venture capital firm.

Additionally, the skills gained through the Georgetown MBA leadership curriculum, from teamwork to managing diverse teams, prepares students to make an impact when they enter the workforce.

2. *What are some of the key features/highlights of your MBA program that make it unique?*

Georgetown McDonough prepares students to become globally minded, principled leaders ready to address the most significant challenges and opportunities facing business and society. To support this mission, Georgetown's MBA program has a number of unique features and initiatives:

Executive Challenge: This experiential learning opportunity is a day-long simulation of real world executive presentations and board meetings and serves as the final exam for the Leadership Communications core course. The entire first-year MBA class works in teams to role play three cases with more than 100 executive-level alumni who return to campus from around the world for this experience.

Global Business Experience: In this required capstone course, student teams partner with executives from multinational organizations like Citi, L'Oreal, and Lamborghini to consult on complex business challenges facing these organizations. The students begin their work remotely, but also travel to the company's country to finalize their research and review preliminary findings before delivering a final presentation to the company leadership. Topic areas can include, but are not limited to, market entry, finance, supply chain, e-commerce, marketing, real estate or entrepreneurship. Each year the locations change but past locations have included Abu-Dhabi, Accra, Berlin, Cape Town, Hong Kong, Madrid, Mumbai, São Paulo, Lima, Shanghai and Tel Aviv.

International Festival: Washington, D.C., is one of the most global cities in the world, and our classes reflect that diversity. As an MBA program, one of the ways we celebrate our global diversity by hosting an annual International Festival led by students. Out MBAs share their food, music, dance and culture with the entire student body. This is one of the most popular events of the year.

Intensive Learning Experiences (ILEs): These elective courses are taught in a span of one to two weeks and require a project deliverable. Many of these courses are taught by practitioners working at local area multinational companies or from Georgetown professors from other disciplines within the university. Examples of ILEs include Data Visualization; Mobile Apps; The Business of Water; The Startup Factory; Mad Men is Just Part of It: Advertising Campaign Development from Start to Finish; Social Entrepreneurship; and Energy Policy in the Age of Climate Change.

Hands-on Learning Experiences: Students can gain academic credit for completing a project for an organization like The World Bank/IFC or Nestle. Last fall, Georgetown McDonough added a consulting project to the Managing the Enterprise course, where students consulted on management and human resources issues for the Washington Metropolitan Area Transit Authority. Additionally, some classes have built in projects with local entities like our Design Thinking class, which completed a project with the embassy of the Netherlands.

Access to Employers: Washington, D.C., is home to numerous national and international headquarters for businesses, nonprofits, and multilaterals, making it easy for employers to visit campus. Most recently, Amazon announced its HQ2 location in the D.C. metro area, and Nestle recently moved their headquarters here. Additionally, the MBA Career Center partners with many of our student clubs to organize national and international career treks to places like New York, San Francisco, London, Colombia, Israel, Mexico and Tanzania.

Service: Georgetown is the oldest Catholic, Jesuit university in the United States and was founded with a strong ethos of "women and men for others." Throughout the Georgetown MBA experience, students have the opportunity to become Community Fellows if they volunteer over 100 service hours during the program (the Class of 2018 volunteered 4,700 hours collectively).

3. *What defines a strong candidate for your school? What do you look for when admitting students?*

We want critical thinkers with an executive presence who are driven, motivated and professionally accomplished individuals. We want people with a global mindset, grit and determination; people who are committed to a rigorous and transformational program and have a generosity of spirit. We seek both diversity in terms of who will be in our class as well as where they will go after they complete their MBA.

4. *How do you help international students chalk their career paths?*

Our career support is designed to benefit our domestic and international students and tailored to meet their individual needs. Our career support is structured around three key areas: the summer start, career coaching, and industry/function alignment.

Summer Start: Our Career Development Curriculum and summer career onboarding program are outstanding. Starting in June the summer before they arrive, students participate in our Summer Webinar Series and produce a career portfolio. This includes an accomplishments record, value strategy, career inventory, résumé, cover letter, networking strategy, target company list, and interview prep. At the end of the summer, incoming students will have a McDonough-approved résumé in hand and ready for the MBA journey.

Coaching: Our team of certified career management coaches have deep industry experience and work one-on-one with each student to help them achieve their career goals. Together our students partner with a coach to work through the Personalized Job Search Framework: career portfolio, industry/function/geographic target(s), target company list, and networking tools.

Industry/Function Alignment: Our model is aligned by industry and function. Practice leaders and coaches manage relationships with students, employers, and alumni for the spaces they represent. Students can expect to have alignment across the McDonough career experiences.

5. Is there any financial aid available to international students? If yes, who is an ideal candidate for this?

All applicants to the McDonough School of Business are automatically considered for merit-based scholarships and do not need to submit any additional materials to be considered. Additionally, we have a scholarship reconsideration process to reconsider admitted students who may not have received scholarships initially. Finally, we provide a list of external scholarships and private lenders to all admitted international students.

6. What are some of the common mistakes you see frequently on applications?

A few mistakes that I've seen over the years:

Including names for other universities in essays. We know you're likely applying to other universities to maximize your chance of success, but it looks sloppy if you include a wrong name and it makes it seem like Georgetown isn't your number one choice.

Answering the first "tell me about yourself" question with a very long response. It should be no more than two minutes. In general, answering with a response longer than two-three minutes is not ideal.

7. Your final word of advice for students.

Do as much as you can to connect with the community. Watch webinars, connect with alumni, go to recruiting events when we come to your city, read blogs, and talk with current students. The more research you do about a school and its culture, the more likely it will be that you can then make an informed decision. This is a mutual decision for both the MBA Admissions committee and you to choose your next family. Washington, D.C., and Georgetown are very inclusive communities for international students and we welcome you to get to know us better.

The University of Texas at Austin, McCombs School of Business

Name: Rodrigo Malta

Designation: Managing Director, MBA Recruitment and Admissions

1. Students want to earn an MBA for multiple reasons. What do you consider to be strong reasons for doing an MBA? Why should one get an MBA?

On a macro-level, the biggest, most pressing issues that humanity faces like food security and climate change will require individuals who can work cross-functionally and take on leadership roles. By attending the Texas McCombs MBA program, you will get both the technical skills and leadership skills to be successful in our ever changing world. You will be able to manage teams of individuals who come from various backgrounds and who have diverse expertise. By attending our program, you will have a transformative experience.

You will be able to pivot into your dream career, company, or geographic location. Our MBA will unlock your full potential to take your career to the next level.

2. What are some of the key features/highlights of your MBA program that make it unique?

The Texas McCombs MBA program has many unique characteristics. I will highlight three:

Location: No other top business school is located in Austin. We are the source for talent for the city and our business school is located in the central business district. Austin is an extremely vibrant city with businesses moving here every day and it is also a great place to live.

Experiential learning: We give our students the ability to get hands-on experience both inside and outside the classroom. Our MBA+ projects are micro-consulting projects where our students work for a company like Deloitte or Microsoft on a problem the company is currently facing. Our Fellows Programs also allow our students to go very deep into a particular discipline. To name two—we have Venture Fellows where our students work for a Venture Capital Firm in Austin. We have Texas Venture Labs where our students work directly with startups. There are many more as well.

Flexible curriculum: We want our students to customize their experience so we limit required classes to basically the first semester. After this, students can choose from a plethora of electives and even take classes outside of McCombs.

3. What defines a strong candidate for your school? What do you look for when admitting students?

When reviewing an application, the admissions committee takes several factors into account. The McCombs Admissions team will evaluate each application holistically. The main parts evaluated are (in no particular order):

- Work experience—which includes your résumé and your professional references
- Extracurricular activities
- Education and academics—which includes your GMAT/GPA
- Essay responses
- Your interview (by invitation only)

There are no fixed criteria or weighted portions of the application. Each aspect of your application should reflect what you will contribute to and learn from the McCombs MBA program. Stronger candidates are those who are able to portray (both in the written application and in the interview) why they want an MBA, and particularly why Texas McCombs is their preferred school. We also look at a candidate's leadership potential, ability to work and collaborate with others, and their willingness to contribute positively to the Texas McCombs community.

4. How do you help international students chalk their career paths?

The career conversation typically starts in early August with a required career management workshop for new International MBA students. We have a team of dedicated career management advisors who will work with students as soon as they arrive on campus to prepare them for the competitive US job market. In addition, during the first semester, all MBA students take a Strategic Career Planning course, where they work on their résumé, networking and interviewing skills, elevator pitch, and discuss their desired career path.

Career management advisors are available every step of the way for one-on-one appointments. In addition to the advisors, we also hire students during their second year to serve as Career Fellows. These Career Fellows just lived the internship recruitment process and thus provide valuable information about the industry or function first years might be pursuing.

We also find that our international students benefit greatly from our communications coaches. These are professionals in the field of communication, and our students receive eight hours per semester of included communications coaching while they are enrolled. These coaches can help not only with things like interview skills or personal brand development, but can also work with international students to overcome any cultural differences that arise during the US job search process.

5. *Is there any financial aid available to international students? If yes, who is an ideal candidate for this?*

We understand that earning an MBA is an big investment in your future. To make your MBA more attainable, we provide merit-based recruiting scholarship to candidates.

Awards range from $5,000 to full tuition and are distributed to applicants who have demonstrated a superior record of academic merit and professional accomplishments. No separate application is necessary, since every applicant is automatically considered for recruiting scholarship during the admissions review process.

Each year, an average of 45 percent of admitted students have received financial assistance.

6. *What are some of the common mistakes you see frequently on applications?*

No matter how many times people review elements of an application, there are always a few mistakes that creep in. Here are a few questions to consider that may help you avoid a mistake in your application:

- Did I spell the name of the business school correctly? (Similarly: Am I pronouncing it correctly?)
- Did I make sure that the business school name listed in my essay is in fact the business school I'm applying to?
- Does my essay answer the prompt?
- For my video essay, did I stay within the time limit?
- Does my essay include research about the school?
- Are my MBA goals clear and to the point?
- Is my résumé one page with revealing details about my leadership, impact and contributions?

7. *Your final word of advice for students.*

Be yourself. Ensuring you put forth your story in an authentic way differentiates you from other applicants and improves your chances of admission!

The University of Michigan
Stephen M Ross School of Business

Name: Meredith Hartmann
Designation: Associate Director of Full-Time MBA Admissions
Function/Role: Admissions committee member and recruiter for the Indian Subcontinent

1. *Students want to earn an MBA for multiple reasons. What do you consider to be strong reasons for doing an MBA? Why should one get an MBA?*

We see most candidates wanting to get an MBA to make a career pivot—they've been following a certain career path and come to a point when they're ready to make a change. An MBA is an excellent choice in this scenario because it is in an extremely versatile degree wherein you develop the skills, experiences, and network you need to work in a new field.

Even if a candidate doesn't want to switch careers, the management and leadership skills one hones during an MBA program will be useful in today's ever-changing career landscape. The MBA is a clear signal that the individual is skilled, adaptable, and knowledgeable across industries.

Further, an MBA will enhance a candidate's network in tremendous ways. While the program itself is a stepping stone to that first job after graduation, an MBA relies on her or his network for a lifetime. Access to a large, active, supportive alumni network is one of the greatest benefits of an MBA.

2. *What are some of the key features/highlights of your MBA program that make it unique?*

Three main things that make an MBA from Ross stand out. The first is our emphasis on experience-driven learning: if you learn best by doing, Ross is the place for you! Our premier experience is the multidisciplinary action project or MAP. For seven full weeks during the first year of your MBA experience, you tackle a real business challenge for a sponsor company. Projects span all geographic regions, functions, and industries, so it's a great way to explore something new or strengthen skills for an intended industry. The rest of the curriculum is built around the experiential learning model—there is no shortage of opportunities to get real, in-depth experience. Another feature that makes us stand out is what we like to say: "Go Blue, Go Anywhere". We say this because our graduates go everywhere, both in terms of geography and industry. About two-thirds of our graduates accepted positions in Chicago or one of the US coasts, and about 9 percent launched their careers internationally. We see our grads go into every industry as well—nearly 60 percent of graduates went into Tech and Consulting. We also place a significant number of graduates in Healthcare, Consumer Packaged Goods, and Finance. In short, whatever industry you aspire to, wherever you'd like to work, the Ross MBA can help get you there. Ross also features an extremely close-knit community. There is such a strong community culture here that students are eager to venture outside their comfort zones to learn something new or follow their passions knowing they have a great support network to back them up, whether they succeed or not. You don't see many sharp elbows at Ross—peer support is a hallmark of the Ross experience, from the classroom to recruiting. This holds true for after graduation as well—an MBA from Ross not only gives access to the Ross alumni network, but the wider University of Michigan network of 500,000+ alums all over the world.

3. What defines a strong candidate for your school? What do you look for when admitting students?

We are looking for similar things to other top MBA programs, the first being intellectual ability, as evidenced by a candidate's standardized test scores and undergraduate GPA. We also look closely at a candidate's professional and personal achievements. When looking to admit students, we want to know what you have accomplished in your current and past roles, and what kind of impact you have had. But that isn't all we want in a Ross MBA candidate. We have heard from top companies time and time again that interpersonal and communication abilities are some of the most desirable skills they look for in employees, and Ross is no different. We are looking for candidates who can communicate effectively with their peers and professional colleagues. Similarly, we are looking for candidates who have demonstrated ability to work in teams. The culture here at Ross is very team-focused, which mirrors conditions in the professional environment. If a candidate has robust team experience, that is an indicator she or he will thrive at Ross. Finally, a strong candidate will be able to demonstrate alignment with our mission and values, where business is the most powerful force for positive change. We are looking for candidates who want to have a positive impact on the world, who fit with our community-driven, pay-it-forward culture.

4. How do you help international students chalk their career paths?

Student career outcomes at Ross are outstanding, and this is no different for our international students! Our Career Development Office has a dedicated international career coach, and support and guidance starts before the student even arrives on campus.

Additionally, international students are helped every step of the way by their peers at Ross—from Functional Accountability Career

Team (FACT) Groups (recruitment interest groups led by successful MBA2s), to peer coaches, to Culture Shock—a student group designed to guide international students through the ups and downs of recruitment.

5. Is there any financial aid available to international students? If yes, who is an ideal candidate for this?

There is! At the time of application, all students are considered for merit scholarships, ranging from $10,000 to the Ross Fellowship (a full scholarship). We recently awarded the highest number of scholarship dollars in the history of Ross for the class of 2019 (up to 35 percent of international students had significant scholarships for this same class as well).

Our scholarships are offered on a merit basis with no extra work on the applicant's behalf required for consideration—all awards are based on your application. Further, we announce all scholarship decisions at the time of admission—you don't have to wait to hear your award.

6. What are some of the common mistakes you see frequently on applications?

Some of the most common mistakes are the easiest to correct—typos! Don't be afraid to have a friend take a look at your application before you hit 'submit'—a fresh set of eyes can make a huge difference.

7. Your final word of advice for students.

Be authentic! Some applicants try to figure out what admissions committees want to hear, rather than portraying themselves genuinely. We want to get to know who you are and what you will bring to the community, and you want to find the best school for you. Putting forth your most genuine self will help you get to where you're meant to be.

Duke University, The Fuqua School of Business

Name: Shari Hubert

Function/Role: Associate Dean of Admissions

1. Students want to earn an MBA for multiple reasons. What do you consider to be strong reasons for doing an MBA? Why should one get an MBA?

I think there is room for all types of degrees, and life-time learning opportunities, throughout the longevity of your career and life. Depending on your age and stage and how your priorities and options shift and evolve over time, you can leverage an MBA degree to continue to learn and build new skills, refresh current skills or pivot into a totally new direction. As your career evolves, you may find that you need a broader toolkit or want to advance beyond the individual contributor role or beyond your current employer. For international students, global mobility is definitely a great reason to pursue an MBA as it allows you to reset, while increasing your marketability and compensation potential all at the same time. Many who seek it want to apply their technical knowledge to organizational challenges, or develop as a manager or leader with greater scope of responsibility. An MBA helps you think critically about organizational issues and challenges, and is a universal credentialing that is well understood and valued by employers regardless of industry, sector, function or region of the world.

2. What are some of the key features/highlights of your MBA program that make it unique?

At Fuqua, we are extremely focused on making sure business education remains relevant. We will continue to listen to industry about the skills they need and adapt accordingly—such as in data analytics. Our programs in big data focus on not just finding key insights, but also applying them in a particular business and communicating their value.

We will also continue to adapt curriculum to focus on the current challenges facing our students as future business leaders—We have a very popular professor, Aaron Chatterji, who teaches a cool course called "CEO Activism." He's one of the few academics who has studied the effect on a company when a CEO speaks out and if CEOs actually have any influence on public opinion about issues. We also have a world-renowned scholar on diversity and inclusion, Ashely Rosette, who just launched a new course called Gender and Leadership.

We are developing more courses to focus on business as tool for building common purpose through triple threat leadership capabilities: IQ (Intelligence Quotient), EQ (Emotional Quotient) and DQ (decency quotient). More emphasis on having an entrepreneurial mindset, and equipping our students with managing in an era of fast technological change.

3. What defines a strong candidate for your school? What do you look for when admitting students?

Our students very much contribute and are accountable for their respective transformations from day 1. We look for applicants who really understand our culture, can see themselves thriving here and demonstrate that they have taken the genuine time to get to know us throughout the application process, and therefore really want to be part of our unique community. We intentionally seek to bring in a diverse student population—truly representative across experiences, backgrounds, cultures, beliefs, nationalities and various demographics—with the intention of broadening our collective perspective and facilitating more innovative thought and discussion.

Our students are driven to achieve but understand you go further as a team than alone, they persevere and have grit that makes them able to weather tough times, while still thriving and learning and contributing; they understand the power and confidence that comes from being humble and being open to learn from others; and they are genuinely happy to be part of our community.

4. *How do you help international students chalk their career paths?*

Our Career Management Center is a team of 30 professionals with industry and functional expertise who collaborate with students as well as potential employers. The CMC works with students to oversee all aspects of their job search. Your career management team includes: Career coaches with industry specialties, a coach who also works closely with international student programming and resourcing, a programming team that helps students master complex career search techniques, and other specialists who work across department lines—helping you identify synergies and career options you never considered.

There are seven Sector Directors who cover every industry our students are interested in going into. They work with students (for internships and full-time opportunities) and employers and make connections that increase our students' ability to access great job opportunities. There are 70+ Career Fellows, who are 2nd year students who mentor and coach 1st years to support them through their career journey as well.

Beyond career services, we have a global Fuqua network that is enriched through our infrastructure (regional teams, Global Executive MBA residencies, Global Academic Travel trips that takes Duke and Fuqua to other parts of the world.) The MBA experience both inside and outside the classroom exposes students to globally diverse perspectives on doing business and working in teams. Some of the Career Center's work is based on the Culture Map, which helps students more effectively understand how cultural differences impact international business. Our alumni career services includes coaching support regardless of location, and our job postings and events are also not exclusive to those in the US.

Finally, we have an International Office at Fuqua, as well as Duke Visa Services at the university level that help our students with OPT. We also are unique in that we have an attorney who is available to our students for questions beyond the norm about visas and can even work with companies to process the H-1B paperwork if the company does not already have an attorney. Finally, another competitive advantage our students have access to is our new MSTeM second major, which has become even more popular, with 31 percent of the class (up from 25 percent in the first year) completing the requirements. This additional credentialing coupled with obtaining a job that is STEM approved, enables our students the opportunity to graduate with 3 years of work authorization and increased chances at an H-1B.

5. Is there any financial aid available to international students? If yes, who is an ideal candidate for this?

Yes, all students who apply for admissions are automatically considered for merit-based scholarships, ranging from partial to full-tuition. If an applicant is awarded a scholarship, he or she will be notified in the admissions offer letter. To qualify for merit-based scholarships, we look at the same criteria for admissions—work experience, essays, recommendations, and academics/test scores. There is no formula and it really depends on the holistic achievements of the individual relative to the strength of the applicant pool, so will vary each year.

We also have competitive financial aid options for our students. We offer both cosigner and non-cosigner loans for international students from a recommended list of lenders.

Students who qualify for non-cosigner loans, can borrow up to 90 percent of the cost of attendance (minus other aid; scholarships, sponsorships or other loans). We also post on our website a list of external funding sources that students may want to look through as well on their own.

6. *What are some of the common mistakes you see frequently on applications?*

Avoid being trite and superficial in completing your essays, and I would also focus less on your professional accomplishments in the 25 Random Facts essay, as we can read those through your résumé or another part of the application form. Some people have a difficult time getting to 25 we know, but we recommend including context around how does that fact drive your ability to be a better, different, or a more unique Fuqua MBA. We want the insights behind the random facts, but also how they shape who you are today. It is also okay to infuse humor in your facts. Talk to your friends and family to get ideas of what might be appropriate or interesting to share, as these individuals tend to really know you—the good, bad and ugly.

We are genuinely interested in going beyond just test scores or any single data point—and as such we take our essays and the interviews very seriously. We are looking for people who share our belief that business can change the world for the better and possess the humility and leadership skills to bring out the best in others. That match all starts with sincerity and authenticity.

Don't be afraid to be somewhat vulnerable in your essays as those are always most interesting.

Treat everyone in the process with respect; use good judgement and be self-aware of when you are coming on too strong or over communicating.

7. *Your final word of advice for students.*

Enjoy the self-reflection that is part of the overall process of applying to business schools. Have humility throughout the process. Don't rely solely on your test scores or spend countless hours retaking the GMAT/ GRE at the expense of focusing on true and authentic engagement with the school. Remember to treat everyone in the process, no matter at what point in the process, with dignity and respect.

The Hong Kong University of Science and Technology

Name: Towni Lao

Function/Role: Assistant Director, Marketing and Admissions

1. Students want to earn an MBA for multiple reasons. What do you consider to be strong reasons for doing an MBA? Why should one get an MBA?

Technological breakthroughs are reshaping the way we do business. Even top consulting firms like McKinsey, BCG and Bain are struggling to get talents who can bridge technology and business. Therefore, it is important for you to get an MBA that equips you with the digital competencies, leadership prowess and business acumen required to survive in tomorrow's workplace.

2. What are some of the key features/highlights of your MBA program that make it unique?

Global Reputation: Ranked in the world's top 20 for 10 consecutive years by Financial Times, HKUST MBA is widely regarded as a top business school in Asia and our worldwide recognition speaks for the quality of our students and education.

International Experience: You will study with a diverse group of talented individuals who represent over 90 percent non-locals and more than 20 nationalities. Our global exchange program allows you to spend a whole semester at one of our 60 school partners, such as Columbia, LBS, NYU, Berkeley, Chicago, Cornell, etc.

Asia Focus: Our strategic location and regional business expertise will give you an indisputable edge to succeed in the region. We offer Asia-focused courses and career treks where you can explore real-world challenges faced by business leaders. With Hong Kong's open work visa policy and our strong recruiter connections, it will be easy for you to find the desired opportunities after the MBA.

Business meets Technology: You can choose from over 70 courses in six career tracks, including Finance, Consulting, Management, Marketing, Entrepreneurship and Business Tech and Analytics, the last of which features new courses on the business application of disruptive technologies like AI, Blockchain, Big Data, Fintech and Machine Learning.

3. What defines a strong candidate for your school? What do you look for when admitting students?

HKUST MBA, we aim to bring together a diverse group of students who will benefit from and at the same time able to contribute to our community. Given the selectivity of our program and the emphasis on case studies and teamwork, we are looking for candidates with an open mindset and leadership potential to succeed in our cross-cultural and functional setting.

On the other hand, it is equally important that what we offer matches with your own needs and objectives. For example, if a candidate is interested in developing his career in Asia or appreciates the importance of technological innovations in business, we will consider that candidate to be well suited for our program given our school's strengths.

4. How do you help international students chalk their career paths?

Our Career and Professional Development Office works in partnership with our students to realize their career aspirations. As soon as you join HKUST, you will be assigned a career coach who will help you formulate an ideal career strategy, share professional advice and insights on your target job market, and introduce relevant career opportunities to you throughout the program.

A variety of career events like recruitment talks, the MBA Career Fair and overseas career treks are also organized throughout the year. We also arrange many career-related workshops like Professional Networking Skills and Case Interview Practice for Consulting Careers so as to enhance our students' professional capabilities.

5. *Is there any financial aid available to international students? If yes, who is an ideal candidate for this?*

We offer Merit Scholarships ranging from 10 to 50 percent of the tuition fee to top students admitted into our full-time program. The ideal candidate for our scholarships should be well-rounded, and is able to demonstrate strength in their academic background, professional achievements, leadership potential, interview performance, etc.

6. *What are some of the common mistakes you see frequently on applications?*

We understand that some candidates might need more time to prepare for their GMAT test score—however, it would be ideal if everything is ready when the admissions committee review your application as first impression matters and you can present your entire profile to the school and show that you are well prepared.

Also, we sometimes see very generic answers to essay questions on career goals and reasons for doing an MBA. To differentiate your application from others, you should be as specific as possible and conduct more in-depth research on your target school and job field.

7. *Your final word of advice for students.*

Getting an MBA is a life-changing investment, which is why it is important to maximize the value of the time and effort you put in. At HKUST MBA, you will finish your study and join the workforce again in just 12 or 16 months. With the relatively intensive schedule and workload, it would be best if you already have clear goals on what you want to get from the program so that as soon as you start the MBA, you can focus your time and energy on courses, networking activities and career opportunities that matter the most to you.

During the MBA, you will meet a lot of different people from various industries and companies, which may open new doors for you and change your mind about what you want to do in the future. It is good to be flexible and keep an open mindset to maximize your opportunities.

Rotman School of Management
University of Toronto

Name: Imran Kanga
Designation: Director, Recruitment & Admissions, FT MBA
Function/Role: Recruitment and Admissions

1. Students want to earn an MBA for multiple reasons. What do you consider to be strong reasons for doing an MBA? Why should one get an MBA?

The two most common reasons for students looking to do an MBA is to switch their industry and/or function, and career progression into senior management within the same industry they are working in currently.

2. What are some of the key features/highlights of your MBA program that make it unique?

Rotman's focus on research and collaboration with the government and emerging industries make it a truly unique proposition for students. We have research institutes in areas like behavioral economics, corporate governance and strategy, diversity and inclusion, gender equality to name a few. We are also investing heavily in Fintech, AI and machine learning so that students in our program will be able to master these emerging trends and lead organizations through the changes and complexities these emerging technologies will bring in the near future.

3. *What defines a strong candidate for your school? What do you look for when admitting students?*

It might be a bit cliche but we are really looking for intellectually curious, passionate and well-rounded students. We see our students as change agents in our communities and in business locally and globally, so we look for students that have demonstrated strong academic ability, leadership potential and community involvement

4. *How do you help international students chalk their career paths?*

Throughout the two years students will go through a rigourous career focused roadmap which will include industry advising, individual career coaching, alumni mentorship, leadership development and self-development to help them with getting internships and full-time job opportunities in Canada.

5. *Is there any financial aid available to international students? If yes, who is an ideal candidate for this?*

Yes there are merit scholarships available to strong applicants. The average scholarship amount is around $25,000.

6. *What are some of the common mistakes you see frequently on applications?*

Students misrepresenting themselves and students not representing their best selves in the application due to lack of preparation.

7. *Your final word of advice for students.*

An MBA is a wonderful opportunity that will propel your career to new heights, it will broaden your perspective and open doors to a world of opportunities. It will also challenge you and push you to get out of your comfort zone and can make you very uncomfortable. My advice would be to keep an open mind, roll with the punches and give it everything you've got because the more you invest in the experience, the more you will get out of it. Get involved in as many activities as you can outside the classroom and focus on building your network and relationships.

I wish you the very best as you embark on your MBA trajectory. Remember the words of Lao Tzu, "A journey of a thousand miles begins with one step."

Thank you for reading my book; you are now one step closer to your destination.

Acknowledgements

In life, nothing of significance is achieved alone. Behind every person, there are support systems: loved ones, friends and colleagues who help you push through and achieve your goals and dreams. I extend my heartfelt gratitude to every person who has nurtured me.

First, a special mention to Dr Gita Piramal for her constant mentorship and believing in me, sometimes more than I believed in myself. Her astute guidance comes at critical points in my life and pivots my trajectory completely—she is a true genius!

The foundation for everything we do in life is set at school and in our early years. This book is dedicated to all the teachers, mentors and influencers who have made me the person I am today. To mention a few, Anita Billimoria, Ms Darasha, Ms Munshi, Ms Taraporewala, Ms Anjuli Kaul and all the other wonderful teachers at the JB Petit High School in Mumbai. A huge vote of thanks to the many amazing professors at Carnegie Mellon University and at Harvard Business School for the lessons in math, statistics, management and life!

Additionally, I extend my thanks to Ms Contractor, Jehangir Palkhiwala and Kalpesh and Purvi Kapadia who taught me the fundamentals of accounting, balance sheets and business in differing proportions. Also, Mr Shekhar Gupta, who enlisted me as a columnist for The Indian Express in my mid-twenties, giving my confidence a huge boost. His articulation, memory and eye for detail continue to amaze and inspire me.

Also, a special mention to my guardian family at college and my guardian angels today, Pratik and Grishma Nanavaty, who have stood by me like pillars.

Through all the phases of life, my family has been an intimate and constant source of strength. My parents, siblings, cousins and relatives have all, in equal measure, bolstered my ambition and reveled in my successes. A shout-out to the Jain & Kagzi families and my doting sister and brother-in-law, Shalini and Samir Goenka, who held me in their palms until I learned how to walk.

Cicero considered friendship to be among the most intimate bonds one could share with another human being, and I concur. I have been fortunate to find a supportive group of friends who have been with me through thick and thin. A heartfelt thank you to Umme-Aiman Merchant, Krupa Shandilya, Jayati Vora, Jahnavi Martinoni, Risheen Reejsinghani, Meha Jhaveri, Sahiba Kaur Sethi, Vishal and Ratna Goenka, Radhika Shastri, Zeeshan Suhail, Sejal Kuvavala, Manoj Gursahani, Shital Mehhta, Sudha Sharma, Josh Crooner, Camille Richardson, Anjali Pratap, Farhanah Akikwala, Abhishek and Shreepriya Karnani, Jignesh and Aanchal Jhaveri, Ritesh and Ami Kothari, Ruhana Hafiz, Sohil and Aparna Chand, Abbas Merchant, Manish and Yogita Chokhani, Anupriya Chowdhary, Nivedita Hattangadi, Avinash Ananda, Azeem and Simran Zainulbhai, Chaya Momaya, Arshiya Singh, Aditya and Bhavna Talwar, Anuj and Utsah Kohli, Harbeen Arora, Vinay Rai, Dhananjay and Sonal Lodha, Harsh & Maitreyi Parikh, Raj and Ritika Parikh, Dhruv and Avni Samal, Suren John, Millie Mitra, Hrishikesh Desai, Nikunj and Tina Saraf, Kaneez Surka, Pratik and Puja Parekh, Rajesh and Vinita Jain, Siddharth Tata, Saloni Doshi, Chetan and Shivani Vohra, Shelly Garg, Tara Deshpande, Leeza Mangaldas, Divya Nachani and many other friends for standing by me through the years—your friendship means the world to me! To my entire class at J B Petit, class of 1997, and Section J, Harvard Business School, class of 2010—thanks for your support, you guys rock!

Finally, I fundamentally believe that teamwork makes the dream work. A group of highly talented counselors and team members have helped immensely in shaping this book:

Developmental Edits
1. Kovid Gupta
2. Gayatri Pahalajani

ReachIvy Experts
1. Grishma Nanavaty
2. Gaargi Desai
3. Aparna Maroo Jain
4. Shyam Gursahani
5. Suman Barua
6. Ameya Bhangle
7. Ananya Jain
8. Madhav Pathak
9. Udit Bhatnaga
10. Niyati Dave

ReachIvy.com Team (Past and Present)
1. Nishreen Darukhanawala
2. Suchitra Nair
3. Delia Frank
4. Varsha Chalke
5. Khushboo Ganatra
6. Juhi Tiwari
7. Sonalee Parekh
8. Garima Rathi
9. Dhwani Rajani
10. Rinal Jain
11. Abel Gonsalves
12. Simran Khurana

ReachIvy.com's Global Advisory Board
1.   Vijay Makwana, MBA, Insead
2.   Aaron Chadbourne, MBA, Harvard Business School
3.   Rushabh Kapashi, MBA, Harvard Business School

Research Partners
1.   Chandini Sehgal, HDFC Credila
2.   Nikhil Lasarado, Prodigy Finance

Legal Advice
1.   Reeti Choudhary

Jaico Publishing House: Akash Shah, thank you for believing in me and this concept. As a pioneering alumnus of Columbia Business School, Akash's personal experience and expertise formed the guiding pillar of our book. Special thanks to Reena Jayswal for assisting us with her rich knowledge of the complex reader base India boasts of. Her meticulous editorial feedback, attention to detail and eye for simplifying language helped us finely tailor the content of the book.

Many thanks to Satyendra Nair for helping me conceptualize the book's content and structure. His editorial guidance has been invaluable for the book. Every sentence, phrase and word in the book went through his scrutiny and that has made all the difference!

About the Author

Vibha Kagzi holds an MBA from Harvard Business School and a Bachelor of Science from Carnegie Mellon University. She has also pursued courses at the University of California, Berkeley, London School of Economics, Indian School of Business and Xavier's Institute of Communications. She is a certified Leadership coach from Coach for Life, USA. At Harvard, she co-wrote a case for the Negotiations Department, which has been incorporated in the teaching curriculum at the school.

Vibha's professional experience spans finance, fashion, media and public relations. She has worked in New York for BlackRock Securities, an asset management firm, spent time with her family business in the fashion accessories industry and helped to establish a California-based hedge fund in India.

Vibha has been featured extensively in the media, with articles and quotes in *The Economic Times*, *The Indian Express*, *DNA*, *Your Story*, *Business Standard*, *She the People*, and many more publications. Vibha's insights on career guidance, studying abroad, and education have been aired on popular radio channels such as Radio One and Radio City. She has created a niche on Quora as well, where she is recognized as an expert in the 'study abroad' space with almost two million views (and counting!) to her answers.

Vibha has completed a yoga teacher's training course, is a certified open-water diver, is proficient in French and has traveled extensively, visiting over 60 countries across six continents. She is on the executive board of the Harvard Club of Mumbai and on the Carnegie Mellon Admissions Council.

Vibha has been invited to speak at and has also been felicitated at several prestigious forums, including IIT Bombay, IIT Delhi, Teach for India, Citibank, YPO, NHRD, Indian Merchants Chambers, IEEE WIE Leadership Summit, top colleges, schools and corporations across India and globally.

She is on a mission to provide holistic guidance to young individuals who aspire to reach leading universities and determine their career paths. Given her dedication and perseverance, she was awarded the Woman of Excellence plaque at the 2018 Women Economic Forum and the 'DivHERsity Champion' title from Jobsforher.com in 2019.

Vibha brings her myriad experiences and expertise to ReachIvy. com and synthesizes her learning for the reader in this book.